D0933572

# CHINDIT
# AFFAIR

The manuscript of *Chindit Affair* was
re-discovered by the author and journalist
Brian Mooney, and he and Antony Edmonds
edited it for publication

# CHINDIT AFFAIR

## A MEMOIR OF THE WAR IN BURMA

### BY
### FRANK BAINES

Pen & Sword
**MILITARY**

First published in Great Britain in 2011 by
Pen & Sword Military
An imprint of
Pen & Sword Books Ltd
47 Church Street
Barnsley
South Yorkshire
S70 2AS

Copyright © Frank Baines, 2011

ISBN 978 1 84884 448 3

A CIP catalogue record for this book is
available from the British Library

Typeset in 11 on 13pt Times New Roman by
Acredula

Printed and bound in England
By CPI

Pen & Sword Books Ltd incorporates the Imprints of Pen & Sword Aviation,
Pen & Sword Family History, Pen & Sword Maritime, Pen & Sword Military,
Wharncliffe Local History, Pen & Sword Select, Pen & Sword Military Classics,
Leo Cooper, Remember When, Seaforth Publishing and Frontline Publishing

For a complete list of Pen & Sword titles please contact
PEN & SWORD BOOKS LIMITED
47 Church Street, Barnsley, South Yorkshire, S70 2AS, England
E-mail: enquiries@pen-and-sword.co.uk
Website: www.pen-and-sword.co.uk

# Contents

# Maps

## Burma, 1944

The area in Northern Burma where the Chindits 111 Brigade operated behind enemy lines from March to July 1944.

# Operations of III Brigade, Burma, 1944

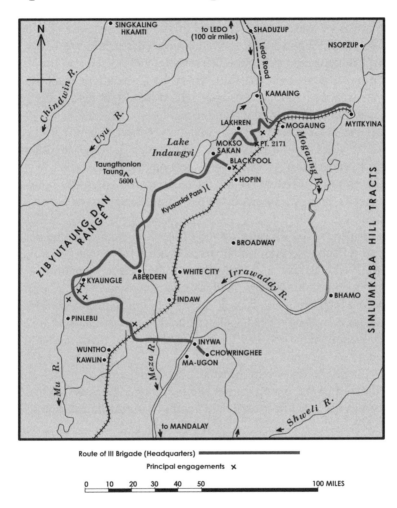

The route 111 Brigade marched through enemy-occupied Burma, and the main points of engagement with the Japanese. Out of 2,200 men who started the campaign, only 119 were fit to fight at the end.

# Foreword

It was summer in 1943 in the middle of India. We were training for the extraordinary operation that Frank describes in this book. At Brigade Headquarters we were a small band of officers and we came to know each other very well. When Frank arrived I realized I would not easily forget him. He had come to us by an unusual route, and indeed had little right to be with us. 'I have come,' he said, 'from the Camouflage Pool where the sedge has withered and no birds sing.' His words, quoting a poem by John Keats, had a ring of their own and defined him.

Whatever the circumstances – and they varied fearfully – there was always a zest and a spilling of words with Frank, in which he emptied his feelings; his heart was – it seems – always on display.

Read his story. It is like no other account of war. He hides nothing.

He shocks, and says things that I was afraid to say in my account of the campaign.

But he also moves. His description of the dire situation at the end of the operation reflects everything that we felt with a force that I have not seen matched – exhaustion and despair and the fearful conditions, and a despising of our commanders. And he gives a picture of the land in which we moved which brings it all back. In his relations with his Gurkha troops his frankness – a happy word – shows him at his most unafraid. I saw how close he was to them, and saw his grief when one of them seemed to have received a fatal wound.

How deeply he felt – with heart and head contending.

At the end of the operation his life took uncertain ways. What he has described as his love affair with the Chindits had fulfilled so much of him. It is all here.

I will remember Frank when other more ordinary folk have disappeared down the sink of a failing memory.

Share my delight that war has so many faces.

*Richard Rhodes James – Cambridge, January 2011*

# Introduction

Frank Baines was in many ways an improbable Chindit. At the outset of the Second World War he was a sailor, not a professional soldier, and he was homosexual. But he had a winning way with people – he could care for and lead men – and he was adventurous and courageous and had boundless energy. Although the Chindits faced almost insurmountable challenges and were tested to their very limits, they were not all hewn from hard rock. Many of them were simply men who were called upon to do extraordinary things; Frank was one of these.

Frank Baines's entire life was an adventure. It is not surprising that one moonlit night in early March 1944 he found himself flying in an American Dakota from India into Japanese-held Burma with a bunch of Gurkhas armed to the teeth. In this book, which he left unpublished, and which has only recently been rediscovered, Frank describes graphically how he got there, and what happened to him and the men with him. But before reading it you should know a bit about who he was, and how he came to be there, and what became of him afterwards. It won't spoil the story; it adds important background.

Born in London in 1915, Frank was the son of a prominent architect, Sir Frank Baines KCVO, who designed what is now the Headquarters of MI5 and saved the medieval roof of Westminster Hall. He also bequeathed Frank a visual eye and taste for controversy. Frank's mother was the daughter of a yeoman farmer from Staffordshire. Frank himself had a blissful childhood, much of it spent in the southernmost Cornish parish of St Keverne, and some of at Oundle, a typical harsh boarding school of its time – from which he fled. After school, Frank went to sea, sailing to Australia and back on one of Gustav Erikson's Finnish four masted grain ships, the *Lawhill*, and then working his passage to South America. At the outbreak of war, Frank enlisted as a gunner in an anti-aircraft battery in East Anglia, but was later transferred to India for officer training. He saw action as a junior artillery officer on the North-West Frontier and was then assigned to Kirkee Camouflage School, near Pune, where he became a camouflage instructor in Urdu.

Frank thirsted for action, and in June 1943 he wangled a transfer to 111 Brigade, which was to become part of General Orde Wingate's crack force of Chindits. He was seconded to Brigade Headquarters as Staff Officer, Grade III (Camouflage) with the rank of Staff Captain, and thus embarked on one of the defining experiences of his life.

By that time, General Wingate had achieved fame leading a long-range penetration expedition behind Japanese lines deep inside Burma and demonstrating that the British – reeling from a string of humiliating defeats across Asia, and with the enemy at the gates of India – could indeed fight the Japanese in the jungle. The Chindit operations have always sparked controversy. There is even disagreement about how they acquired their *nomme de guerre*. Some believe it is from a corruption of the name for the mythical Burmese lion, the *chinthe*, which guards Buddhist temples; others that it was after a figure of Hindu mythology; others, after the Burmese word for Griffin.

If the military achievements of the Chindits in their first sally into Burma remain questionable – Wingate lost one third of his men – the propaganda effect was nevertheless electrifying. Winston Churchill, an ardent proponent of commando operations, recognized this and was all the more prepared to overlook Wingate's very evident eccentricities. The Chindit leader often wore an alarm clock around his wrist, which would go off at times, and a raw onion on a string around his neck, which he would occasionally bite into as a snack. He liked eating boiled python. He would also go about without clothing. Lord Moran, Churchill's personal physician, wrote in his diaries that 'he seemed to me hardly sane – in medical jargon a borderline case'. Notwithstanding this sometimes bizarre behaviour, Churchill took Wingate with him to the Quebec Conference with America's wartime leader Franklin Roosevelt in August 1943, where Wingate persuaded them to equip him with a far bigger force for a second Chindit operation. It was in this operation that Frank took part.

Frank talked of his 'love affair with the Chindits', and for rest of his life he was obsessed and traumatized by his experiences fighting in this unorthodox force behind enemy lines. He saw himself essentially as an amateur among hardened professionals, but he acquitted himself bravely and shared all the ghastliness of the five-month campaign. He also behaved in an unorthodox way: he fell in love with one of his Gurkha riflemen. Frank tells his Chindit story in this book, which he started 25 years after the war, and on which he was still working until shortly before he died in 1987. Frank's account of his service with 111 Brigade is factual and brutally honest – but it has been only in the accounts of others that his courage, his cheerfulness and his readiness to face the enemy have fully come across.

Frank joined 111 Brigade at its jungle training camp near Lalitpur in Central India in June 1943, an area which provided ample scope for jungle warfare training. The Brigade had little use for him as a camouflage expert, but they took him on initially as the Animal Transport Officer and then permanently as Orderly Officer commanding Brigade Headquarters defence platoons. He was given command of two platoons, each of fifty Gurkha riflemen, and it was leading them that Frank went to war in Burma. They were mostly little more than boys, but they were brave soldiers. One of them, Dal Bahadur, who was probably only 16 at the time, became Frank's orderly; and Frank fell in love with him.

Frank served under Major Jack Masters, an extraordinarily able and aggressive officer with a brilliant but chequered career and a searing intellect, who was to be in the thick of some of the bloodiest fighting and, after the war, as John Masters, to go on to be a best-selling author. Masters would write more than 20 novels, including *Bhowani Junction*, which was made into a film, as well as a number of autobiographical works of which one of the most celebrated is *The Road Past Mandalay* – which includes his own account of leading 111 Brigade.

Born in Calcutta in 1914 and trained at Sandhurst, Masters came from a long line of Indian Army officers and public servants; and, although he did not know this until much later in his life, he was part Indian. He saw action as a young adjutant with his Gurkha regiment, the 4th Prince of Wales, in three countries in the early stages of the Second World War – in Syria, Iraq and Iran – and he was then posted to Staff College at Quetta, where he fell in love with Barbara Rose, the wife of one of his fellow officers. To have become involved in a divorce in the socially uptight British Raj would have meant Masters's resigning his commission; the couple took furtive holidays together, and finally Barbara left her husband and bore Masters a child out of wedlock, all stirring minor scandal. It was when she was pregnant with the child that Masters was posted as Major to 111 Brigade.

Frank was the junior officer in charge of the Brigade Headquarters, and thus his experiences with the Chindits were centred on Masters, the Brigade Major, who was ultimately to be set an impossible mission. At Brigade Headquarters Frank had a ring-side overview of the campaign. He also saw action in the field.

Wingate's original plan was to insert his specially trained Brigades into Burma, and harass Japanese communications and threaten the rear of their army in Upper Burma by waging guerrilla war. The bulk of his Chindit forces were flown into Burma in early March 1944, an air armada that was code-named Operation Thursday. But Wingate was killed in a plane crash on 24 March shortly after the start of operations – some continue to believe that it was not an accident – and his original plan was abandoned for something far more ambitious. The American second-in-command in South-East Asia, General Joseph 'Vinegar Joe' Stilwell, who now effectively took overall command of the Chindits, wanted more fighting on the ground to support his thrust into Burma from neighbouring China. Stilwell sought above all to open up a supply route from India through Northern Burma into China. The new objective was the capture of the strategic town of Mogaung. But this meant redeploying lightly armed troops, who were trained and equipped for mobile hit-and-run operations, to dig in and engage with the enemy – far from the front, without big guns, and relying entirely on air support.

Masters, promoted in the field to command the Brigade in place of Brigadier Joe Lentaigne, who was flown out to replace Wingate but was no match for Stilwell, was ordered to occupy and hold a strategic area, perversely code-named Blackpool, a low spur rising above the paddies and jungle close to the main north-south rail and road supply routes to Mogaung. At various stages during the campaign, other Chindit Brigades occupied similar strongholds – code-named Aberdeen and White City. Despite its name, Blackpool was no holiday – it was perilously too close to the main Japanese forces and to their big guns. For 17 days and nights, and during the onset of heavy monsoon rains, the Japanese repeatedly attacked and shelled the block, killing two hundred of the defenders and slowly reducing the redoubt to a sea of bloody mud. Reinforcements promised from 14 Brigade never arrived and the airstrip vital for their survival was finally overrun. Masters's men were literally pounded into defeat. When he finally gave the dazed order to withdraw on 24 May, Masters had also to instruct orderlies to shoot 19 stretcher-cases too badly wounded to be moved.

The defeated Brigade got away from Blackpool into the jungle hills because, miraculously and inexplicably, the Japanese did not pursue them – why, has never been properly explained. But that was not the end of the campaign. Stilwell, who privately despised the British, demanded more. Masters regrouped his battle-shocked and by now mostly sick soldiers, and was ordered to attack from the west and take a hill known as Point 2171 overlooking the valley and railway line to Mogaung – an action in which more of his men were killed and wounded. This engagement lasted from 20 June to 5 July.

By the time 111 Brigade quit Burma at the end of July 1944, Masters's original force of 2,200 had been depleted by death, wounding, capture, malnutrition, malaria, dysentery, general sickness, desertion and madness to just 119 fit men – eight British officers, a score of British soldiers and 90 Gurkhas. They had endured and survived five months of the utmost hardship, each losing between thirty and forty pounds. Frank was one of those eight officers – one of the last men standing in 111 Brigade.

Three of the officers have published accounts of the Brigade's campaign – *The Road Past Mandalay* by John Masters, *Chindit* by Richard Rhodes James, and now *Chindit Affair* by Frank Baines. Frank's account throws new light on the leaders of the operation and tells a soldier's story from a highly charged and unusual perspective of an officer on the battlefield in love with one of his men. There are several more accounts of the Chindit campaigns which record the fate of the other Brigades – including Brigadier Mike Calvert's vivid account of his 77 Brigade – but no other story so closely connects with the raw nerves of the men who fought there and recreates so well the sensations of being in the jungles and hills that devoured nearly all of them.

Frank was a rebel and a non-conformist. After the war, and partly as a result of his harrowing experiences with the Chindits, he spent three years as a Hindu monk in a Himalayan monastery. He then moved to Calcutta, where he set up a successful business repairing tea chests and became a journalist on the Calcutta *Statesman*. He returned to England in the mid 1950s and transformed himself into a successful author – publishing four books, including *Look Towards the Sea*, an acclaimed account of his Cornish childhood; *In Deep*, the story of his sailing voyage to Australia; and *Officer Boy*, a chronicle of his early days in the army in India. Late in life, when he was aged 62, he cycled back to India from his home town of Coggeshall in Essex, and on his final return to England in 1984 he set about the redrafting of his Chindit story. It still mattered so much to him. He died in 1987, and the typed manuscript of this book was one of his few remaining possessions.

The draft lay forgotten, stored in a cupboard by Frank's literary executor Dan Samson, until I read it when I began to research Frank's life. I realised at once that this was a remarkable account of one of the most extraordinary campaigns of the Second World War. I set about preparing it for publication, together with Antony Edmonds, who brought an indispensable rigour, deftness and sensitivity to an editing project that was quite challenging.

So here it is, Frank's story, and the story of the men he served with – above all his beloved Gurkhas, and, among the others, Jack Masters; Briggs, 'Briggo', the Signals Officer who returned to work as a customs inspector; Major John Hedley, the Intelligence Officer, who became a housemaster at Bromsgrove School; 'Chesty' Jennings, the RAF Squadron Leader, who co-ordinated incoming airdrops and supervised the building of airstrips; Lieutenant Lawrence Alexander Wilson, 'young Lawrence', killed in action at Blackpool, aged 21; Brigadier Joe Lentaigne, who ended his days as one of the only serving British officers in the post-independence Indian army; Mike MacGillicuddy of the Irish Reeks, also killed in action; Richard Rhodes James, the Cipher Officer, who became a housemaster at Haileybury College; Major Frank Turner, the Transport Officer; and Doc Desmond Whyte, the Battalion Medical Officer, who was nominated by Masters for a VC, and returned after the war to medical practice in Northern Ireland. At the time of writing, Rhodes James is the only one of these officers still alive; and I owe him a particular debt of gratitude for his assistance and advice during the preparation of the book for publication.

*Brian Mooney – Coggeshall, March 2011*

# CHAPTER ONE

# 111 Brigade

My love affair with the Chindits began in a prosaic fashion. I was seconded from my duties as an instructor in field camouflage at the Army School near Poona to 111 Brigade, and posted to Brigade Headquarters as Staff Officer, Grade III (Camouflage) with the rank of Staff Captain. It was June 1943.

During the rail journey to take up my new appointment, I had plenty of time to meditate on its nature. 111 Brigade's role had been presented to me by the Commandment of Camouflage School as, in effect, a suicide mission. The object of training was to have us ready for action by November 1943. We were then to march unobtrusively through the Japanese front lines and, by avoiding engagements, penetrate into the heart of enemy-occupied Burma. There we were to blow up bridges, demolish railway stations, liquidate ammunition trains, ambush commissariat columns, in such a way that we would create maximum confusion. It was inevitable that I spend some part of that journey reviewing my chances of survival.

I was already acquainted with some of 111 Brigade's more general aims and objectives. In the light of this information I could not but accept the fact that my chances seemed pretty slim.

111 Brigade were a comparatively new outfit hastily put together by General Wavell in one of his last administrative acts as Commander-in-Chief before becoming Viceroy. Their formation was undoubtedly intended as an expression of Wavell's confidence in the Wingate concept. They were what was known as a long-range penetration group and were modelled on General Orde Wingate's original 77 Brigade, with which he had effected the first penetration into Japanese occupied Burma.

The Brigade was constituted of four battalions under the command of Joe Lentaigne, the Brigadier. Each battalion was divided into two independent columns under separate management. The lieutenant colonel in command of the battalion invariably took charge of one column; a senior major the other.

Our battalions, and the columns into which they were divided, were as follows:

2nd Battalion King's Own Royal Regiment  –  41 Column, 46 Column

1st Battalion Cameronians  – 26 Column, 90 Column

3rd Battalion 4th Prince of Wales Own Gurkha Rifles – 30 Column, 40 Column

4th Battalion 9th Gurkha Rifles – 49 Column, 94 Column

The Brigade thus constituted was designed to operate on its own, under Lentaigne's independent leadership. The object of our training was to have us ready by November. We were then to march unobtrusively through the Japanese front lines and, by avoiding engagements, penetrate the heart of enemy-occupied Burma. There we were to blow up bridges, demolish railway stations, liquidate ammunition trains and ambush commissariat columns, in such a way as would create maximum confusion. It was hoped that this would impair Japanese efficiency as well as tie down in the centre of Burma forces which would otherwise have been better deployed along the frontier with India.

Just before my train pulled into Lalitpur in the Central Provinces, which was the railhead for all 111 Brigade's training operations, it ran through a monsoon rain-squall. Lalitpur station appeared sacked and ravaged. It was scattered with broken branches and bruised leaves as if abandoned after an enemy onslaught. In contrast, its carefully tended flower-beds still looked as if laid out for kit inspection. The rows of rigid zinnias regimented as for a CO's parade were magnificent in their scarlet tunics. I took it as a good omen – and I could not but feel reassured by this augury.

I was not, however, anticipating being received with enthusiasm. In those days a Camouflage Officer was still a rare bird and was regarded with coolness. It was difficult for infantry officers to take to one. I had to be prepared to be rebuffed, if not refused permission to land at all. To add to my anxieties, I was having a much trouble coping with an aspect of my own personality. I was anticipating taking up my duties with the Gurkhas, memories of whose endearing young charms had stayed with me since I first saw them go into action on the North-West Frontier. These memories had far too ardent a relish not to presage dangers in the future.

This was a difficult situation. Yet I was determined to get away with it. I was much less prepared than formerly to surrender to social conformity. I judged that success in getting accepted by 111 Brigade would depend on luck and on there being some sympathetic officer on hand to appreciate my less evident qualities.

My plan was to suggest that I was an officer with a little more to his credit than just the boring background of an Army School of Instruction – possessing talents in other directions than being able to display dried flower arrangements in tin hats. My aim would be to convince whoever interviewed me that here, in my person, was a spare officer they had not expected, and were not indeed entitled to, whom it would be folly to reject when they could, with my wholly willing co-operation, utilize me for dozens of other purposes having nothing to do with camouflage.

I had been the sole passenger to alight. A relaxed young sergeant came swinging briskly towards me, his boots crunching crisply over the finely granulated stone chips spread across the platform. The smile of welcome which illuminated his innocent English face was homely with pleasure. He was obviously delighted at being able to exercise a bit of authority. He was displaying, at the same time, a splendid indifference to the approving glances darted in his direction by a group of crudely brazen hussies draped provocatively at the windows of the third-class wagon. He could not but have been aware of them and I calculated, on that account, that he would display equal *sang-froid* on the field of battle.

They, for their part, were in the process of giving his physique an appraisal which was chillingly meticulous. They were speculating pleasurably about the size and shape of his small-arms equipment. He smelt characteristically of sunburnt sweat and soaped flesh. Both his forearms were magnificently tattooed.

I threw these vile creatures on the train some filthy remarks about their fathers, their husbands and their lovers, and they vanished behind the shutters with lewd giggles.

A heavy scent of tuberoses pervaded the air. The scent and the scene were so far removed from sober Camouflage School Mess and Poona Officers' Club that they made me feel even more insecure than usual. They conjured up images of Benarsi courtesans panting with exhaustion from carrying the over-ripe fruit of insupportable bosoms, or temple dancing girls with scarlet palms and hennaed feet, loaded with gold ornaments and smothered in suffocatingly scented garlands.

These thoughts tempted me to surrender to more personal sensual images. Again I visualized what might await me in the persons of the young Gurkhas.

Until then, I had managed during my career in India to insulate myself fairly successfully from the debilitating gales of libido. Now I felt exposed to them, just as I knew that the preoccupation of soldiers with such bodily things as sweat and salt and sex and shit and toil and blood would fall inevitably within the ambience of operations to be undertaken by 111 Brigade. The scent of the tuberoses, somehow reminiscent of the sickly-sweet stench of death, the sinister banter of the women, the smell from the sergeant's armpits – these were the first intimations I received of the sore spots to be laid bare.

I was dressed up as if for going into Poona. My uniform was one of which I was excessively proud. It emphasized subtle distinctions by its inconspicuous departure from standard patterns. It was embellished here and there with those insinuating little refinements which gave an air of added elegance to the appearance of every young officer. In the crook of my arm I carried, like a knight his helm, the prized possession of my exaggeratedly pretentious solar topee. It was doubly precious to me on account of the fact that, in the Bombay Presidency, all the Governor's *aides* carried one. It was unlike the missionary model, Mark III, associated with the late Dr Livingstone and the Emperor Haile Selassie, as immortalized by General Wingate, and it exemplified, instead, the whole Army School of Instruction approach to war, with its emphasis on gracious living. In front of this young sergeant, with his utilitarian excellence, it made me appear perfectly ridiculous.

The engine puffed spasmodically and the train pulled out. I had been up at the front. Coach after massive coach rolled past me, giving their passengers the opportunity of getting a really good look at me. I felt myself caressed, crushed, cauterized – even controlled – by the hundreds of eyes which observed me with intense, cautious and yet evasive curiosity. It disappeared in the direction of Jhansi, steaming down the long tunnel of over-arching greenery with a slight wobble, like a self-conscious drunk placing each foot before him over-confidently yet insecurely.

The young sergeant and I had been watching it as if hypnotized. I felt as if it were bearing away the whole burden of my past experiences. He smiled and saluted me. We shook hands like blood brothers.

'111 Brigade, sir?' he enquired brightly.

'Yes. But how did you know I was going to be on the train? I might just as easily have taken the next one.'

He laughed good-humouredly. 'We meet every train, sir. Nothing personal. Rear headquarters are always sending down an extra bit of equipment or some technical officer. What is your particular line, sir – if I may be so bold as to ask the question?'

'It's camouflage,' I said, feeling dreadfully inadequate.

'Very interesting,' he commented without a hint of patronage. 'I shall look forward to attending some of your lectures, sir!'

We jumped into a 15 hundredweight truck and bowled down the clean, red, rain-washed roadways. After a minimal suggestion of shanty-town bazaar, the jungle closed in.

Flocks of green parakeets, as iridescent as humming birds, swarmed about sour smelling fruits rotting on the trees of an orchard. Groups of naughty monkeys, like rude little boys, made obscene signs at us from the side of the road as we flashed past. Occasionally we glimpsed an expanse of lake. The waters lay as polished as pewter, placidly reflecting a sky that alternatively looked luridly threatening or as lifeless as lead, according to the density of the cloud-cover.

Sometimes a deer – one of the great, red Indian *sambhur* – bounced out of a thicket and bounded along the grass verge of the road beside us. The countryside swarmed with game. The only thing it appeared conspicuously short of was humans.

Presently we arrived where 111 Brigade Headquarters was encamped. A large, muddy pond extended for a quarter of a mile along the side of the road, in the middle of which some water buffaloes were enjoying a wallow. From over the tops of a tangle of various shrubs, conspicuous among which was the prickly, ubiquitous *lantana* with its characteristic smell of cat's piss, there could be seen the pitch of several mud-coloured tents. Their prevailing tone, I noted professionally, blended so well with the surrounding terrain that it did not look as if a camouflage officer was needed.

'Will you be staying with us permanently, sir?' enquired my sergeant.

'Honestly, sergeant, I don't know. It rather depends on the Brigadier.'

'Well, in any case, sir, I don't doubt you'll be wanting to ditch that solar topee. The stores tent is over there. The quartermaster will fix you up with a battledress, a pair of boots, and a bush hat. Also he will see to the storage of your personal possessions.'

'All the officers' gear is stored to Rear Headquarters at Gwalior,' he added, casting a dubious eye over my magnificent Asprey suitcases embellished interiorly with cut crystal bottles, ivory brush-backs, and solid silver fittings (relics of my father), so soon to become food for the white ants.

'For the time being then, sir, I'll wish you the very best of luck and leave you. I hope we shall renew our acquaintance shortly. The officers' mess is over there. You report your arrival to the Brigade Major. His tent is behind that *baobab*.'

He gave me another perfect salute and left me quivering with trepidation. I made my way along a filthy footpath churned up by hoof prints and fouled with mule-droppings towards my first confrontation with Jack Masters.

I had no idea what to expect. My conception of staff-officers was extraordinarily hazy, composed principally of images of dandified subalterns from old copies of *Punch*. I half imagined that Jack Masters might be a chinless wonder like Bertie Wooster.

I approached the tent. A trestle table had been placed like a barrier across one end of it, just behind the tent-pole where the flaps folded back. From beyond it glared out the somewhat caustic countenance of a man prematurely aged (for he could not have been much older than I was) by responsibilities, and pale from years of perspiration and heat exhaustion.

It turned out that he was about twenty-eight. He was so pared to the bone by overwork, however – almost humming with the strain of too much tension and as tight as a bowstring – that I appeared mentally and physically quite flabby by comparison, and as inexperienced as a babe. The cast of his features was predominantly intellectual. His whole personality was ablaze with the flame of striking intelligence.

Already, for so young a man, it seemed that deep speculation and profound thought (for it never occurred to me at the time that his haggard look might have something to do with unhappiness) had furrowed his brow and gouged out the eye-holes. From their sockets, a pair of opaque sepia brown eyes gave little away. Currents of placidity and ferocity alternated. Emotive yet innocent, his expression evoked the patient ox rather than the volatile satyr – and yet there was something too of the centaur (I am thinking of Cheiron). Masters looked at the world with a satirical eye, and yet saw it also as his oyster.

He had a high, broad, bony cranium on which the hair grew rather sparsely and was cared for untidily, and he wore 'bugger's grips' – at least they developed into 'bugger's grips' during the later stages of the operation (a sign, no doubt, that his progressive disenchantment with headquarters had succeeded in alienating him from the conventions). On this occasion of our first meeting, however, they were embryonic, and his moustaches orthodox. The only indication that they would subsequently develop into 'handlebars' were the tufts of unshorn hair which grew, quite isolated, high on his prominent cheek bones, like hardy alpines. They made him look deliberately and inflexibly unhandsome.

He was, with the solitary exception of General Wingate, the most uncompromisingly inelegant regular officer I have ever met.

As we confronted each other across his office table and I performed the ritual gesture of saluting authority, he gazed at my face so fixedly, but with such a cool, level look of appraisal, yet without hostility, that I half imagined something fearful must have happened to it, like feathers sprouting instead of whiskers. We looked at each other in complete silence, with wary circumspection.

I decided to break the silence, and introduced myself: 'Baines, sir. Reporting for duty from the Camouflage School for ...' – and came to an abrupt halt. I had no idea, as a matter of fact, what I had been posted to 111 Brigade for, except to be a nuisance and importune GHQ with pet schemes for clandestine operations – something which I did not feel at liberty to disclose to Jack Masters in case it gave him an unfavourable insight into my ungovernable independence.

In the ensuing pause, made quite painful by my lack of self-confidence, my incapacity to handle the situation became so patent that Jack Masters was impelled to sum it up by saying 'Precisely' in a bleakly amused tone, and with a weary facial expression.

This galvanized me into a sort of desperate fluency. It seemed a good idea to begin again. I cleared my throat, and determining not to be put off by the deliberately discouraging pantomime across the table, I repeated firmly, 'Reporting for duty, sir,' adding forthrightly, '*Any* duty! And please don't let the fact of my being a Camouflage Officer turn you against me!' My tone was abrupt, and indeed the remark had been intended as a challenge.

'Whatever gives you that idea!' said Masters, looking taken aback. 'You mustn't go around expressing such a preconception. I have absolutely no bias against a Camouflage Officer. Has something I've said given you any indication that I might be partial?'

'No, sir. Certainly not, sir. Only some people are inclined to resent it.'

'In that case, disabuse your mind that I might be one of them. And don't credit me with other people's thoughts without proper evidence.'

'Very well then, sir. Certainly, sir. And please forgive me for the unworthy suspicion.'

The glance he gave me in response to this pert reply showed a certain surprise. No doubt he was unused to being treated quite so cavalierly. Suddenly he looked quite young – almost human – and I realised with a surge of relief that I would be able to identify with him. He was searching for the notification of my posting. He found it, read it, and then asked me how I proposed to handle my assignment, giving me a fair opportunity to fire off a personal statement.

'That sounds perfectly reasonable,' he said. 'You shall have all the encouragement to do as much instructing as you want. I shan't put any obstacles in your way. But, of course you understand, I hope, that I can't take you in with me. If I killed one of their Camouflage Officers, GHQ would never forgive me.'

My face fell. That gave him an indication of how to proceed and he pursued his advantage relentlessly. 'I never asked for you in the first place,' he continued. 'GHQ just sent you down on their own initiative. Not that I'm ungrateful for small mercies.' He looked at me with the contempt a miser would reserve for a Salvation Army collecting box. 'I'm happy to have all the help I can get. But you see, this brigade is a newly formed organisation. There are positively dozens of officers besides a Camouflage Officer who are absolutely indispensable to me, but whom I'm without, whereas I can get along without a Camouflage Officer quite easily.'

I saw this as pretended candour. There was a pause.

'You weren't expecting, were you, to come in with us?'

'Well – er – yes.'

'What a pity' he murmured to himself. 'And such enthusiasm! There's an Animal Transport Officer I want – could do with someone to take charge of Brigade Headquarters defence platoons – want an officer to organize rations – investigate distribution of loads – work out duty rotas. All the same, I can't take you in with me.'

He shook his head with mock ruefulness.

In my desperation I began to tremble and stammer.

'What?' he demanded furiously.

But I was unable to say a thing.

'Do you,' he barked, 'know anything about pack-animals?'

'Pack-animals? Why – naturally. I'm an expert on pack-animals!'

'You are? Then why didn't you say so, if you're so keen to come in with us?'

'Mountain Artillery is famous for it!' I said.

'In that case I might be able to use you. The circumstances are entirely different. Of course it would mean your shelving your camouflage responsibilities temporarily. Would you object? Would you be prepared to do that?'

'Oh no, sir! Oh yes, sir! Not a bit!'

'It would have to be done, you understand, quietly – without GHQ's connivance.'

'Certainly, sir.'

'Well, then,' he said, stretching out his arms over his head and pushing his legs out under the table as an indication of dismissal, 'that puts a completely different complexion on the matter. You'd better go down to the stores and get yourself kitted out. The quartermaster will allocate you a tent. I'll have to speak to the Brigadier, of course, to secure his permission.'

'So – you'll take me?'

'Temporarily, yes. But you'll have to prove you can make yourself useful.'

'Thank you, Brigade Major, sir. I'm very grateful.'

I withdrew hastily through the *lantana* scrub towards the quartermaster's tent before I should say anything further that might make him change his decision.

That evening, as a symbol of having started on a completely new career with 111 Brigade, I consigned my topee to their muddy waters. It slipped slowly out of sight as if unwilling to leave me, floating away sadly on the surface of the filthy pond and out into the dank obscurity of the dark, hot night like the vanishing ghost of my camouflage commitments.

In its place, I put on my head the coveted Gurkha hat, cocked rakishly sideways. Then I entered the Brigadier's mess tent in order to make the acquaintance of the other officers who were at dinner. They were a craggy lot. The greenish glare of the pressurised kerosene gas lamp revealed a selection of countenances, hard-bitten and unhandsome.

They had come in and dumped themselves down and gobbled up the food without an atom of ceremony, encouraged apparently by Brigadier Joe Lentaigne to get their snouts into the trough in this inelegant fashion. It bespoke a deliberate disregard for traditional officers' mess manners which betokened disenchantment, I suppose, with the ballerina school of behaviour.

Joe Lentaigne himself was like a great gaunt, belligerent, battered vulture. He talked with a slight lisp on account of his front teeth having been bashed out while he was leading his battalion during the retreat from Burma. He was full of coltish, middle-aged fun in a galumphing, carthorse kind of way, although neither was he without subtlety. Periodically he used to allow himself to surrender to an infectious, boyish sort of high spirits which he was not too pompous to translate into juvenile exploits, for he loved dashing around in jeeps and terrorising junior officers into accepting hair-raising joy rides.

In the middle of the meal, a great big floppy moth blundered into the tent wall from outside with a sombre thud. It bulged out the canvas as if someone had thrown a cricket ball at it. Then a huge, heavily carapaced cockchafer, armoured with hirsute claws like a crab – its blades whirring as noisily as a gun-ship's wings and every hair-follicle rigid – zoomed through the tent-flap on a helicopter errand and hit against the lamp with a crunch like the crushing of an empty match-box. It fell into the soup tureen with a plop, its wings flailing like egg-beaters. Everything reeked of damp.

Sometimes, on a special occasion, Joe Lentaigne could be lured by Briggs, the Signals Officer, into soliloquizing on strategy and tactics, and Rhodes James, the Cipher Officer, would sit sadly gazing at him through his thick lenses, his head cupped in his hands. Alternatively Geoffrey Birt, Engineers, or John Hedley, Intelligence, or Chesty Jennings, Squadron Leader RAF liaison, might twit Doc Whyte ironically about some spurious medical problem.

The pressure lamp would hiss and the mosquitoes whine and drone like dive-bombers; and Joe Lentaigne would warm to his theme of long-range-penetration groups as potential aggressors in hit-and-run tactics. This was the only sort of conversation ever exchanged, except in rare moments. Social intercourse was as good as non-existent. My first impression of them was of a dedicated group of ungracious puritans.

You felt that the jungle, just outside the mess tent in the velvety blackness, wanted to ingest you. The heat was stifling and unmitigated by any breath of freshness. Sometimes there would pass across the camp, like a wet caress, the hot, soft suspiration of a shower.

As we broke up for the night to seek our beds and got to our tents, I noticed the hurricane lamp which was burning in the Brigade Major's tent, like a beacon. It denoted that Jack Masters was still labouring over the all but intractable problems posed by our unorthodox composition.

I fell into a drugged sleep, punctuated by short bursts of light automatic fire from his comradely typewriter.

# CHAPTER TWO

# Mule Problems

So, for the nonce, I became the Animal Transport Officer.

I also became the officer commanding Brigade Headquarters defence platoons. This was a situation I was to retain for the duration: it had the unenviable reputation of being on the periphery of the social system, appropriate only to Second Lieutenants.

The Brigade Headquarters defence platoons were pariah platoons, dropped-out-of-favour children, little runts of the piglet litter, and they suffered both from a sense of being neglected as well as from feeling unwanted and unloved. I felt I had a duty to make up for this in some way.

But I still had no idea what those poor children could have done that was sufficiently dreadful to deserve the stigma of my leadership. Perhaps they had simply become scapegoats for some unseemly battalion frolic or folly? Whatever it was, it failed to reveal itself further. In fact, they became so docile that I grew extravagantly devoted to them.

Brigade Headquarters was a body consisting of specialists highly vulnerable to surprise attacks from unpredictable quarters. It must have amounted *in toto* to a string of about fifty load-carrying mules and riding ponies and a column of about one hundred men. To prevent attack, and as a precaution against being overrun, they invariably attempted during actual operations to attach themselves to one or other of the fighting columns held in reserve. There were bound to be, however, occasions when this could not be managed.

In the event of finding themselves unprotected and unsupported – as when manning a perimeter at night when they went into harbour, or providing certain patrol and reconnaissance duties inseparable from a defence role – they were allocated two defence platoons of fifty men. These were drawn in equal proportions from the 3/4 Gurkhas and the 4/9 Gurkhas.

I was their commander and masqueraded under the name of Orderly Officer. The Orderly Officer – for such indeed was the high-sounding title Masters had invented for me – was to be smuggled in amongst the senior officers, the proved experts and the professional foot-sloggers, to be a sort of maid of all work and universal dog's body. There was no official place for me on the allocated establishment.

Let nobody think, however, that I was disappointed at being assigned to this humble position. I was tickled pink. But before Masters could arrive at such a crucial decision and confirm me in my appointment, I had to prove to him that I could indeed make myself useful.

I threw myself wholeheartedly into this challenge, but with such eagerness that I actually became a casualty before the Brigade even got away from its Lalitpur training-ground.

I had arrived at the Brigade Headquarters coincidentally with some new mule-harness which had been specially adapted to accommodate our heavy radio sets and the generators upon which our communications depended. Briggo, Lentaigne and Masters were impatient to see this equipment tested.

As we were about to evacuate our present camp and set off into the unknown for our longest and most realistic training exercise, the matter was urgent, for the whole purpose of the exercise was to set up a radio communications network and try it out under realistic conditions.

It was into this situation that I blundered while making my way towards the mule lines on the morning after my arrival. I was intercepted and brought to heel by the small, moody group composed of the Signals Officer, the Brigade Major and the Brigadier, who were looking rather despondently at a large well-formed mule.

'Baines,' said Joe Lentaigne, 'come over here and give us the benefit of your advice.'

I had shown signs of attempting to circumvent them out of a feeling of delicacy, on account of Briggo's appearing to be holding forth vehemently to Lentaigne.

'I'm sorry, Brigadier,' I heard him say, 'but I'm only your Signals Officer. I've never touched a mule in my life. Moreover I decidedly reject your contention that I have anything whatsoever to do with loading these radio sets. My job is solely to operate them and ensure that they're kept operational. It does not include having any truck with transport.'

'But Briggo,' Lentaigne said mildly, 'what are we going to do if you refuse? Somebody's got to make the attempt to get them onto the brute's back.'

'I'm afraid I shall have to pass on that one as your responsibility, Brigadier. Why, the fact is, sir, this is the first time I've been near enough a mule to examine one; and what I see I don't like. One touch of those hooves, and your Signals Officer will be a goner!'

He pointed to the hard, horny, narrow little feet, diamond-hard like flints and steel-shod. The animal under inspection shifted uneasily as if kicking was much on his mind.

Lentaigne sighed long-sufferingly and glanced obliquely through his steel-rimmed spectacles at Masters. Masters glanced obliquely at me.

'Is there something you want? Are you looking at me?' I asked ingenuously.

'That's right!' they replied in chorus.

'Are you having me on?'

'Absolutely not!' said Lentaigne. 'We simply want someone to supervise loading these radio sets.'

'Good heavens!' I replied. 'Is that all? I thought you wanted something serious!'

I was astonished at their diffidence.

Briggo gave me an appreciative stare. He obviously considered that my being a candidate for martyrdom and subsequent canonization made me more palatable. The three of them exchanged guilty looks.

'I'm sure it will be perfectly all right and you'll be able to load up easily,' the Brigadier responded encouragingly, with the chilling kindliness that freezes the blood. 'Jack here tells me you're a mountain gunner and I know from experience how competent they are with pack animals.'

'Please sir,' I begged. 'Don't expect miracles. Something may go wrong, for, after all, I've been away from Mountain Artillery for more than a year. All the same, I promise you I'll do my best. I don't see why we couldn't accustom this mule, or – if not her – then some other, to carry the radio sets.'

'Mighty good of you!' he responded amicably.

'Will eleven o'clock do? I've one or two routine duties I ought to attend to. After that, I shall be at your service.'

'Certainly, certainly,' they replied eagerly.

'Take her away, then,' I said to the mule-driver. 'Have her back here about eleven!'

This conversation succeeded in breaking up my concentration on my duties. Grateful for the momentary reprieve before being sucked into the daily routine, I glanced around. This was the first occasion for over a year that I had been under canvas and out in the open. It was glorious to be communing again with nature. I sniffed up the scents, savouring their freshness and the ravishing smells of herb and shrub. I gulped down the early morning air, so different now at sun-up to the heavy damp air during the downpour of the previous evening which had imparted so joyless a flavour to my induction.

Sparklets of moisture were scintillating on every grasslet, and the sun was flooding the forest glade with light. A mist was rising from the ground in humid heaps and the sun's rays were plunging through.

The spell was broken by the unmistakable stink of a military jakes drifting into my nostrils.

I changed course abruptly. I was captivated by the prospect of fifteen minutes' private prayer before starting my duties, and searched out that little hessian enclosure discreetly set aside for the use of officers.

It was enchantingly placed, charmingly remote, and concealed from observation by a profusion of pink-and-orange flowered *lantana* in pink-and-orange perfection. It consisted of a huge trench. Already at this early hour – for the sun was not yet decently risen – great bluebottles were landing in it with resounding thuds, and from its dark depths, cooled a long age in the deep delved earth, a distant but diffused roar was issuing from a disturbed hive. Despite the liberally sprinkled doses of lime about its lip, some of the largest and most determined flies I had ever seen were rooting about among the rotting turds like rutting elephants tearing at teak logs. As I sat down and disturbed them, they rose up, brushing my bare bottom with the soft patter of their tiny wings, and zoomed off towards the side-lines.

Occasionally during the day, while pursuing your lawful avocations in other parts of the camp, you might look up and observe them – these passaging bluebottles like swarms of migratory swallows – in the very act of crossing the desolate places between one protein-rich play-ground and another. Extraordinarily enough they neither inconvenienced nor disturbed us.

All the same, I couldn't help but subsequently ask the doc.

'Isn't it unhealthy?'

'Not a bit of it. No self-respecting bluebottle is going to abandon all that lovely, fresh shit in favour of these filthy mess sausages.'

On this first occasion, with trousers remorselessly entangled around my ankles, I was struggling to perch on the whittled, white *sal* pole which was the only provision for comfort, when I heard footsteps approaching through the mud. I had become vitiated with luxury at the Camouflage School and so was unused to such interruptions. I was just at the point of proportional balance and about to launch into the orison of the day from the Book of Common Prayer, so I was incapable of flight. In stalked the Brigadier.

He dropped his trousers without the bat of an eye. It completely ruined the set canticle. Something of my frustration must have imparted itself to him. He turned to me politely and with exquisite solicitousness enquired, 'Do I disturb you?' as if asking after my health.

'Not at all, sir. Absolutely delighted!'

***

Not in the best of humour after this encounter, I resumed my attempt to achieve the animal transport lines and put in an appearance at the morning *malish*.

This, I ought to explain, is a ritual levée according to a standardised, traditional pattern. It is scrupulously observed wherever a unit occupies itself with animal transport. *Malish* is the Urdu word ordinarily used for sausage, but in this context it refers to grooming. The attendance of an officer elevates the event into something like an act of Divine Worship. I decided to put in a formal personal appearance and thereby give my new charges an opportunity of getting used to me.

When I arrived at the mule lines I was astonished by what I found.

They were performing – could it have been for my special benefit? – with a verve that would have done credit to a band of dancing-boys. Indeed it was such an overt display of concupiscence that I concluded that they had guessed my sexual proclivities and were putting on this show with the object of testing or tantalising me.

A cast of thousands, or so it seemed to my over-eager impressionability, was hammering away at the climatic number – although I could not make up my mind whether they represented Eleusinian *mystae* or Bachic celebrants. They were accompanied by the entire complement of Brigade Headquarters defence platoon as chorus.

They were almost naked. Some – with the exception of their huge military boots and their regulation ball-cloth of wrestler or *sadhu* – were completely so. They were of many sizes. Some were tall and willowy like the Long Elizas of Chinese porcelain. Others had hollow, concave chests but massive thighs and huge calves. Others again displayed the squat, pugnacious physique associated with load-carrying coolies.

They came, moreover, in all varieties of colour, from the milky white of cottage cheese, through creamy Camembert, to rude Cheshire with its russet, rustic red. They looked good enough to eat.

I swallowed convulsively. The undisciplined screams from tortured taste-buds were rising, and I glanced apprehensively about to see if anyone had noticed; but they seemed sublimely unaware that a monster of depravity had penetrated their paradise. The scene was disarmingly innocent. It was as if there had never existed a Puritan conscience this side of Eden.

The mules were standing about, tethered to shrub and tree. I was appalled to notice that they had not been cleaned. I pointed at the dirty organ of one of the mules and shouted at the boy who stood nearest – he could not have been more than sixteen.

'Here! Clean that down! Fetch a bucket of water!'

'*Hussoor* (excellency)!' he said, in token of assent, leaping smartly to grab a bucket. He made as if to dash off, apparently tickled to death to be singled out for this unattractive service.

'Hold on a minute!' I shouted after him, on impulse. 'Come back!'

He returned, crestfallen, and stood before me, a picture of dejection.

'I'm sorry,' I said. 'I didn't mean to shout at you. I only wanted to know your name. You see, this is my first *malish*. You're the first rifleman I've spoken to.'

He positively beamed.

'Dal Bahadur, *huzzoor sahib*, Chettri.'

It was quite irregular for whoever had been in charge of the mules to have allowed them to remain in this condition. Their pricks should have been washed and dressed and tucked away out of sight long since. I called, accordingly, for the offending havildar, in order to deliver the appropriate dressing-down. He was of the very highest caste, a fair-skinned *thakur* named Thaman Bahadur. I expressed my disapproval of the mules' condition in no uncertain terms – after all, an officer has to find something wrong when he takes over command from a previous incumbent!

He rasped out an order at the top of his voice. His face betrayed no sign of pique. Indeed it was without change of expression. All the boys seized buckets as Dal Bahadur had done, and rushed off with them into the jungle to fill them at the famous Brigade Headquarters filthy pond.

Within the space of seconds they were back.

Immediately they set to cleaning down the less attractive parts of the mules' anatomy. They did this with such care and detail that I felt a fool for ever having mentioned the subject. I began to suspect that I was deliberately being made to look ridiculous. So I would have been, had they been Sikhs, but not with Gurkhas, who are without malice.

'For Heaven's sake,' I blurted out to Thaman Bahadur. 'That's enough, I beg of you! I'm sorry I ever mentioned it. I don't want them to make an exhibition of it.'

The mules were squealing and bucking and kicking. The Gurkhas were squirting with barely suppressed giggles. The manoeuvre was being accomplished with a torrid commentary. Moreover the place reeked to such an extent of ammonia fumes exhaled from the mule-piss and the horse-dung – and everybody was in such high good humour – that I sought to dampen down these excessively high spirits. I dreaded that the Brigadier might put in an appearance and demand to know the cause of the confusion. He would probably attribute it to my inability to keep order.

'Please, Thaman Bahadar,' I pleaded. 'You've had your revenge and I feel thoroughly chastened. Now do try and get your men at least to look a little more serious. This is intended to be a fatigue. They are not supposed to be enjoying it!'

'Huzzoor!' he assented sternly, the gleam of a smile dawning tentatively across his wooden features as he realised that I was being funny. He barked out another order, and the smiles on the faces of his men disappeared on the instant.

By now it seemed as if I might be establishing, unsteadily, some sort of moral ascendancy. The Gurkhas were all at their tasks, brushing down and grooming away assiduously – some of them were so diminutive that they could scarcely reach up to put on a head-halter – and the muted hum of a disciplined and controlled activity began to make itself apparent. It was like the purr of a precise and perfectly maintained piece of machinery. I began to feel rather self-satisfied, as if I had adjusted it all by myself.

Thaman Bahadur and I were strolling back and forth, deeply engrossed in the problem of which mule to select for the Brigadier's demonstration. Suddenly an impish face popped over the back of a mule and gave me the most decided, diabolically impudent young wink. Before I could respond, it disappeared behind the mules – we had passed by in our perambulations, and Thaman Bahadur was engaging my attention. I was so astonished that I wondered momentarily whether I had been the victim of a hallucination.

17

I reacted to it by finding myself completely and unpredictably committed. It has not generally been my good fortune to be on the receiving end of such an unmistakable come-hither signal, and it bound me with bonds as unequivocally as a magical invocation.

I got rid of Thaman Bahadur as quickly as I could, and returned palpitating to the place where I had been propositioned.

The men all had their heads tucked into the mules' flanks, brushing and blowing away furiously. I could not for the life of me detect which one of them it had been. Who had dared distinguish me with that discreet, dashing, disengaged sign? Whoever it was, he was obviously not risking revealing himself again. I deliberately went around the near side of each mule to see if I could get a diagonal view of the culprit.

No luck! Still, I am practically certain it must be *that* one! I decided to sail close inshore and risk coming to grief on the rocks. If my challenger could be provocative, I too could be daring.

Now, if there is one thing I am confident of performing correctly, it is the grooming routine according to the traditional formula of a stable. I had always maintained a horse of my own and I had been scrupulously drilled by a succession of grooms in the strict techniques of looking after it. Consequently I can pick up a brush and walk into a grooming session with confidence.

I did so now, trusting to God that I had picked on the right fellow.

'Here, Comrade, hand me that brush!'

The young man withdrew his head from beneath the mule's belly and slowly straightened up. His face wore that self-conscious, slightly bemused smile which I later learnt betokened uncertainty. He was obviously expecting to be reprimanded.

'Good heavens!' I exclaimed. 'It's Dal Bahadur!'

'So his excellency recognises me!'

'Who,' I said, taking the brush and curry-comb from him and fumbling embarrassedly with handfuls of fingers, 'could ever forget you?'

He had not expected this! My simple, out-of-hand acceptance evidently baffled him. He said nothing and contented himself with looking mysterious.

Presently I plucked up the courage to blurt out, 'Did you wink?'

'What?' he replied, with a show of imperturbability.

'Did you wink at me just now – as I passed by, I mean – as I passed by with Thaman Bahadur?'

'So!' he hissed with a pretence of passion. 'That's what they're up to!'

'W-w-what?'

'The shameless young riflemen are making eyes at his excellency – and his excellency is flirting with them!'

'Certainly not,' I declared. 'It was nothing like that.'

I got under the mule's belly and put in some devoted work with my brush. Dal Bahadur maintained a discreet silence.

'Well, did you?' presently I persisted. 'Did you?'

He adopted such an equivocal attitude, it was hardly removed from coquetry!

'Would it have displeased his excellency if I did?'

'No,' I said, 'certainly not,' adding as an afterthought, '*Sulti!*' This was a Gurkhali term which I had heard the Gurkhas using on the North-West Frontier. 'If you had winked at me, I should certainly have been flattered.'

'So you dare call me that!' he responded almost explosively, his eyes sparkling like planets.

'If it has offended you, I'm sorry.'

'It is very intimate,' he said. 'Perhaps his excellency doesn't understand. It is only used between lovers.'

He looked suddenly shy and bashful.

'His excellency is surely making a mock of me.'

***

It was soon eleven o'clock.

Gossip about my forthcoming trial by ordeal seemed to have seeped out to the entire training establishment. Word of it had been brought to the mule-lines by the muleteer whom I had told to return at the eleventh hour for the demonstration. That was even before I put in an appearance at the morning *malish*, where I had my first experience of commanding my Defence Platoon Gurkhas and when, under my orders, they had playfully washed down the mules. I had distinctly caught one of them, Dal Bahadur, giving me a wink.

Muleteers and defence platoon riflemen were drifting in from every quarter, in ones and twos, like rustics towards a country fair. They cautiously examined the pitch as they passed with the discrimination of a selection committee or a long-established Board of Governors. They added such an exaggerated aura of unconcern to the elaborately constructed excuses with which they bolstered their airs of injured innocence when challenged, that it was well-nigh impossible not to be disarmed by their manner as well as half-deceived by their transparent cunning.

But I felt sufficiently radiant and relaxed to be generous towards my public. I did not feel inclined to insist that admission was only by invitation. The Brigadier and his consorts arrived to a fanfare of trumpets and processed to the royal box. A casual signal would start the entertainment.

The scene was set. The sky had cleared. The clouds had momentarily vanished. The sun beat down with abrasive candour. I retired to my corner calmly enough, as befitted a famous animal-tamer. I wanted to await completion of the various formalities before launching into the final flourish.

In that noonday silence – the hour sacred to Pan – when every living creature had retreated to the shelter of whatever shade was available and where, in the villages, the pie-dogs lay panting in the shelter of the walls, prostrate with exhaustion, the activity within the Brigade Headquarters encampment area could not but strike an observer like myself, who had been able to withdraw slightly from it, as having a perverse aspect. It went contrary to the dictates of nature.

It was indeed difficult to deny that such activity exemplified, in the most unflattering manner, that obstinate cussedness of mankind, who insists on imposing his personal will on circumstances, no matter how inopportune they are, while relaxed nature walks her own unaided way into the shade and accommodates herself to the fact that sleep is the only answer to climatic inclemency.

In front of me, in the little jungle clearing where the contest was to take place, Havildar (Sergeant) Thaman Bahadur was arranging the loads on the ground with the help of the four tallest riflemen – selected on that account from the defence platoon in order to be able to reach up to mule height. They looked a bit lost in the full blaze of the sun. The perspiration was pouring from under their hats on account of their shaven heads, so it is hardly surprising that they were not enthusing over their work. I abandoned my place in the shade to saunter over to see if my presence could inject a bit of enthusiasm.

I suddenly wanted to make a howling success of it. The demonstration was, after all, designed to prove my mastery of men and animals.

I had from the beginning always been somewhat mystified by the sense of daring which accompanied this simple operation. The movement to be completed was the easiest in the Mountain Artillery drill book. It was one which my Sikh gunners could have performed a dozen times in a dozen minutes without considering themselves in the least dashing.

It consisted of selecting two loads of approximately equal size and exactly equal weight – in this case, the radio transmitter and its generator, or perhaps a couple of boxes of accumulators – and placing them on the ground with a space between them. The mule would then be led into this space like a ship into dock, so that, as soon as the order was given, the loads could be hoisted up and hooked simultaneously on either side of the pack-harness. 'Simultaneously' was the operative word, for of course if one side was loaded earlier than the other, the unbalanced weight – something in the nature of 280lbs, if I remember rightly – would hopelessly disarrange the pack-saddle and greatly upset the mule. It had to be a swift, swinging, co-ordinated, concerted movement on the part of the men, two each to a load.

Mules, being unable to speak, have only one method of expressing their disapproval – to kick their load, and sometimes their muleteers and mule-loaders, to pieces.

Given a simulacrum of simultaneity, however, and the whole operation was dead easy. The muleteer simply had to stand at the head of the mule, with his two hands on either side of the snaffle and the reins looped loosely over this arm, ready to throw himself into the mule's path if it should show signs of bolting.

Smartly I assembled my little squad and told them all this. They were singularly unresponsive. Being the tallest among the riflemen seemed to have taken everything else out of them. I wondered, after all, whether I had been right to be so self-confident.

One of them, Rifleman Agam Singh, appeared so listless that regretfully I had to replace him as being constitutionally unsuitable. I called in, instead a sturdy, sombre-browed, dark-skinned young lance-corporal called Shiv Jung.

At the last minute, evidently sensing my disquiet about the men, Havildar Tulbir Gurung took the place of lance corporal Tej Bahadur Gurung, and Havildar Ganga Bahadur took the place of Rifleman Bhim Bahadur. Then Havildar Thaman Bahadur suddenly stepped forward and took the position which was being competed for by Riflemen Gopal Bahadur Rai and Man Bahadur Limbu – a pair of boy-inseparables whom nobody would dream of parting from each other.

With the exception of Shiv Jung, I recognized that I was left with a detachment of havildars. It was rather disconcerting, as it always is when top people stoop to menial labour.

Stifling my disquiet, I sent for the mule. She turned out to be a great big placid creature with a velvety muzzle and docile eyes – or such was the impression which registered on the surface. It was at this point in the proceedings, however that I received my first protest from the subconscious: it was not going to go well; I had been too sanguine about the outcome.

The mule gave me a look full of indignation which only too plainly indicated what she intended. She resented being disturbed at this noon-tide hour for a detachment of havildars and she did not intend to put up with it, not even if his excellency the captain-sahib himself should personally take control of the lead reins.

How strange that she should have expressed herself thus intuitively! When she arrived on the scene, I had already decided I could not in all conscience further postpone taking part personally in the demonstration. I advanced, accordingly, in order to take up the position of first muleteer and key mule-driver.

Looking back on the event, the temptation to suspect some sort of secret conspiracy between the havildars for my discomfiture is very compelling. However, I absolve them from any complicity. What they did, I am convinced, was done out of simple sense of duty. It was just unfortunate that the incident did not turn out better.

The five of us adopted a position of readiness, and I glanced guardedly towards the Brigadier. He nodded. I said 'Up!' tersely, and the men doubled themselves over the loads and straightened up, elastically flinging the 280lb boxes acrobatically into the air. There was a cavernous clunk as the hooks engaged and the mule stood there, slightly staggering, with approximately 600 lbs of radio equipment in the saddle.

If ever I saw an expression of amazement come over an animal's face, I saw it then. It was replaced by an expression of consternation, followed by one of resentment, finally malice. She obviously thought we were going to get the better of her and get away with it.

'Steady on, old girl; it can't be as bad as that!'

My remark was entirely inadequate as an attempt to calm her. She let out an outraged squeal of protest and immediately started bucking.

It was all up. Once they do that, the loads flop up and down against their sides, encouraging them to even greater demonstrations of resentment, and the process does not stop until they have disposed of everything.

'Look out!' I yelled to the havildars. 'It's all up with us!'

I motioned them to move aside as the loads began to come adrift like the shifting cargo on a sinking liner.

'Take care; she'll end up getting you!'

She had started off with a little kick – nothing more than a girlish caper. Having done this two or three times and in this manner satisfied herself of what she was capable, she really let fly with her heels. A sod of impacted earth shot off from her hooves and hit the Brigadier in the midriff. I too was forced to abandon ship, for once you have gazed into a mule's mouth with her lips turned back you lose all stomach for closer acquaintance.

Presently the radio set was sent flying into the air to a groan of dismay from Briggo and the uncompensated-for load on the other side pulled the pack-harness loose until it slipped down past her ribs where it simple lowered itself in a dignified manner to the ground and then fell off, leaving the mule standing with the harness underneath her belly, grinning slightly with those great big yellow teeth of hers, but otherwise without an ounce of malice.

I approached her cautiously and repossessed myself of the reins. Thaman Bahadur loosened her girths and between them the havildars readjusted the pack-harness. She made barely a move, nor hee-haw, nor whinny, nor neigh of protest.

'Well!' said Briggo dispiritedly, 'I suppose that settles it!'

'Not at all!' interposed Lentaigne.

'Then what do we do now?'

'We simply try again.'

'I don't know' said Briggo dubiously, 'if my sets will stand up to this hammering.'

'I don't see why not!' exclaimed the Brigadier tartly. 'That's what they've been designed for.'

'Again?' I queried.

'Again,' nodded the Brigadier.

'Are we ready?' I asked the others.

'Yes, ready sahib! Yes, ready!'

'Up!'

'Clunk' went the loads as they engaged on the hooks. The pack harness creaked disquietingly. The mule stood her ground, absolutely still. I was not deceived, however, by her absence of movement. I noticed in those eyes an unnerving glint of intelligence, denoting a brain as calculating as any chess player's.

Quite deliberately yet unhurriedly she began to kick. It was not the panic reaction of a confused beast. It was the result of complicated processes of mature logic. She was, moreover, big. Doubtless all her muleteers had been as terrified of her as I was. It must have given her considerable confidence.

Suddenly her face registered a most marked change of expression. She changed her tactics. She decided to bolt. It was something which I had not the slightest intention of allowing.

'Hang on to her!' the others were shouting. 'Hang on to her!'

She started off by adopting the short trot. It consists of head erect, ears pricked, eyes blazing. It is always indicative of an obstinate, angry mule on a rampage, and I was too familiar with the symptoms from my time in Mountain Artillery to want further demonstration of them. At the last moment, it is true, Thaman Bahadur flung himself at her head-harness in a desperate attempt to stave off disaster, but she shook him off.

I put both arms around her neck affectionately, raised my feet from the ground and curled them across her withers, and dedicated myself either to our dying together or to my going down with the ship.

There is no doubt that the position I adopted must have had a singularly constricting effect on her freedom of movement. It was evident immediately that she had decided on a strategy for ditching me.

She made straight for a thorny bush. I, on the other hand, having my back to her line of direction, could not see what was coming. But by this time I was committed. I was faced with the alternative either of hanging on and taking the consequences, or of falling off and foundering beneath those flailing hooves, which would not scruple to kick me to pieces. Naturally I hung on.

She went through that bush like one of those automatic, armoured, mine-exploding floggers they used to employ for clearing paths through mine-fields in the Western Desert. It neatly ripped every stitch of clothing off me.

I heard a gasp of awe go up from the spectators. Out of the corner of my eye I saw Lentaigne and Briggo start in my direction with a jerk of dismay but Masters, I recall, remained as indifferent as if watching a professional circus.

For my part, I simply surrendered myself to the rhythm of the ride and to keeping my arms round her neck and my feet round her shoulders. I could rely upon the fact that, with a 600lb weight on her back and me draped round her foreparts, it was not going to be easy for her to continue to be sprightly.

True enough, quite soon I noticed that she was flagging. She had done enough damage, God knows, what with my hat hanging on one branch and the remainder of my clothing on another. Now I felt reasonably secure she would be content to surrender her independence. She might legitimately give up without in any sense comprising her integrity.

24

Both my short puttees were also unravelling from around my ankles and eventually what I had vaguely feared – or hoped for – happened. She got them entangled around her legs.

She faltered; recovered; faltered again; and then came down on her knees and her nose with such a bang that she precipitated me several yards in front of her. Her load came off her back and bowled forward like a Barnes Wallis bouncing bomb and came spinning towards me on steel reinforced corners until it came to rest, with stunning numbness, on my already much lacerated right fore-arm. I didn't feel it. The whole limb had simply gone dead like frozen mutton.

Briggo, Lentaigne, Masters, Thaman Bahadur and the rest now arrived. They had tracked me with Red Indian cunning by means of my trail of torn rags. They found me sitting on the radio set with the reins already gathered in my hand (it is needless to state that they were broken). The creature and I were gazing darkly into each other eyes, having somehow arrived at a deeper level of comprehension.

'Load up!' I managed to say crisply, as the rest of the team staggered up.

She had had enough. Her flanks were heaving, her big was champed, her neck was flecked with foam and her nostrils were red and distended.

'Quickly!' I said impatiently, fearful lest she might recover her spirit of waywardness.

But she had absolutely and finally submitted.

They loaded the radio set and the generator awkwardly enough and she made not a movement of protest.

I handed the reins to the muleteer. 'Lead her away.'

'Are you OK?' people now asked.

I knew what was in their minds, without their telling me. My fellow officers were beginning to wonder, ashamedly, whether I might not perhaps be a little better than, or at any rate not quite so awful as, on first acquaintanceship they had imagined.

Early one morning about a week later, Brigade Headquarters set out. The other columns had left several days previously and we were to rendezvous with them at a spot two hundred miles distant and there fight out a mock battle – two of our columns out of the four having been detailed to act as enemy.

It was to be an exercise to end all exercises, designed not only to test the radio communications and set up new frequencies, but also to weed out every unassimilable element. I prayed that I might not be one of them. During the interval since my mishap with the mule, my injured arm had deteriorated to such an extent that I wondered whether I possessed the stamina to put up with the pain and inconvenience.

The previous night I had been assailed by self-doubt, coupled with an onset of fever which I imagined to be a recurrence of the malarial attack I had sustained while on the North-West Frontier, but which was actually caused by the tissue-damage inflicted by that transmitter falling on top of me. It had been a night of such electrifying bone-ache that I felt as if I was being hung, drawn and mentally tortured.

Now, as dawn seeped across the sky and penetrated the phantom-ridden corners of my tent, I welcomed its advent with renewed courage. I raised my fever-grizzled head, sweat-saturated, from its pillow, gingerly nursing my inflamed limb. It would be up to me to take full advantage of this opportunity for 'making myself useful', as Masters had demanded, and I was determined that no mere physical handicap should prevent me exploiting it. I was hell bent on achieving the coveted distinction of becoming a recognized member of 111 Brigade, come what might.

I dragged my body from off the palliasse and staggered out into the light. The effort was so great that I almost capitulated. The thought of a clean hospital bed was undeniably tempting. As I walked past the medical unit, however, I determinedly rejected all inclination to succumb.

A convoy of transport was lined up along the roadside and squads of demented Rice Corps (RIASC) sepoys were defiantly demolishing our tents and piling them feverishly into the backs of lorries. It was the last we should see of them, or our beds.

I paused for a moment to watch the medical marquee come tumbling down. Doc Whyte appeared to be away at breakfast, but I was astonished to see Dal Bahadur securely established there.

He was sitting on top of one of the ready-packed *yakdans* (square leather boxes), exchanging the time of day with the Gurkha medical orderly who had been left behind on duty.

It seemed like one of those fortuitous occasions which cannot be entirely dismissed as coincidence. A shudder of joy shot through me. I saw that I could turn the moment to my advantage.

The pair of them, fair-skinned and fine-boned as delicately featured porcelain figures, looked like wayward children pitilessly evicted by a ruthless landlord. They jumped and saluted me.

'What on earth are you doing here?' I smiled.

'I'm just here, sahib,' replied my little friend (for such I can hardly avoid calling him), 'to help Krishna Bahadur with the medical *yakdans.*'

If I could engage his sympathy, this would be an opportunity of utilising this friendship with Doc Whyte's medical orderly to cadge some pain-killing drugs while the doctor was absent.

'I don't suppose you could help me!'

He smiled back at me extraordinarily sweetly. Dumbly I exposed my gangrenous limb.

It was a dreadful wound and stank horribly. At the sight of it, he went as white as a sheet. His huge brown eyes clouded with concern instantly. Wordlessly I put myself at his mercy. I supplicated him with joined palms like a professional beggar. We all three remained thus mute while he and the medical orderly examined the swollen flesh but scrupulously avoided touching it. Suddenly he took the pulsating member between both of his hands with incomparable gentleness. Shivers of anguish like tongues of molten flame shot up and down the surface of my skin. A rainbow appeared amongst the shimmering globes of St. Elmo's fire, followed by a peacock; then a salamander; finally, the twelve apostles.

Then I raised my head, and we gazed at each other as if we had been together been through some massively traumatic experience. He was dripping as much sweat as much as I was.

'You'll have to come back and show it to the colonel-sahib.' His words sounded dull and inadequate.

'If only,' I replied, 'you could wangle me some pain-killers!'

He glanced depreciatively towards the *yakdans* and made fluttering gestures in thir direction.

'They're packed up,' he said, as if they had contained an imprisoned spirit or bottled djinn.

I sank dispiritedly to the ground, depleted by pain, frustration and disappointment.

Before I had time to despair, however, his defences suddenly collapsed. He threw himself down beside me and his fingers explored the locks of the *yakdans* as if he would release them through very urgency.

'The keys!' he murmured desperately. 'They're with the colonel-sahib. He's having his breakfast.'

'Go and get them, both of you! Say someone wants some headache powders.'

In my insistence, I leaned towards him. He was gnawing his knuckles. I grasped him, with my hands incongruously placed on his delicate shoulder-blades. I felt his limbs articulating loosely beneath the pressure of my exploring fingers. Turning him around, I gave him a gentle shove.

They trotted off as obediently as little boys.

While they were away, I probed the lump under my right armpit, and gloomy thoughts began to circulate. Then Krishna Bahadur returned. Without further ado he opened a *yakdan* and gave me from his bountiful store a boxful of blissful pills – enough to have kept me high for the whole exercise. I downed three of them in an instant.

Brigade Headquarters loaded up and moved out. I stood at the side of the track and shielded my eyes against the rising sun while the long line of muleteers – some grinning facetiously – filed past me. I was watching to see if I could intercept a signal from Dal Bahadur. As he went past, he shot me an ambiguous glance. It was too cryptic to be susceptible of interpretation.

To all intents and purposes that ends everything I am able to recall about that exercise. Of course I was found out. After flogging up hill and down dale in a haze of pain and rugs for the best part of a fortnight, I finally collapsed and was carted off to hospital and given a scolding for having improperly manipulated those pills out of Doc Whyte's medical orderly. Indeed Doc Whyte was so cross that he threatened to have me court-martialled.

Dal Bahadur remained behind and I received no news, during that trying period, of what had happened to him.

I was away in hospital, and recuperating on sick leave, for a couple of months. I was lucky with my arm, for I narrowly missed having it amputated. There had been an evening in Lucknow when the surgeons had decided to cut it off. That same night, by an extraordinary stroke of good fortune, it began discharging its purulent matter. On the following morning, the inflammation was so reduced as to make draconian measures unnecessary.

# CHAPTER THREE

# Ready for War

I returned to active duty, keenly anticipating a joyful reunion.

I found that the situation with regard to 111 Brigade was completely changed. When I left, we had been an enterprising, talented, autonomous force with an amateurish predisposition towards extemporisation. Wingate had not had time to hammer home his message. On my rejoining the Brigade (it must have been towards the end of October) he had cemented his influence with Churchill at the Roosevelt conference in Quebec, and building on that astonishing success, he had turned everything to do with long-range penetration into a larger dimension.

The new scheme was to form a Chindit division under Wingate's operational control comprising upwards of 23,000 men. Wingate was promoted to Major General. Not only had he succeeded in prising this huge number of men out of the nerveless control of GHQ, but he had also obtained the use of a sort of private air force.

Joe Lentaigne was not unnaturally aghast at having his independent command snatched away from him. Nevertheless, I took the trouble to reassure myself that this reorganisation met with the wholehearted support of all hands.

The positive influence Wingate was having was convincingly demonstrated within half-an-hour of my arrival. The Brigade was undergoing a series of joint inter-column exercises near Jhansi. For this purpose, the columns were grouped fairly closely into a single catchment area round the shores of a considerable lake.

Brigade Headquarters was encamped where the road from Jhansi ran across the large embankment, called Dukma Dam, which held back this body of water. I was being driven to this rendezvous from Jhansi station by an attached British Service Corps private of indeterminate vintage who was not even a Chindit.

About fifteen miles from our objective, where the road entered an area of dense, virtually untrodden jungle, he suddenly announced: 'We are now entering 26 Column's and 90 Column's training area!' This observation he volunteered quite chattily. I thought he was making a factual statement, like a tour-operator's courier commenting on a noteworthy locality. I was on the point of framing a suitably non-committal response when it occurred to me that perhaps the remark was intended as a warning.

This suspicion was no sooner formulated than vindicated. A couple of shots rang out, followed by several others. A bullet tore through the truck's tarpaulin cover.

My driver immediately pulled the vehicle off the road and drew to a shuddering halt. Then he threw himself onto the floorboards. I thought we were being attacked by dacoits.

'It's only a party of Cameronians out hunting, sir!' he explained, in deference to my terrified expression. 'Last Wednesday they bagged a village water buffalo. The corporal in charge of the detail's a real wild man. He said he thought it was a wildebeest, but it didn't prevent him having to pay fifty rupees in compensation. I only hope they don't contrive to shoot the sacred cows in their enthusiasm – not to speak of the benighted peasants!'

'Will we get compensation if they kill us?' I asked feebly, though feeling decidedly hollow in the pit of my stomach.

'Come with me, sir,' said the driver, 'and I won't let you down!'

It was as if he had taken me under his personal supervision. His eyes were spitting hostile impulses like snapping dogs and in his excitement he practically knocked me senseless with a blow of his elbow to the solar plexus.

'Let's give 'em a confrontation. The General takes an interest in a bit of a scuffle!'

Not knowing in the least what was expected of me – for it was an entirely novel experience – I mutely contented myself with imitating his example. He grabbed a light machine-gun which lay conveniently to hand in the cab of the vehicle, leapt with it into the ditch and crammed fistfuls of live ammunition into the magazine.

I joined him in the ditch. Having myself only just returned from a sort of peacetime establishment, I was unprepared to withstand a siege and not even in possession of a stick.

My companion, undaunted by the presence of an officer at his side to witness his outrageous acts of insubordination, proceeded to discharge burst after burst into the jungle in a display of spirited animosity.

I watched while the scalded leaves trembled in the wake of the white-hot trajectory of his tracer bullets. Complete silence followed. It was as if the forest had been struck dumb by his boldness.

'You've killed them.'

'Not a bit of it,' he complained bitterly. 'Wish I had. Them bastards need teaching a lesson!'

Suddenly I heard a crashing and crackling as of a huge, charging rhinoceros.

'Don't shoot!' I shouted, preparing to run away at the first gleam of bayonet.

I had intended the injunction for my driver. It was taken up instead by our 'opposing forces'.

'Hey!' apostrophised an aggrieved voice, surprisingly close at hand and with a pronounced Gorbals twang to it. 'Watch out what yairr doin' wull yer! That came near me goolies!'

A pale and emaciated face, lean and freckly and surrounded by a ruff of vivid hair which made it look like a recently evolved breed of dog at Cruft's, emerged from behind some tufts of greenery.

'We saw yairr comin',' it announced ecstatically. 'Yairr-r-r ambushed – that's what yairr!'

It then proceeded to perform a sort of tribal dance, similar to the dance I have seen captive storks perform when tantalized by a waving handkerchief.

Finally it threw itself onto the grass verge. It was followed by the remainder of its patrol, their battle-dresses black with sweat, who proceeded to roll and smoke cigarettes unconcernedly.

'What about me flaming tarpaulin!' raged the driver at them. 'What'm I goin' ter tell me fuckin' officer? Yer thinks it's bloody funny, but this is the second time I copped yer friggin' bullet!'

Then he suddenly dropped his voice confidentially, and demanded, 'Any luck?'

The Cameronian corporal glanced at me with extreme distaste and said 'Nay!' with such finality that it was quite obvious the driver would not get anything more out of him.

'It's all right,' continued the driver in a tone of revolting sweetness. 'This officer would never breathe a word.'

Then he turned to me.

'They generally have a little buck, sir. And of course, I sometimes do them the favour of giving them a lift. Yer see, it's worth a joint a' venison for me and me mates. But this time they ain't gonna trust me. Makes yer sick!'

He spat contemptuously.

'Come on then!' he suddenly yelled at them. 'Jump in! I ain't helping yer! Anyway, he's only seconded to Brigades Headquarters.'

It seemed as if this frank admission of my fearful inadequacy would qualify me for membership of their club; and of course it did.

They fetched the deer they had shot, bundled themselves into the back of the truck without further comment, and we dropped them off at their column headquarters.

As we approached Dukma Dam, where was located the nerve centre of this huge concentration of men and weapons, the sight of much purposeful activity astonished us.

First, my attention was drawn towards the sky where the sun was setting in extravagant splendour. Then I looked at the earth, already darkening under lengthening shadows. Finally, I turned to the lake, which lay pallid in the plangent light like polished pewter.

A curious old-fashioned biplane was coming in to land on an improvised airstrip. It was cruising to get up wind. Its First World War silhouette stood out against the peach-pink sky. It was being flagged down by a stocky individual in shorts and a singlet stretched tight across his huge chest, who was plainly recognisable as Chesty Jennings.

A jeep was racing up with frantic haste to come alongside as the plane landed, every so often leaping bodily into the air as it accelerated over a bump, and as it did so, bouncing another item of priceless equipment out of the back – for the strip had only recently been hacked from the paddy-fields by our riflemen using their entrenching tools, and it was still rough and uneven.

My driver had meanwhile pulled our truck up at the top of the dam. From such a vantage point, although I had been all too long absent, the Jehu in the jeep was easily identifiable. That crooked, intent posture, those blazing eyes, that hawkish profile, those smashed-in teeth accentuating the tendency towards nutcracker – all would have been unmistakable even without the red bank on the battered hat which proclaimed its owner's status.

Joe Lentaigne was characteristically indulging his reckless passion for jeep driving and handling the vehicle as if it were Ben Hur's chariot.

Through an open glade to my right a tired patrol from 46 Column was trudging wearily home to camp. They bore slung on a pole between them a deer, trussed up as professionally as by Sioux hunters. I watched as their mates swarmed out of their grass-thatched *bashas* (huts) to welcome them. Some scurried busily to and fro collecting firewood. Others honed knives, built hearths, prepared spits. Their waspish wit drifted up to me in caustic commentary.

Further off, a fatigue party was constructing a timber stockade to surround their camp. It was an exercise in utilising local techniques and materials *in extempore* and was intended as a corral for the little herd of milch-goats they had dubiously come by. They were methodically plunging the sharpened stakes into the portable brazier erected next to the farrier's anvil.

He, clad in his traditional leather apron and with a pair of tongs in one hand and a hammer in the other, was putting a redly glowing horseshoe to the near-fore of a piebald pony. Clang! Clang! Clang! The smell of its scorching hoof rose up like singeing feathers.

Within a reserved plot at the dam's foot, fenced with spiny buckthorn branches to protect it from the stolen goats, three detached British 'other ranks' and a corporal were cultivating a vegetable allotment. These dedicated gardeners had made the soil fertile by the liberal application of human muck which they dug from old solidified cesspits and dried like sulphur. In combination with prodigious quantities of horse dung, this manure had produced vegetables of unmanageable size and shape and of a hitherto unheard of grossness and coarseness. In the gathering dusk, the inky aubergines glowed like polished globules of purple enamel; they hung beneath the leaves like gigantic scrotums. The sinister convoluted tomatoes with their diabolical intestinal shapes looked like fruits of evil. On a fence of bamboo canes to the rear, the huge rioting vines of runner beans would have scared witless any Jack discovering their scimitar-shaped pods on his beanstalk.

Suddenly there sang out from the shore of the lake a cry for help. Everyone within earshot rushed thither.

A comrade was in difficulties. An over-adventurous angler, not satisfied with tiddlers, was wrestling with an enormous catfish. It was an ugly-looking, mammal-featured brute, thrashing away furiously about twenty yards from the bank. It had sought shelter in the shallows by running up the line and then getting itself entangled in quantities of mud-weed.

33

The fish had succeeded in quelling the inexperienced angler, whose yelps for help brought to the scene numerous men, who they threw themselves off the bank and into the water.

From the opposite shore half-a-dozen canoes had launched and were rapidly approaching. Their wet paddles glinted in the weakening sun like warning signals from flashing mirrors.

At the farther end of the lake, an outboard motor craft was manoeuvring, throwing up sheets of spray. Its revving engine sounded like a distant saw-mill. Several DUKW amphibious trucks, crammed with burnished brown bodies, were languidly practising some sort of assault landing or river crossing. They looked like miniature ships momentarily abstracted from an invading armada. Nearer at hand, the glistening heads of swimmers were bobbing up and down in the waves like glass floats.

While I was contemplating this crowded scene, there emerged into the lake from behind a projecting sand-spit a contraption – it was a kind of raft – which could only have been constructed by some Huckleberry Finn. It cruised slowly into view round the screening promontory. Propelled by two Red-Indian-brown protagonists who poled it dexterously forward, it carried plumb in its centre a little wooden hut from whose grass-thatched roof protruded a bent stove-pipe, picturesquely belching out smoke.

The sun had meanwhile set. It was the magic hour of the golden cow-dust. Through the shimmering haze kicked up by their hooves, the men were leading the mules down to water them at the lakeside. This was that twilight time, captured in dozens of devotional paintings of the subject and commemorated in song and story, when Shri Krishna and his cowherd companions lead their herds home from the forest. The acrid smell of horses bit into the nostrils with a pungent scent of embalmers' spices.

In the bat-haunted banyan tree at the water's edge, which harboured ghosts as well as fruit-sucking vampires, the flying foxes were already beginning to squeak and rustle. One by one, their huge bodies dropped heavily out of its branches and flapped lopingly off, to consummate a nightly tryst with the neighbouring jack-fruit trees.

Suddenly from a little temple whose *shikara* was just visible above a nearby mango-orchard, there burst forth the rough timbre of conch-shell horns and trumpets, accompanied by the melodious tintinnabulation of gongs and bells. The local pundit was celebrating the evening *arati*. His Hindu ritual spelt out for me, too, a message: namely that it was time for me to resume my duties.

Shouldering the pack which contained my few belongings, I marched down the slope of the dam to report my arrival to Jack Masters. He looked and behaved so exactly as he had on the first occasion of our meeting that I had difficulty in imagining he could even have moved from his chair.

'Oh!' he said indifferently, as soon as he caught sight of me. 'So it's you!' It was the sort of greeting that you might have given to a debt-collector. 'Glad you're back! Hope you're better!'

'Yes, sir! Reporting for duty, sir! Much better!'

'H-m-m-m!' he said, biting savagely into the end of a pencil. He looked ill and sallow and haggard. 'I want you to get down and deal with the defence platoons.'

He launched characteristically into a sequence of orders. The defence platoons had become perfectly unmanageable. A man called Frankie Turner, who was a Vetinerary Corps Major, had turned up to take charge of the animal transport. 'And I want *you*,' he concluded, fixing me with a gimlet eye that went right through me, 'to practise airdrop recovery, plus the disposition and the lighting of bonfires. Take your men out and do it several times a week, at night, in the jungle!'

'Yes, sir.'

'I'm quite pleased with you. You showed courage in carrying on as you did. I'm going to take you with me. You will be the Brigade Headquarters Orderly Officer. It's a controversial decision. Kindly see that I don't regret it!'

'Thank you, sir.'

Punch-drunk, I was just staggering out when he called me back.

'Oh, Baines, come 'ere. By the way.'

Something awful was coming – if I anticipated it rightly – and I was correct.

'I had to find a temporary orderly for one of the Rear Headquarters officers – I forget 'is name – so I detailed one of your riflemen. Thaman Bahadur'll tell you about it. 'Is name's – what is it – oh, yes – Dal Bahadur. But he'll be back before we go into action.'

'Mighty good of you!' I thought.

Imagine my consternation. What a homecoming! I could have wept from vexation of spirit.

One dazzling bright winter morning about the middle of December, our training suddenly came to an end. A group of column commanders abruptly put in an appearance at Brigade Headquarters, apparently summoned to an important conference.

'What's going on, d'you suppose?' I demanded uneasily of young Lawrence, a platoon commander whose sector abutted mine. It was so distantly located from his own Column Headquarters, however, that he was accommodated in our mess, and he had become my interpreter of the infantry outlook.

'They've come to report progress.'

'Progress towards what?'

'Well, if you want to know, they've come to report to the old Man the fact of our final preparedness. That's what my column commander told me.'

'You mean our training's over!' I exclaimed aghast.

'Looks like it.'

'We're ready for war?'

'You seem surprised.'

'To tell the truth, I hadn't even thought of it. I assumed we'd go on playing at soldiers for ever!'

'Not a hope,' he replied, smiling ruefully.

'Are you ready?'

He shrugged indifferently.

'I suppose so. One gets accustomed to the idea of being committed.'

The distinguished panel of column commanders filed into the mess-tent. Joe Lentaigne preceded them like a Lord Chancellor heading a procession of judges. It was planned to be an impressive ceremony, and it would have succeeded in being so, except for one tiny accompaniment.

A puckish fellow had started prowling through the camp. He was seeking to suborn the troops, and even incite them to acts of insubordination. Now he grasped the opportunity thus offered to spring recklessly into open mutiny.

The spirit of Christmas, that is to say, was abroad. None of us, however, could have guessed he would prove sufficiently daring to attack the senior officers. Imagine our surprise, therefore when he began dispelling the sombre atmosphere created by Joe Lentaigne and wrecking the gravity of the gathering.

After two or three hours of mounting conviviality, there was only one conclusion anybody could come to. The score or so of spectators which any event collects, and who had gathered outside as spies, were able to drift away, perceptibly relaxed. They passed on this conclusion to their fellows: the Lord of Misrule had arrived; the Brigadier had been observed to get quite drunk – although of course, still a perfect gentleman – and everybody was at liberty to follow his example.

About a week before Christmas, Joe announced that 111 Brigade had won first prize in the Divisional Headquarters lottery, and was to be entertained by a troupe from ENSA. The news was not received with much enthusiasm. The various column headquarters were so uncooperative that Brigade was virtually compelled to take over. Joe Lentaigne detailed his staff to stand in and complete the necessary arrangements.

A couple of marquees were erected – one for the males of the troupe to sleep in, and another for the females – while a further two marquees were joined together to form an improvised stage and proscenium in front of which the audience was expected to dispose itself on the slope of the dam, as in a Greek amphitheatre. A row of chairs in front was to accommodate the column commanders and the senior officers.

When all these dispositions had been completed, Lentaigne asked: 'Do you think we ought to put a guard on the women?' He plainly expected, if not Vera Lynn, then at least a bevy of lust-inciting Messalinas.

'Whom do you actually aim to protect them against?' I could not help but enquire. 'I mean, is it from the Gurkhas or the Cameronians, or do you visualize your staff as becoming inflamed with fatal passions?'

'Nobody likes to entertain such a possibility!' said Lentaigne.

'I know. All the same it *is* important. In the first place, the defence platoon would never challenge a gang of marauding Cameronians to a confrontation. They have far too much respect for the British troops to be used with any confidence in opposition to them. In the second place, if it is your staff who you expect to behave in this manner, then hadn't they better sort it out between themselves and leave the Gurkhas out of it?'

I was determined to get the defence platoons relieved of this distasteful chore, and I succeeded.

'One squad of King's Own and one squad of Cameronians to mount guard consecutively.' snapped Lentaigne.

When the theatrical troupe arrived, however, it was plain that we had been over-zealous. Their passion-provoking propensities turned out to be limited. There were five women and five men. Their abject desire to make themselves acceptable was rather pathetic. They became the subject of a little homily from Lentaigne.

'It's Christmas for them as well as for us,' he observed, after someone had made a disparaging remark. 'Consequently I want you to co-operate in making their stay an enjoyable one. I need hardly remind you that they are all ladies and gentlemen. I know none of you will be so discourteous as to suggest that they are other than entirely welcome. Don't forget that they're doing us a favour. How would you like ...' His eye swept round the mess-table and landed on me. 'How would you like, Baines, to entertain a drunken battalion of Cameronians?'

I could not help but find in my heart a deep sympathy for the troupe in its predicament, for any attempt to entertain the Cameronians over the holiday would be to court the direst consequences. With this chilling prospect in mind, we all buckled to create as favourable an impression as possible.

No sooner had we accustomed ourselves to adopting the lady-like manners prevailing among the Anglo-Indian females (for all the floozies were Eurasian), than Lentaigne dealt us a further crippling blow. It seemed that our private, drunken, misanthropic Christmas was to be completely ruined.

'Here! What d'you think of this?'

He entered the mess-tent, flourishing a message-form tantalisingly, his face puckered with mischief.

'Hirohito has abdicated! And the war in Europe is over!'

'My bet,' said Briggo cussedly, 'is that it's another Biblical quotation from the flaming general.'

'What's it say, sir? Are we off?'

'It's from the General. It says: "Request permission eat Christmas dinner Brigade Headquarters mess. Arriving 1200 hours. Wingate."'

The silence that ensued was so solid it could have been quarried.

'Well!' said Lentaigne, 'it's no good looking at me! I'm not responsible. And what's more, I can't even get out of it, so it's useless asking me to. If the General wants to spend Christmas with us, we shall simply have to resign ourselves to it. We could concentrate on making it enjoyable for him.'

His remark was greeted with a mutter of agreement. I don't suppose any of us even knew at the time whether we were being sarcastic or serious. But, for my part, I was perfectly sincere. I was keen to get a close look at this famous personality, and thus worried by any possibility of Wingate's visit being cancelled.

The morning of the fatal day dawned cold and clear. There was not the faintest suspicion of a hitch to mar the final arrangements.

Long before sun-up, I jumped out of bed. The air, as it hit me, was entirely devoid of humidity. There was a continental crispness about it which would not have been out of place in Siberia.

I put on my boots, gathered up my washing kit, and walked to the top of the dam. As I shaved, it was so dry that my lips split and my skin cracked. When I combed my hair, it stood on end and let out crackles of electricity.

All around me, soldiers and sepoys were similarly performing their ablutions – the Gurkhas trotting out to the *trutti khanas* grasping their little brass *lotas*, the King's Own and Cameronians clutching their folded sheets of bog-bumph. with that quiet concentration and dignity which always betokens men at their morning devotions. Their actions had about them such rightness that in the dawn they appeared singularly beautiful.

It was going to be a beautiful day, for both Christ's birth and the General's visit. Imperceptibly the sky began to be tinted with streaks of apricot. Suddenly the sun got up. Absorbed in my toilet, I hardly noticed. In the cookhouses below me, dozens of turkeys were being slaughtered and stripped of their feathers so that we Christians could consume their flesh. At my feet, the water of the lake was still. Only one or two languid fish rose in it, breaking the surface with their bubbles.

The cooks began beating the bottoms of their billy-cans with wooden spoons and from various parts of the camp there arose, like a bacchic Evoe, the invocation indicating that tea was up: 'Come-n-gerrit! Come-n-gerrit.'

I felt as if I was watching some ritual celebration on the morning of a bloody battle. It made the nearness of our departure for the war zone loom menacingly closer.

In a mood of absorption, I descended to my tent. If today was going to be a ceremonial occasion, I felt impelled to put on something special. I selected my most bleached battledress: even as long ago as that, faded denims were fashionable. Then I nipped smartly across to the mess tent in order to procure myself a breakfast before the morning run started on the tinned hamburgers.

What was my astonishment to find the whole tribe already in occupation. Breakfast was in full swing. It was characterized by a twittery expectation which would not have been amiss in a church outing of pensioners. But whether to attribute this to the promise of Christmas or to the General's visit was problematical.

Joe Lentaigne was seated at the centre of the table like Christ presiding over the Last Supper. On either side of him were two of the fluffiest of the floozies, leaning all over him in a variety of abandoned attitudes – in fact, one was practically reclining on his bosom. They were both clutching huge sheaths of gladioli. Lentaigne had had these flown in by light plane from New Delhi specially for the occasion.

The other three females sat at a little distance, fingering their flowers murderously, as if they would willingly ram them down their rivals' gullets. What was astonishing about the scene, however, was that all the girls were exhibiting a dazzling display of *décolleté* that could only have been intended for the General's benefit.

Everybody was downing double-brandies with their breakfast coffee and in addition Lentaigne was plotting confusion to his superiors by offering his two leading ladies certain hints with regard to deportment – which amounted to nothing less than an invitation to seduce the innocent General during the interval allowed for lunch. Being actresses, they were responding enthusiastically to his encouragement.

Most of those present seemed half-drunk already, and, since the day had started early and it was obviously going to be a corker, I hastened to join them and began downing double-brandies myself. Within a very short time I was as exhilarated as the rest of the company and perfectly indistinguishable from them in my behaviour.

'Is a General really important?' Desiree was lisping in that impromptu baby-blue voice, putting on a beautiful imitation of an ineffectual dumb blonde being dizzy.

'Very,' Lentaigne replied, revelling in all the attention he was getting. 'He carries us all in the palm of his hand – all our destinies!'

'Ooooo,' said the one called Antoinette, applying the automatic self-hug to her middle and making her breasts pop out of her bodice until they practically showed the nipples.

'I hope you're duly impressed,' said Lentaigne, spraying them with spit as if they had been infected with aphids.

'Ooooo, certainly! Of course I am. But do you think he'll like me?'

'Love you,' suddenly interjected young Lawrence with a gush, going scarlet with embarrassment in the process. He shot out the remark like a bullet, opening his mouth too wide in the first instance, then snapping it shut as if it were a Venus fly-trap.

Such a daring observation from our youngest member was greeted with a gasp of admiration by we others.

'Who said that?' demanded Lentaigne, veering round as if on a pivot. 'Whoever it was, I heartily endorse it!'

'You mustn't be inhibited by his rank,' Briggo interpolated, also blushing furiously like a schoolboy.

'He's said to be rather a puritan,' I put in priggishly. 'And to be easily deterred by the sight of a lady's bosom. He'll probably want to exorcise it with bell, book and holy water!'

'Oh dear! Do you think I ought to cover it up?'

I was about to say 'Well, just a bit,' when Lentaigne jumped into the breach.

'Not at all,' he said imperiously, glancing down with admiration at the dusky protuberances, which gleamed back at him indecorously. 'Keep yourself just as you are, m'dear. You are going to help us through an appallingly difficult situation, and if you hadn't arrived out of the blue we should've had to send for you. You are going to act as the perfect catalyst.'

I don't think Heloise, or whatever she was called, had the slightest idea what he meant. I could not help wondering, all the same, how Wingate was going to react. It was a pretty testing experience to submit him to – to place him at lunch between two such outrageously bold hussies.

After breakfast, Lentaigne decided he would like us to put in an appearance at the church parades. I chose the Catholic mass, celebrated among the Cameronians. I knew the sight of all those young soldiers kneeling bareheaded in the dust like so many Sir Galahads would appeal to me irresistibly.

It was an impressive service, but there was one odd circumstance. Padre Galt terminated the proceedings with a blessing. As the nature of the celebrations was essentially bellicose – something like blessing the men and their weapons in order that they should be successful in shedding blood – I was considerably taken aback to hear Padre Galt then suggest to his communicants that they ought to 'be fruitful and multiply'. I had expected us all to be expelled from his presence with the injunction to 'go forth and kill'. It was somewhat of a disappointment to discover that our tribal religion had degenerated so far into squeamishness

By the time all the church parades were over and we had reassembled in the mess, it was eleven o'clock. The hour of the General's arrival was drawing relentlessly nearer. Brigade Headquarters began frantically fortifying themselves against it with noggins of gin.

It was obvious that unless something was done to relieve the tension, there would be an explosion.

'Who's for a joy ride?' asked Lentaigne. 'We've still got time, before we get down to the airstrip!'

'I am, sir!'

'I am!'

'To the airstrip, then!' rollicked Lentaigne, in a tone of voice appropriate to a shore-leave matelot setting course for a licensed brothel.

Young Lawrence and I flung ourselves into the jeep and a lot of others tumbled on top of us. At a touch of his foot on the starter, the engine juddered into life. The tormented cogs of the gears engaged, the tyres bit into the tingling dirt, dust flew from under her tortured wheels – and the jeep shot across the open ground in front of the mess to the smell of scorching rubber.

She had screamed, on first starting, like an anguished log in a saw mill. Now the motor seemed to adjust to Lentaigne's mood, which was essentially rhapsodic, and to settle instead for a full-throated throb.

'Do a little trip!' yelled Lentaigne into my ear, confidentially. I was sitting up in front.

'Yes, sir!' The vehicle trembled ecstatically.

'Do a tour of the camp!'

'Certainly, sir!' It squirmed responsively like a voluptuous courtesan.

'Eh?' he barked, looking at me questioningly for some sort of confirmation, as if I had failed to answer.

'We're right behind you!' I shouted at the top of my voice.

Taking advantage of Lentaigne's invitation, about eight of us had clambered in. An additional two were accommodated on the bonnet. They managed to maintain themselves by clinging to the windscreen – which was down – like shipwrecked mariners to the bottom of an upturned boat.

I found myself crammed into one of the front seats between an unfamiliarly elevated Rhodes James on the one hand, and the gear-lever on the other. It was such an awkward position that every time Joe tried a racing change he put his hand on my genitals.

We zoomed to the top of the dam, turned right, and flew along a road that led into the depopulated countryside. Groups of soldiers were promenading along it in a sedate and respectable manner. Their well-scrubbed faces and immaculately clean uniforms recalled childhood memories of chapel-going Sundays in Cornwall along the roads leading to Zion and Bethel meeting-houses.

The sight of this jeep-load of drunken officers driven by their demented Brigadier screaming along the roads and kicking up clouds of dust must have awakened in them other, latent, possibilities. They were fully to redeem them before the day was over. For the moment, however, they simply saluted us.

But since Lentaigne persisted in turning the jeep at the end of the lane and zooming back over the same course, it began to dawn on the soldiers that this was a game – and that maybe they were even expected to participate in it.

They started cheering him every time he made a personal appearance. And we in the jeep, of course, cheered back. I don't know whether the whole thing was a pre-planned operation, or whether it simply occurred to Lentaigne spontaneously. Suddenly he stopped. The soldiers clustered round curiously. He stood up. Someone said, 'Good old Joe!', without much conviction.

Lentaigne launched into the classic declamation of a General addressing his soldiers.

'Men!'

There was a startled pause. One can only assume that everyone was composing his face into a suitably reverent expression.

As a rule, Lentaigne was not much given to haranguing the troops – not even on the eve of the battle. In this instance, however, some overriding necessity for mobilising public opinion or a buried instinct for community relations must have prompted him. He repeated the same manoeuvre, and the same speech, in various parts of the camp.

'The General arrives in a few minutes. He's coming to spend Christmas among you. Get down to the strip. Don't fail to give him a rousing reception!'

'Very subtle move, if I may venture to say so,' I hazarded approvingly, as we stormed back.

'Do you really think so?' he replied. He sounded gratified.

'Certainly. The General cannot fail to be impressed. It will be like one of those spontaneous demonstrations so dear to the heart of Supremo!' I was referring to Lord Mountbatten, the Supreme Allied Commander in South-East Asia.

'Look here, Baines, that's really too much. You'd better shut up! Keep your sarcasms for the General's lunch!'

One more perilous swoop down the slope of the dam, and we sped off in the direction of the airstrip. Lentaigne could not but be pleased to see that it was tightly packed. His appreciation of the circumstances had been magnificent. As our jeep shuddered to a halt, the soldiers came surging forward to see who was in it. They were like the crowd outside a Leicester Square cinema for the premiere of some notorious film. They would not neglect even the most nondescript arrivals, let alone Lentaigne's red-banded hat. To his credit, he resisted indulging in histrionics.

His sole concession to the gallery, as he descended from the jeep, was to say, 'The General will be here any minute. Give him a cheer, boys, as he gets down from his aircraft.'

It was enough. It perfectly exemplified the image of a strong, silent commander. A huge air of expectation prevailed, almost of exaltation. I personally felt breathless with excitement. The tremendous quantities of drink I had drunk, the perfect sunlight, the crisp blue sky, this auspicious day (it was still Christmas, however much we might have lost sight of the fact), the impending visit – all conspired to produce an impression of occasion that was hard to resist.

In addition, Lentaigne's final words about the General getting down from his aircraft had conjured up an imaginative picture. I was unconsciously led to expect something charismatic. Completely ignoring the nature of the air strip (which was only 100 yards long) I assumed that the General would be travelling in something with four engines. If I had been aware that there were aircraft in existence with more, I would probably have insisted on six. An engine being a sort of status symbol in my mythology, I naturally expected the General's plane to have at least as many of them as the Old Cunarders had dummy funnels.

With this concept in mind, I began scanning the sky, searching for that streak of silver which would be carrying the General from Gwalior.

Several minutes before, a tiresome buzzing noise had become apparent. It preceded form an impertinent little plane – obviously a spotter of some description – which had been reconnoitring round and round taking propaganda photographs, doubtless for publication in the SEAC newspaper.

Now it was preparing to land, right in the flight-path of the splendid sky-bird which might at any moment appear overhead like the gigantic phoenix from an Arabian Nights fairy-tale. It touched down, shot into the air, bounced, came again to ground clumsily and finally taxied towards us. The performance was so unprofessional yet at the same time casual and painless, that I mistook it for something entirely non-official.

All the soldiers, with Lentaigne at their head, started forward. I, on account of my obtuseness, got left at the back. By standing on my toes, however, I was just able to see the smallish figure who descended and now stood at the centre of the throng with a disdainful as well as apprehensive expression on his face while Lentaigne greeted him. He looked totally unlike his photographs, and indeed quite different from what legend had led us to expect. Yet there could be no doubt about it – this was General Wingate! The impression he created was both considerably less than, and at the same time more – infinitely more – than his myth.

Initially, I felt inclined to give way to disillusionment. The wildest stories about his looks and his deportment were current. Consequently I felt cheated when he appeared clean-shaven without his missionary topee, and with no visible sign of the razor-slash across his throat as proof of the assertion that he was an attempted suicide. He was, moreover, conventionally, even neatly, dressed in a beige-coloured khaki-drill officer's uniform of impeccable cut.

I then looked more closely. Wingate was short in stature, but possessed of a massive Imperial Roman head. His face was rather flat, but his features were broadly, even boldly sculpted. They recalled one of those cadet-college sand-tables in imitation of an undulating landscape suitable for tanks. His was the sort of face, however, which in spite of having been much fought over, had not yet surrendered to the scars of battle. It was deathly pale – almost disfigured. As a matter of fact, he had been desperately ill and was only just risen from a sick-bed, but I did not know this. His pallor made him look as if he had been indefinably cannibalised.

His expression was of a deliberately assumed sternness and implacability which did not ring quite true. Though it, however, two trapped eyes, like holes burnt in a piece of snow, peered with the beseeching intensity of a tortured animal. They were seeking sympathy and requesting compassion, and failing to find it.

How in God's name, I thought, did such a noble individual manage to get itself incorporated on earth? The face was the face of an archangel, although fallen and indefinably besmirched. It retained however, all the traces of its sublime origin in that it was obstinately and loftily handsome.

Surrounded by the encircling soldiers, his eyes cast diffidently to the ground lest one uncontrolled glance form them should light upon somebody and frazzle them to a cinder, General Wingate listened modestly to Lentaigne's welcome.

Young Lawrence and I walked soberly back to camp. Once you have been granted a flash of insight like this, it is bound to be rather thought-provoking. We were accompanied on every side by groups of soldiers, others also reflecting on their first impressions.

Young Lawrence himself kept repeating, 'What did you think – what did you make of it?'

In reply I could only grunt. What on earth was it, I wondered, that made the man so conspicuously arresting? Glimpsed for a moment in the midst of the crowd, he had towered above all of us without the aid of a single expansive gesture. Powerful people like Joe Lentaigne and Jack Masters paled beside him, while lesser men faded into complete insignificance.

Whatever it was – this unquantifiable – it put a completely different complexion on the quality of the forthcoming operations. They became, suddenly, much less like a routine manoeuvre of military logistics performed by mercenaries, to which crude level the exigencies of warfare so often reduce a crusade, and they became, instead, inspiring. It was possible to imagine them in all their unveiled glory spilling from the fount of God, in which virgin form Wingate must undoubtedly have conceived them.

But judging from the way the troops spent that Christmas, you would never have thought so. Our own little luncheon party at Brigade Headquarters, of course, went splendidly. The General turned out to be a considerate guest. However, that was the only place in camp where such urbanity flourished. All around us the lofty tone of the morning degenerated into one final alcoholic orgy before we departed for the war zone.

# CHAPTER FOUR

# Into the War Zone

On 11 January we took a train to Assam.

The Brigade's disappearance form the Jhansi area was supposed to be accomplished with the strictest secrecy. Of course, the secret leaked out. The occasion even sparked off quite a demonstration.

During our stay near Jhansi, which is a big, teeming, almost entirely Indian town and the centre of the Administrative District, we had formed a wide variety of relationships. In particular, there had developed a close rapport between the British 'other ranks' and some of the locals.

It was to deceive these people, and deny them the opportunity of gossiping about us, that security precautions had been instituted.

'You're to say goodbye to nobody!' Jack Masters had ordered us. 'So get out of your heads that you're going to indulge in affectionate little farewells on the eve of battle.'

Everyone was, as a consequence, tight-lipped for several days before our departure.

Biting back the lump in my throat and reining in a certain amount of manly emotion, I finally managed to assemble the defence platoons into two transport trucks and get them down to the station all in one piece. The time of our departure was fixed for that evening at six. Brigade Headquarters was joining the same train as one of the Gurkha columns and one column of the King's Own.

Our enlisted Brahmin cooks and camp-followers had left us. We took with us, however, a week's supply of provisions, together with our cooking-pots. They were to serve us on the train during our five days journey across India. I detailed Havildar Ganga Bahadur, also a Brahim, to cook for the platoon at our various track-side halts, and directed him, immediately on our arrival at Jhansi station, to set up the men's *langra* (cook-house) on a plot of ground adjoining the station yard. I wanted the defence platoons to have a good meal before we departed.

It was the occasion of rather an unpleasant incident which was to have a sombre termination in days to come. I had always prided myself on my sensitivity to Hindu prejudices. Particularly was this so with regard to their eating habits which are hedged about with many restrictions. I had always scrupulously observed every obligation and interdiction. I cannot therefore account for my relaxing my precautions in this respect with regard to the Gurkhas. Perhaps it had something to do with Dal Bahadur, in that I had unconsciously come to consider the Gurkhas as my friends.

At all events, once you allow an orthodox Brahim to entrench himself behind any of these religious regulations – as I had innocently done in getting Canga Bahadur to cook for us – you are sunk.

It is an officer's duty to ensure that proper arrangement are made for his men to be fed, and it is his privilege to inspect and sample the food which is served to them. I now determined on doing so. Foolhardily – it was done in a fit of genuine abstraction – I strode inside the sacred circle inscribed to ensure that no unorthodox person approached the food, and thereby contaminated it.

Nobody said a thing. I thought, however, that I detected a faint chilliness on Ganga Bahadur's part. But it was only afterwards, when it was too late to rectify my mistake by cooking a second meal, that I learnt that Ganga Bahadur had insisted on all the food being thrown away on account of my having desecrated its ritual purity. The defence platoons, in consequence, went hungry.

Rightly or wrongly, I saw in this incident an attempt to unload on me an unjustifiable amount of opprobrium and an attempt to subvert my authority. I decided that I should have to watch Ganga Bahadur closely. My suspicions led to a most unfortunate misunderstanding between us which resulted in irrevocable consequences.

Our coaches were now drawn up alongside the principal platform. The men were mustered, paraded, roll-called, and then received the order to get on the train. Railway officials were busily checking details, but there was no sign of onlookers. It appeared that our security precautions had been a success. I reported to the Brigade Major's compartment that Brigade Headquarters was present and correct and ready for departure. Masters was deep in *Pilgrim's Progress*.

So that appeared to be that. My responsibilities were temporarily in abeyance. I could relax. I strolled down the platform, cautiously observing how the various ranks were adapting themselves to the situation. The train, with its confined quarters, had the character of a troop-ship. It was interesting to see how the different people established the atmosphere of their own space.

Masters, with Intelligence Officer John Hedley and Doc Whyte, had already made his compartment seem like the hub of the universe. It was military command-post, scholar's study and religious oratory all in one, and was littered with books such as –prominently and perhaps symbolically – *Paradise Lost.*

Next door, in a coupé (a small, two-bunk compartment), Joe Lentaigne had taken out his false teeth. He looked like an exhausted infantryman who has at last been able to remove his boots.

In my compartment, we juniors – Burmese Intelligence Officer Smithy, Rhode-James, young Lawrence and I – were demonstrating our own ethos. In spite of my admiration for Masters and all that he stood for, I regret to say that we never managed anything more impressive than an imitation of the Lower Remove at Greyfriars.

Chesty Jennings occupied a compartment with Briggo, Geoffrey Birt, and Frankie Turner. As they were all technical officers, it became like one of those clinical cubicles you find in huge edifices given over to the Civil Service.

The defence platoons were accommodated in a great, bare, third-class wagon at the back. They had stripped to their vests and underpants and were crawling all over it. They had rapidly split up into card-parties and the cry of bid and counter-bid, plus the soft slap of cards, indicated that gambling was in full swing. It was strictly against Military Regulations, but it kept them out of other, worse, forms of mischief. I shrugged indifferently and hurried to my own compartment.

We were evidently on the brink of departure. Up forward, the engine driver was leaning out of his cab and in the rear the guard, standing well clear of the train, had under his arms his furled flags. It seemed rather sad to be leaving so furtively.

From the station concourse, a tall, elegant, gentleman approached He was flanked on either side by two others. Their entrance was so carefully contrived and its timing so critical, that it was inconceivable that it could have been unplanned.

I stood irresolutely on the platform, undecided whether I ought to arrest them. What were these civilians doing in the station precincts – were they coming with us?

Suddenly form behind me on the train, one of the King's Own Riflemen – better informed than I was – exclaimed brutally: 'Christ! It's the District Commissioner and the Deputy Collector. I seen 'em in the Club. That other one's the Superintendant of Police. If those bastards 've come to see us, we must be important! We're obviously done for! We're finished!'

'Good luck – best of luck – goodbye,' these officers repeated, passing down the length of the train and saluting every one of us – British 'other rank' and Gurkha alike – with their cordial good wishes.

Lentaigne snapped-in his false teeth – his jaws closing over them like a vice – and scrambled out to do the honours.

But the climax of the occasion was yet to come. From behind the station fence, and drifting within the station concourse there suddenly appeared – at a wave of the Commissioner's stick –the whole population of Jhansi's principal bazaar. Each one them was carrying his tiny tribute of a single flower; or some, if they could afford it, a glowing marigold garland. The effect of such an unwarranted gesture by the common people, whom we British had always affected to despise, was overwhelming. I for one, surrendered to it unconditionally – to so many flashing, fleeting glances, and to so many darkly gleaming, velvety skins.

They came forward with that half-cringing, half-abject self-abasement which, in the humble Indian, has become habitual.

'Why, Mahoboob, you old bugger! What the hell're you doing here?'

'Stiffen me, if it isn't Juggat! Hey – Juggat Ram, come over 'ere, me little beauty! What's this you got? A *flower*? Well, I'll be buggered! Here, stick it in me button 'ole for us, will yer? No – 'arf-a-mo! I'll stick it be'ind me fuckin 'ear. That'll tickle yer!'

'What do you make of it?' I said, turning to young Lawrence.

'Never seen anything like it,' he replied. 'It's touching!'

The words were hardly out of his mouth, before a diminutive urchin – a shoe-shine boy – came up and presented him the most beautiful tuberose garland. Lawrence doffed his hat reverently and offered him his neck.

'No – don't,' I blurted out, horrified at the symbolic gesture. It was too late. The ritual act was accomplished.

I regarded him with renewed respect. It must be wonderful to be thus chosen by the revengeful goddesses – the Furies. But did he realize the significance of being garlanded like this, like a sacrificial beast?

The only indication I received was that he was blushing.

'Do you know 'im?' I asked, accusingly.

'Never seem 'im before in my life!'

The guard was shrilly blowing his whistle.

'Come on, let's get in!'

The departure bell in the station concourse was tolling. The engine let out several brief, impatient shrieks. The crowd disengaged itself. Young Lawrence and I clambered in. Suddenly the lights came on: inevitably, our departure had been delayed and it was night.

'Well, lean out,' I said irritably, 'and say goodbye to your admirer!' He did so and threw him a silver rupee.

The boy salaamed elaborately. '*Khuda afiz*! God's blessing on the sahib! Sahib come back!'

Where are we – *ham kahan pahunchgaya*?' Smithy shouted down at the section of bridge-guard sepoys posted beside the track, as the train edged past them.

They were not very communicative. It was against their orders to give away information. On a second, more imperative command, however, one of them did condescend to yell back 'Kalpi!'

It sounded like 'Balls to you!', but Smithy promptly responded by replying, 'Then this river must be the Jamuna!'

Faintly a voice confirmed, 'Han, sahib!'

We were all astonished at Smithy's accurate geographical knowledge. Readjusting the windows, we returned to our bunks. I remained for a long time hypnotised by the drumming of the wheels over the track, then finally succumbed. The train dawdled along at its maximum speed of 40 mph and I fell asleep lulled by its thundering clanks.

I awoke with a start some time later, all my senses alerted. The train was ominously silent. It was so still that it could only have come to a halt. Raising the leather blind and lowering the window pane, then the mahogany ventilator slats and finally the steel shutter, I peered out. The chill, damp air of dawn struck at me, and a penetrating cold invaded the compartment.

We were drawn up at an uncannily deserted railway station. It was brilliantly illuminated and so solitary that is seemed insulated against everything human. Under the glare of the arc-lights it looked like an abandoned stage. A few old timetables pasted to a wall attracted my attention, giving hours of departure for place like Mymensingh or Monghyr. A clock opposite proclaimed four, but it was obviously a prop. Elaborately dressed and decorated, the place was waiting silently for the actors. I recognised that I was in a dimension of atemporality, unconnected with duration.

Time seemed to have stood still at that sidereal platform – an anonymous siding on the branch line to no man's land. The great expresses might thunder through to Calcutta or Delhi and all the onlookers wave, but we would remain eternally arrested at this unidentified junction. There was an analogy with my personal predicament and of our present situation: we were to pursue our tiny private war remote from the main operations and denied even the recognition of ever having influenced them.

I groped under my bunk for some slippers, put them on, and ventured warily out. Prowling around this empty lot and peering into the compartments full of hissing sleepers made me feel peculiarly disembodied. The eerie atmosphere was doubly accentuated by everyone on the train having succumbed in frozen suspension, as if struck by a hypnotic spell.

A figure materialised floatingly at the far end of the platform and flowed undulating towards me. I assumed that, if not a ghost, it must be a railway employee.

'Babu-ji! Hey, babu-ji – excuse me!'

'Yes sir?'

'What station is this please? Where are we?'

'Have you come off the train?' it demanded suspiciously, looking at the train with surprise and at me as if I had descended from Jupiter.

'Yes, of course I do! Where do you think I came from?'

'I'm sorry, sir!' he said, recollecting himself. 'This station is Canpur'.

He meant Cawnpore, of course, but he pronounced it according to the Hindustani fashion.

'It's no secret and I don't know why I hesitated. Your presence slightly confused me. The passengers do not usually alight from the first-class compartments in the middle of the night.'

'No? Well, I'm restless. I wanted someone to talk to. Everyone seems to be asleep. What time is it? Is that clock right?'

'Do you know which way the train is routed?' he said, ignoring my question.

'I know it's routed as far as Lucknow.'

He glanced uneasily down its length, as if wanting to say something. Towards the rear, some of the shutters were open and the windows were lowered. A pair of defence platoon feet protruded from one of them, challenging the train's anonymity: they conspicuously sported their army boots. Most of the remaining windows of the train were closed and their shutters firmly in position, but it was evident that it must be a troop-train. It wore that air of secrecy which is inseparable from military security.

'Are you an officer?' the babu said, with sudden directness.

'Yes, of course I'm an officer,' I said impatiently, although it was by no means obvious. I was wearing a peacock-blue Dacca silk *lunghi* and gold-embroidered, Punjabi-style slippers. Over my shoulders I had thrown a Kashmir shawl, Indian fashion. I must have looked like nothing on earth.

'I've never spoken to one,' he said in open admiration, 'though of course I've always wanted to. I've seen them from a distance. Oh, please sir, won't you tell me where you're going? You can confide in me. I admire you British!'

He was plainly prey to an extraordinary excitement. I had the wit to realise that he must have been a Tantric, a worshipper of Kali, and that he was conceiving of me as the ultimate sacrifice – the human!

I retained sufficient presence of mind to gesture vaguely. 'Over there! To the east, I suppose! Where else are all the troop trains going!'

Then my composure cracked too.

'To the front – to war!' I said tersely. 'That's where I'm going!'

He positively gasped with suppressed pleasure.

Having left Jhansi about seven o'clock in the evening, we crossed the Jamuna at Kalpi at midnight and reached Cawnpore at four, arriving at Lucknow at dawn, around six o'clock. We then proceeded, still in a north-easterly direction, to cross the Gogra river at Bahranghat into that rather wild and depopulated countryside which slopes down from the Himalayas to the Gangetic plain and which is known as the *terrain*.

Throughout the whole of one night the train forged across the district of Gorakpur. At dawn our locomotive was still steaming steadily eastwards at thirty miles an hour. Everyone slowly awoke.

I don't know what means of communication were established between the officer commanding the train on the one hand and the guard and engine driver on the other. Perhaps they simply relied on their intuition. At all events, when the desire for tea, for a wash and shave, for obeying the calls of nature, had reached overwhelming proportions, the engine would pull aside into some wayside halt.

A sleepy station master issued from the main building, officiously buttoning himself into his uniform. From the windows of his adjoining cottage his wife peeped cautiously out, her curiosity so great that she did not even bother to veil her face. His children, boiling with suppressed excitement, clustered coyly around the door, their sloe eyes heavy with Collyrium. Soon, overcoming their shyness, they raced down the track to confront the unfamiliar soldiers with demands for chocolate, sweetmeats and *paisa* (coins of small denomination).

A convoy of bullock carts bumped across the level crossing, the exhalation of oxen-breath hanging hauntingly in the cold air. A heavy dew condensed over everything, saturating the bundles of maize-stalks lying on the ground and dripping from the eaves of the railway godowns. An *ekka* trotted smartly past, its passenger sitting immobile under the canopy like the Buddha. Fleetingly, my nostrils picked up the lovely rank nostalgic smell of unwashed horse.

Around the train itself, all was purposeful activity. Several physical functions had to be crammed within the narrow hour she remained there, principal among these being, of course, evacuating and eating. As the lavatory facilities of the train were inadequate for such a huge complement of soldiers, the orders had gone out to reserve them exclusively for emergencies. The lavatories were therefore kept locked and the keys deposited in charge of the NCO commanding each coach. It was imperative, therefore, for all ranks to take the opportunity presented by the morning and evening halts to have their mandatory crap. Before the train had even come to a halt the soldiers had swung down from it and gone swarming off across the fields with their packs of bog-bumf and their brass *lotas*.

The Brigadier advanced towards me down the track.

'Morning, Baines.'

'Morning, sir.'

An enamelled mug containing his false teeth was in one hand, while in the other he clutched around him an extremely grubby dressing-gown. He was followed by his orderly, who carried a galvanised iron bucket.

'All out – everyone out!' ordered the NCOs in charge of the coaches, which the fatigue parties were already beginning to sweep out.

To the rear of the train had been attached a large, five-hundred gallon tank. This was now the object of our attention. Ganga Bahadur was there with the cook-house orderlies, drawing water for cooking the rice and the pulses. He stripped off down to his loin cloth and bathed almost naked in the cold water in these icy conditions – for the sun was not yet up – in order to ensure ritual purity for his cooking. I could not help admiring him for his devotion to detail.

We walked with Thaman Bahadur around the sidings in order to choose a suitable spot to set up the *langra*.

'This will do, sahib!'

Thaman Bahadur sent the orderlies racing back to the defence platoon coach in order to bring up the rations, the cooking-pots, and the firewood and kindling.

'Here' I said helpfully, 'you can use these bundles of maize-stalks to start the fire with. They are quite dry in the middle.'

Tej Bahadur was building three hearths with some bricks – one for *ccha*, one for *dhal* (pulses), and one for *bhat* (rice). We were not going to bother about *roti* (bread) as this was an early attempt at establishing a temporary cook-house and we were not yet very good at it. If we were not all back on the train in an hour, when it was ready to start, the officer commanding the train would forbid us to continue with our cooking. That meant we would all return to iron rations – a prospect none of us particularly relished.

'Come on, Tej Bahadur,' I couldn't help saying irritably. 'Get a move on! You are not building Jugatnath's temple at Puri!'

Up forward, the locomotive – a fine specimen – was also the object of attention, but not on account of a veneration for antiques. Some brilliant extemporiser had discovered that the boiler possessed a tap. He dashed back to get his mess-tin and tea-bag. Then, greatly daring, he opened the tap. The result was a beautiful jet of boiling water – and glorious pot of tea. By the time I arrived on the scene, the whole of the King's Own column was brewing up and Jack Masters had tacitly condoned the activity by having a shave. The engine-driver and fireman were beaming indulgently from their cab and there seemed no point in not joining in. I returned therefore to my compartment to get my razor.

Meanwhile, concurrent with these activities, the local inhabitants had foregathered. They were obedient to that impulse common among unsophisticated peoples to assemble like a herd of cows in the presence of anything unfamiliar. First to line the fence running along the railway siding and behind the godowns were the children. They stood there, observant, patient, well-behaved and obedient, staring seriously at the activity going on and apparently enchanted to discover that they could understand it. Thus they followed the tea-making, the cooking, the ablutions – even the trotting-out to have a crap! – with a delightful and intelligent interest, no doubt secretly relieved to discover that we possessed these activities in common!

Just before we completed our preparations for departure, their elders appeared inside the fence. They were led by the village headman and the local pundit. They enquired of the Gurkhas who was top man, and then duly approached Joe Lentaigne. They laid at his feet, in token of goodwill and as a humble offering, a small basket containing some locally produced *gur* (unrefined balls of brown sugar) and some dark brown and incredibly diminutive eggs. With a deep obeisance, Joe accepted them.

The locomotive shrieked imperatively in token of departure. The soldiers shouted and waved their hats. The children replied, eagerly enough it is true, but nevertheless I thought a trifle sadly.

*\*\*\**

And so we ran on into Northern Bihar and crossed the Gandak River between Sonpur and Hajipur, just north of its confluence with the Ganges at Patna. Then we proceeded along that river's north bank into northern Bengal. We went through Dinajpur and on to Amingaon, where we disembarked. We crossed the Brahmaputra by ferry, got into a train again at Gauhati, and proceeded as far as Silchar, near the Assam-Manipur frontier. This was our destination.

I remember the place clearly and the time exactly. It was eleven o'clock. There was no station and certainly no reception committee. We simply bundled out of the carriages and fell in on the edge of the railway embankment. Then we set off for the mountains that were visible in the distance, up an unsurfaced dirt track.

It was a very different sort of country from what we had been used to, inhabited by a very different sort of people. I realized immediately that we were truly in South-East Asia.

One or two men with markedly Mongolian features regarded us indifferently as we pounded past them, but this might have been due less to hostility than to the natural demeanour of these peasants. Their rudimentary huts, built on stilts and with steeply pitched thatched roofs, were obviously constructed to withstand completely different climatic conditions to those in central India.

Everything was made of bamboo. This exemplified that feeling of strangeness which was inseparable from operations in this theatre. The soil too was in startling contrast to the gritty, red laterite of the Central Provinces. It was grey in colour, and, when crumbled between the fingers, of an extraordinary soapy consistency. I recognized it as a product of that powdery Gangetic silt which I had read about but never actually encountered. Now it was sifting up my nose and down my boots. Assembling the defence platoons into some sort of ragged formation, with one of them going on ahead of Brigade Headquarters as advance guard, and the other bringing up the rear, I trudged in the wake of this huge column through the dust and was soon indistinguishable from it.

The path we were marching on has since turned out to be quite notorious. It was the famous Silchar-Bishenpur track. It was one of the few means of egress and ingress to and from the Manipur basin, although then barely jeepable. It had first come into prominence two years earlier, when it had been used by the Government as a means of marching to India the thousands of refugees who crowded into Manipur from Burma. In this capacity too, little more than a month after we marched down it, it attracted the attention of the Japanese during their onslaught on Manipur in mid-March, 1944 – namely as a means of forcing a passage into the Gangetic plain. Silchar is only 350 miles from Calcutta. They sought to penetrate it, but they never quite achieved this. I think Bishenpur, at the Manipur end of the track, never actually fell.

Much remained, along its 120 mile length, to tell the tale of the 1942 civilian evacuation. I vividly recall its atmosphere of sickness and death. And particularly I recall the great, deserted, desolate, camps. The casualties, who died there and left their unburied bones for the bamboos to grow through, peopled it with their ghosts.

The seven days of our journey along it, however, proved far from unpleasant. The weather was perfect for forced marches, and we were in splendid condition. The trek also proved useful as a rehearsal for real operations. All Brigade Headquarters officers had a chance to shake down and form some sort of unit.

At last we were alone with each other as we forged our way into the hills. The fences of split bamboo, the houses on stilts, fell away. Silchar was an obscure blob, hazed in dust. We were isolated at last from all external preoccupations.

Hour by hour we mounted higher and higher. Away ahead we could see the loftier peaks. The air grew thinner and rarer. Sometimes a large cloud would condense from the damp atmosphere and squat on a summit like a bee on a flower. The track unrolled tirelessly eastward, and we marched equally tirelessly along it. It was marvellously exhilarating to have left behind us the foetid air of the plains and to be climbing at last towards the high sierras where the forest grew.

The transition from open countryside to jungle was made suddenly. For about half-an-hour, while the afternoon drew on towards evening and it was becoming dark, we had been approaching this peculiar obstacle. From far off it looked like a sort of grassy-topped fence. As we came nearer, however, it became clear that what had seemed comparatively insignificant was in fact a vast, ever-continuing wall of giant bamboo. The clumps were growing so close together as to be absolutely impenetrable but for the track.

In face of such a majestic barrier, the chatting soldiers fell quiet.

We entered a kind of gothic cathedral. On every hand vistas opened up through nucleated chapels into arched crypts. Boyhood memories of the Adelphi Arches surfaced, of wandering among ageless foundations deep beneath buried buildings, as between the gnarled roots of forgotten civilisations.

As it grew dark, the Gurkhas cut branches from the bamboos and made torches. Their weird light conjured hellish phantasms out of gloomy corners.

Our staging-post was one of the 1942 civilian evacuee camps. The place was in a shallow depression beside a narrow river. Some big, old rain trees grew there, and the bamboo had been cleared.

The blaze from the soldiers' camp-fires lit up the boles of the rain trees, and flickered on their lower branches. Occasional snatches of conversation drifted over to me as I made my way towards Brigade Headquarters command post. The men were contented with themselves and their officers. All was well. I squatted down and hoped to pass the evening peacefully listening to Jack Masters reading *Paradise Lost*.

All at once I was alerted by the melon shape of Tej Bahadur's face appearing within the circle of firelight. It wore an expression of dismay. He caught my eye and beckoned me. Careful lest I break Masters's spell, I got up cautiously and left. There were three or four of them waiting anxiously for me out of earshot.

'What is it?'

For reply, they simple dragged me by the wrist. When I arrived where they were leading me, I found Ganga Bahadur. With a dramatic gesture, he led me forward.

The place he directed me to was among some short, feathery bamboos. At first sight I could not appreciate what it was he was indicating. The light from the spluttering torches was anything but constant and cast enormous, distorting shadows.

'Look, sahib! Look!' Ganga Bahadur kept saying, at last actually stamping his foot.

I looked long and searchingly, and then I saw. It was quite a shock. I saw a skull. It perched, slightly tip-tilted, on the end of a sprout of bamboo. Its sagging jaw hung yawningly open. Somewhere near at hand the dry stems of some plants were clattering together, as if its teeth were chattering. The skull regarded me from a rather rakish angle.

I bent down carefully and examined it. Its accompanying skeleton was still intact. The bones had been kept in position by the tatters of a cotton print dress. They were disposed near the stones of a hearth built to support a small cooking pot, and indeed a rusty tin kettle lay at a short distance.

Here was undoubtedly a victim of the 1942 Burma evacuation, but whether dead from poison or natural causes or murdered by dacoits for ornaments or money, it was impossible to tell. I looked at Ganga Bahadur and shrugged. There was nothing we could do except bury the bones.

'Detail a fatigue party and bury them immediately.'

'Very good, sahib.'

'We shall need something to wrap them in. If we're not careful, they'll fall apart.'

Everyone remained silent.

'I know,' interposed Tej Bahadur.

'Well, what?'

'There are some strips of hessian put up round the *pie-khana* (lavatory). We could wrap them in that!'

'Good idea! Go and get it!'

So we buried those pitiful remains in a roll of lavatory burlap without even saying a proper prayer over them. Then I retired to my bed.

From high in the nearby hills came the trumpeting of wild elephants. I lay on my back, gazing up at the stars, and a shudder of awe shot through me. It was a response to all this grandeur – the open sky; wild creatures trumpeting majestically; imponderable death.

So we descended to Bishenpur. It must have been about 24 or 25 January. The Japanese offensive against Manipur was even then impending, and in exactly two months Wingate would be dead, but no shadow of these forthcoming events disturbed the placid serenity of our arrival.

We were met by a Lieutenant Colonel Staff Officer from IV Corps just below the little hummock where stood the Bishenpur *Dhak* bungalow. I still find it difficult to visualize this modest dwelling as being the focal point around which the vicious battles for Bishenpur hamlet raged. It seemed too folksy to be associated with real warfare.

The same might be said of the Staff Officer. His self-exculpatory remark upon allotting us the ghastly elephant-grass swamp upon which to make our first camp quickly became a classic in the Brigade Headquarters anthology.

'I know you chaps love to creep away on your own into the jungle!'

Our arrival was, indeed, greeted by no more forceful comment. Lohtak Lake gleamed dully in the distance. A formation of geese flew overhead honking, and hundreds of wild duck arrowed across the opalescent sky in different directions, pursuing a mysterious itinerary which somehow emphasized our isolation.

It was incredibly lonely. That night I was bitten so badly by mosquitoes that it took me two days to open my swollen eyelids. I also made the acquaintance of blood-sucking leeches.

As Brigade Headquarters Orderly Officer, I was occupied principally, during the initial stages of our stay in Manipur, with routine duties. We moved camp several times into a more salubrious locality. Security was drawn tighter and tighter. There was precious little opportunity for observing, as I should like to have done, the very interesting local inhabitants. A foray into Imphal was out of the question. Nevertheless, under the almost *zenana*-like seclusion, I could not but be aware, from indiscreetly dropped asides and overhead hints from conversations, that great events were unfolding, situations developing, and plans maturing towards fulfilment. What sort of package would ultimately evolve from all this furtive activity had as yet, however, to make itself apparent.

From the official histories it appears that the decision to fly 77 Brigade and 111 Brigade into their respective theatres of operation within Burma had already been taken. We ordinary officers of 111 Brigade Headquarters, however – I refer, at any rate, to myself – were unaware of this. I was under the impression that our Special Force staff were still seeking a route for us into the Indaw and Wuntho areas via ground penetration through the front lines of the Japanese 15th Army. But, as January wore away and passed into February, it became increasingly evident that they were not going to find one.

I had no idea, however, what grand scheme was likely to replace this. Not in my wildest flights of fancy would I ever have hit on what actually happened. Although, in my subordinate position, such considerations were far above me, I could not insulate myself entirely from tiny twinges of anxiety about the ultimate outcome. It was obvious to the least significant among us that things were boiling up to a crisis.

Young Lawrence's offer, therefore, to accompany him on a trip in a fifteen-hundredweight truck to the frontier town of Tammu came as a welcome diversion. It was to be in the nature of a jaunt, to give us some idea of what a typical teak-jungle was like. But we never got there. We were stopped some ten miles short of the frontier by an unfordable river. It was just as well. The town turned out to be occupied by the Japs. Maybe this accounts for a strange feeling which I experienced of being observed. Young Lawrence agreed that it was spooky. We turned the truck and fled back.

The next day we set out early in the morning. Young Lawrence occupied the seat in the front of the truck with the driver, as befitted the personage who had signed for it, and I leant over the cab at the back. It was without a tarpaulin and it gave me a splendid opportunity to appreciate the scenery, which was magnificent.

We drove north, passing Lohtak Lake and the unlovely bulk of the Maharaja's palace on the further shore like an ugly, nineteen-thirties hospital block, and crossed the Manipur River at Imphal. This put us into the eastern sector of the plain and on the right track to strike the road for the frontier. We hit it and started to climb. Everything was completely unguarded. The road did not actually enter the hills but ran along the edge of them, about five hundred feet up. It was cut into a rocky escarpment where road improvements were still in progress and there was scant room for vehicles to pass.

We raced along this unsurfaced road at 50 mph, quite oblivious of oncoming traffic. The inevitable was bound to happen. I noticed a little puff of dust approaching from the distance which denoted the presence of another truck. The driver paid it not the least attention. He was too busy coaxing everything he could out of his speedometer.

We rounded a hairpin bend at top speed. The two vehicles skidded to avoid each other amid a squealing of brakes and the smell of burning rubber and screeched to a halt. I raised my head from the floorboards where I had flung myself – or been flung – and gazed incredulously into the truck opposite. There, not fifteen inches away, Dal Bahadur was grinning at me. He was so close I could have touched him.

'Hey!' I whispered, awestruck. 'So it's you!'

'Yes, sahib.'

The simple statement was delivered so saucily that in my ears it sounded like a declaration of passion. I must have made some gesture in reply which was over-emphatic. He looked disapproving. I sat back in the truck, feeling, and no doubt looking, ludicrously dejected. At this he softened.

'I'm coming back, sahib! Sahib! Do you understand! I'm coming back!'

'When?'

'Tomorrow. The Japanese-speaking sahib who I've been with, he's returning to rear headquarters.'

'Don't forget to report to me.'

But there was no immediate aftermath. The next day I awaited Dal Bahadur's arrival fruitlessly – and the day after that too. There was no sign of him. And then an event occurred which pushed him quite out of my mind. The news broke that Wingate had decided to fly us in. From that moment onwards events moved so swiftly that I had no time to luxuriate in personal emotions.

# CHAPTER FIVE

# Lift-Off

It was late afternoon when Jack Masters returned to the mess with news of our impending departure. He had been attending a conference at IV Corps Headquarters. All the top echelons of Fourteenth Army were present, so naturally we expected a decision. For several days the only subject of conversation had been about the various routes into Burma which were available. The general opinion was that we did not favour any of them. 16 Brigade under Bernard Fergusson was already marching from Ledo through country that was proving well-nigh impassable, although the terrain was so awful that the Japs had omitted to patrol it.

For us and for 77 Brigade, things would be different – patrol reconnaissance showed that we could no longer expect to slip through the lines of Japanese Fifteenth Army unnoticed. We should have to force a passage. That meant that our role as guerrilla troops in hit-and-run engagements would be impossible, for we should have been discovered and would be tailed.

Masters, his face looking tense and drawn, threw down his hat.

'Well, what is it?' said Geoffrey Birt.

'What's it to be?' asked Briggo.

He did not answer directly but said something to John Hedley which I failed to catch. He did not wait for our questions, but flew off to his tent.

When he emerged again, he looked more relaxed.

'Sorry to be so abrupt. The fact is – I've really been presented with a poser. I just had to see whether I'd got the necessary reference files. Well, I have!'

We settled down to hear the revelations. And come they did.

'Special Force's organisation,' began Masters, 'was called into being at the Quebec conference and designed to be entrusted to the command of

Orde Wingate for the specific purpose of assisting American General Joe Stilwell's penetration into Burma by Nationalist Chinese from the North Hukuong valley. That purpose is now about to be realized. With this intention in mind, it is proposed initially to concentrate three brigades in the vicinity of Indaw and to attack, capture, and hold it.

'The actual attack will be carried out by 16 Brigade, which is now marching into Burma from Ledo for that purpose. 77 Brigade will assist the operation by interrupting Indaw-Mogaung communications to prevent reinforcements reaching Indaw from the south.

'With Indaw in our hands and effectively isolated, a powerful force will be sitting astride the north-south road and rail communications and within reasonable striking distance of the Irrawaddy. It will be able to block all traffic to Mogaung and Myitkyina from the south and prevent every movement of troops, supplies and ammunition to the Japanese forces facing Stilwell and his Chinese armies in their southward offensive.

'77 Brigade and 111 Brigade will fly in. The operation will involve something like 1,600 mules and 10,000 men. Nothing like it on a similar scale has ever been previously attempted. Advance parties of each Brigade will fly into specially selected jungle clearings remote from the main Japanese communications and concentrations. They will fly gliders, large quantities of which have been obtained by kind permission of Theodore Roosevelt and Winston Churchill. The gliders will be pulled by C-47s (DC3s or Dakotas, as we British called them, but Masters was always noticeably pro-American) – two gliders to each tug. They will contain bulldozers and sufficient men to turn the jungle clearings into fully operational landing strips. They will be released over target and glide down, making forced landings within the area as best they can. Twenty-four hours will be allowed for preparing the landing-strips. On the night after these advanced parties have touched down, the main bodies of the Brigades will begin their fly-in in powered planes. That operation will probably take a further three nights. The whole operation should be completed and tied up within five days – or at the most, a week.

'Thereafter 77 Brigade and 111 Brigade will march each to their separate operational areas and perform the tasks allotted to them.

'Such is the basis of the general plan and it is a good one. But the tiny details are voluminous. In implementing them, I shall have to rely on the help of all of you. There are the plane manifests to work out, the calculation of payloads to prepare – mules, arms, ammunition, men – to say nothing of how you actually hornswaggle a mule inside an aircraft, let alone persuade one to enter or leave it!'

The scope of operations left us agape. It was the beginning of a period of activity in a type of work which was totally unfamiliar. Everything had to be weighed and measured according to the amount of cargo that a Dakota could carry from Imphal to somewhere about Katha, before returning to Imphal empty.

Our landing strips had already been selected and given the code-names Broadway, Piccadilly and Chowringhee – important thoroughfares in New York, London and Calcutta. Broadway and Piccadilly were close together and Chowringhee was intended simply as a reserve field, in case of the failure of either of the others. It was located in the so-called dry belt of the Shweli bend, where that tributary flows out into the Irrawaddy, which in this place is over a mile broad. It suffered from the disadvantage of being on the wrong side of the Irrawaddy. Our theatre was to be to the west of the Irrawaddy; Chowringhee was to the east. Our theatre of operations was just north of Wuntho where road, rail and telegraph communications diverged on the one hand through Pinlebu to Homalin, on the Chindwin, which was an important Japanese supply base for their front line facing Manipur; and on the other hand towards Mogaung and Myitkyina which were the bases for opposing the advance of Stilwell's Chinese army from the North.

As D-Day approached, we were granted the accolade of an inspection by Supremo. The occasion was beautifully stage-managed. The inspection took place at night. I was rather cross about it, as I wasn't allowed to be present. Jack Masters, that wily old bird, was far too cunning to allow a Camouflage Officer to appear in public at a parade of inspection for troops intending to go into battle. As for the Brigade Headquarters Orderly Officer – there was actually no place on the establishment for that high sounding piece of spook dreamed up cunningly to sound and look official; so I just had to be content to remain anonymous.

'All right,' said Masters ungraciously, when I asked him if I could be there. 'But for God's sake keep out of the way. I don't know how I'm going to explain you if you're discovered!'

I had been allowed to march the defence platoons up the field adjoining Tulihal aerodrome where the inspection was to take place, and then I had to vanish. I therefore crouched in a ditch in the wings and watched the inspection with fascination.

The troops assembled at dusk. As it got dark, they moved into position. They were paraded in two ranks in a long line. Supremo meticulously inspected every one of them. Everyone was in full battle kit, complete with extra magazines, spare ammo and grenades. My Gurkhas, I am pleased to say, looked magnificent.

Supremo arrived at the other end of the line in a jeep with the Commander-in-Chief, 11th Army Group, Assam, General Giffard, and Fourteenth Army Commander Bill Slim. Also present were IV Corps Commander, General Scoones, and, of course, our own Divisional Commander, Orde Wingate. Each one of these high-ranking Officers was accompanied by his aide-de-camp. It was a very dressy occasion. As Joe Lentaigne went up to Supremo to report the Brigade present and ready for inspection, every one of our transport lorries – there were over a hundred – switched on its lights. They had been arranged in a semi-circle facing us on purpose to create this special effect. It was like a scene from some old fashioned spectacular, such as Noel Coward's *Cavalcade*.

After about half-an-hour, Supremo's party hove in sight. His performance was perfectly splendid. Every twenty yards he stopped and repeated phrases in Gurkhali, learned by rote parrot-fashion: 'How old are you? How many years service have you got? Is this your first experience of active service? Good luck and God bless you!'

He was wearing the uniform of an admiral. It was snow white. He carried a sword and sported gold epaulettes. After the parade, Tej Bahadur came rushing up to me.

'He spoke to me, sahib! He spoke to me! He speaks our language. Somebody says it's the King. Is it the King, sahib? Tell me! It must be the King!'

'Only a minor member of the royal family,' I replied dryly. 'The King is much more magnificent!'

Our preparations were now almost complete. All that remained was to adjust one's inner attitude. I was lying on the ground one night doing this, gazing up at the moon, when I heard a strange buzzing noise. No sooner had I struggled free of my blanket, than it stopped.

I took a little tour round our bivouac. Soldiers of the defence platoons were lying about indiscriminately. As I stepped among them, rolled up in their khaki blankets like Egyptian mummies consigned to the sand, I was struck by their affinity to carven statues.

The moonlight burnt dappled across them. Young innocents, untouched by the torture of modern life and all its cobwebby implications – how I envied them! Here was Bhim Bahadur, his fascinating humorous monkey features now smoothed out by the soft hand of sleep – perhaps the only one among them with anything approaching a contemporary consciousness.

Here was Tej Bahadur of the surprised expression, his perfectly rounded melon cheek constitutionally exposed to danger of infection by acne – on whose behalf I was always having to break into the medical supplies in order to anoint another inflamed pimple with acquaflavine, for he was very sensitive about it. Here was Agam Singh, tall and lanky and with an extraordinary squint. Here were Man Bahadur Limbu and Gopal Bahadur Rai under a single blanket, their face uptilted and slightly turned towards each other. Gopal Bahadur appeared so young that it would have seemed little short of criminal to have taken him away from his mother, yet he was a plucky rifleman and a superbly stocky load carrier. I had seen him during training with his trousers rolled above the knee and a 62 pound Pack on his back, together with four grenades and a loaded Bren gun, getting carried away by a foaming torrent. Man Bahadur was inclined to be a little reticent – could it be that he was resentful of my attempts to establish contact with him? And here was Havildar Tulbir Gurung. He was a person of very pronounced capabilities as yet quite unextended to their full capacity. He, no doubt, would go far, for he was not above attempting to impress me with his potential. And here was Shiv Jung. He was our only big fellow, standing at least five feet ten in his socks. He was very dark in complexion, and I a little bit scared of him – he had such flashing eyes and such an intense manner.

Now that they were asleep, I could observe them quietly. I loved all of them, I decided, the wicked ones as much as the virtuous.

But who was this? Here was an unidentified form as yet unaccounted for. I stopped beside the anonymous bundle carefully rolled up as if it held something for me. As I did so, all nature suspended its breath. Carefully I bent down and disengaged the enveloping blanket from the enfolding hands. It peeled away like a skin. Underneath was Dal Bahadur. The rest of his face was serene enough, to be sure, but his eyes betrayed that he was very uncertain of his reception.

I slumped down beside him, feeling quite weak and giddy.

'So you've come back!'

'Yes, sahib. I've been here two days, only his excellency took no notice of me.' This was said with unmistakeable asperity.

'Nobody told me. Why didn't you report your arrival as I told you to?'

'I thought the sahib would discover it for himself.'

'Well, even if two days late, I have. I bet that was you singing.'

'Yes, sahib.' He was positively taunting me with his exaggerated innocence.

'Do you want to be my orderly?'

'We are his excellency's slaves, to dispose of as he thinks fit. He has us all in the palm of his hand!'

'Damn and blast your bloody impudence,' I said. 'Do you want to be my orderly or not? If not, you can very easily go back to rear headquarters and become the orderly of another Japanese-speaking officer at once. I'll have you transferred tomorrow. I shall simple declare that you're unfit for active service.'

'I want to be your orderly.'

'Then, quite simply, that settles it. Why beat about the bush? Why didn't you say so at the beginning?'

'I said so as soon as the Captain sahib gave me an opportunity.'

'You didn't.'

'I did.'

'Good heavens!' I exclaimed, aghast at what we were doing. 'Don't let's quarrel. I've only been speaking to you for three minutes.'

'Yes.'

'Then transfer your bedding-roll to my *basha* tomorrow.'

'Very well, sahib. Only his excellency must learn to control himself!'

'And what precisely,' I demanded, outraged by his pert and provocative manner, 'am I supposed to understand by that?'

He did not answer. He merely contented himself with looking enigmatic.

'Look here!' I said, quite broken by such artful coquetry. 'Let's not bicker. Let me confess frankly that I need you. I mean, I need some sort of human support and sympathy quite outside the military obligations of officers towards riflemen and vice-versa. Otherwise I'll never survive these operations alive. They are going to test all of us to the utmost – you too! Surely we can support each other in a comradely fashion? I'll use my influence to secure for you what small privileges and comforts I can. All I ask in return is – well I'm ashamed to say it – all I ask is love.'

I was at once aware how ridiculous the statement sounded.

'Love? I am asking too much! I don't deserve love. I'm sorry I said that. Just be my orderly and brew up. That will be sufficient.'

His reply was surprisingly reticent yet perfectly wonderful. It was true, what he said – I had underestimated him.

'I am not such an ingenuous fellow,' he said, 'as the sahib imagines. I am quite capable of appreciating his excellency's feelings. What his excellency has confided to me does me great honour. Please treat me respectfully. I, in return, would never dream of betraying his excellency's confidence.'

There, under the trees, then, on the eve of battle, with the moon gazing down as witness, and in the midst of our sleeping comrades, we in effect plighted our troth. In spirit, I am sure, neither of us ever dishonoured it.

Thereafter things pushed forward with vertiginous speed towards D-Day – 5 March 1944. One or two events flashed past, but they served more as objects from which to judge our velocity than as events to be chronicled. We at Brigade Headquarters continued to compile plane manifests until the last minute. There was no relaxation in that pressure. We seemed to be sucked towards the vortex of D-Day helpless, like pieces of driftwood floating on a rushing torrent.

The only occurrence powerful enough to arrest this momentum and actually bring it to a halt for a brief period arrived on 1 March. It was Wingate's essay on the stronghold. I remember it being delivered by special messenger from Force very well. It landed with quite a thud.

Habit had accustomed us to being bombarded with heavy literature from Headquarters fairly frequently, but on this particular occasion it seemed too much. We were all furiously busy, and some of us, including me, were behindhand in our timetable. Yet if we did not manage to complete the plane-manifests by target-date, the operation could not go forward.

When the bulky document dropped onto the trestle table where we were working, it was greeted with groans of dismay and irritation. There it lay: Training Memorandum No. 8.

With an expression of extreme distaste, Briggo picked it up. Five minutes later I was astonished to notice that he was still reading it.

'What is it?' I demanded incuriously, expecting to hear that it was the usual flaming manifesto from the infernal General. 'An exhortation – Caesar to his troops on the eve of battle?'

'Actually,' said Briggo with an unsteady laugh, 'this is something quite different.'

'Well, what is it?' repeated Smithy. 'Let's have a look!'

Briggo tossed over the wad of paper. The document was cyclostyled and the sheets were clipped together and bound as a book. There were about half-a-dozen copies contained in the heavy package and we each succeeded in securing one. There and then, in the midst of our pressing work, we sat back and read. I personally approached its perusal with extreme scepticism. I ought to have known better. After all I had met Wingate and been supremely impressed.

I had no sooner glanced at it, however, than I realized I would have to reassess. Imagine a quotation from Zachariah – 'Betake ye to the stronghold, ye prisoners of hope' – staring back at you from a Military Training Memorandum. Yet so quickly did events unfold, that twenty-four days later Wingate would be dead.

In spite of the interruption, we managed to complete our tasks by 5 March. That was the day of 77 Brigade's fly-in. Zero hour for them was at five, just before dusk. It would put them on the ground at the chosen clearings of Broadway and Piccadilly at half-past six. It also meant that we had long stretches of dead water to navigate before we arrived at the rapids.

As that tedious afternoon crawled endlessly towards its climax, I went a little dry in the throat. Similar symptoms of first night nerves were observable among the others. Is it to be accounted for by intuition? Over the mountains to the west, at Lalaghat aerodrome near Silchar where 77 Brigade were assembled, a final, pre-production crisis was racing crazily to confront them – yet all unbeknownst to the rest.

Exactly half-an-hour before take-off – at precisely half-past four in the afternoon – a light plane had landed with the most recently taken reconnaissance photographs. They were studied by all the top brass assembled to watch the take-off – by Wingate, Calvert, Cochran, Air Marshall Baldwin, Slim. They revealed terrible evidence that the Japanese were preparing to oppose us. Piccadilly airstrip had been blocked by what appeared to be deliberately placed teak-logs.

Had the Japanese discovered our intention, or was it purely coincidence? It was impossible to say. The top Commanders at Lalaghat immediately went into conference. Echoes of the uncertainty surrounding this crisis reached us in Manipur by telephone not long afterwards. The operation was off – then it was on –then it was off again. Had we been betrayed? Had we not?

As for myself, having put so much effort into trying to achieve physical and mental perfection in terms of my readiness, I think I should have run amok if all these plane manifests written with heart's blood had turned out to be abortive.

Away at Lalaghat, the conferring and weighing of probabilities lasted until about five o'clock. Then a final decision was arrived at. We of 111 Brigade, however, did not get the news immediately. We waited for confirmation – would it be continuation or cancellation? The suspense was terrific. Finally, after one hour, it came: Operation Thursday (the code name) would go forward; Chowringhee landing strip would be substituted for Piccadilly; detailed orders would follow.

What had happened was this: Chowringhee had originally been intended solely to be used by 111 Brigade's Regiment of 4/9 Gurkhas (49 and 94 Columns). They had been given a special role to operate independently of 111 Brigade on the Burmese border contiguous with the Chinese province of Yunnan to the east. It did not matter to them that Chowringhee was to the east of the Irrawaddy since their theatre of operation was to the east anyway.

All the rest of the two Brigades were going to fly to Piccadilly and Broadway. 77 Brigade was going in first on both strips for a quick build-up of men and weapons. Their operation was to be completed in three days by 7 March. 111 Brigade would then follow them on both strips, the landings to begin on 7 March and end on 10 March.

This plan was now not feasible on account of Piccadilly strip being rendered inoperable. As a compromise, what was suggested and agreed to by the commanders was this: Mike Calvert would fly his 77 Brigade into Broadway only, but accepting a far slower rate of build-up of his force's strength. This in itself was a courageous decision, seeing that, from the evidence available, he had every reason to suspect a Japanese ambush would be waiting for him.

The change, in terms of actual logistics, meant this: instead of the eighty gliders originally scheduled to leave Lalaghat aerodrome on that first night for Broadway and Piccadilly jointly, now merely sixty-one would leave, and these for Broadway alone. This was because Broadway was not thought capable of accommodating more than sixty gliders during a single night. In actual fact, it turned out to be capable of accommodating considerably fewer. In the middle of the night, on receipt of an adverse signal from Broadway indicating that there were difficulties there, seven gliders in flight were turned back.

The first wave of gliders, towed by their powered Dakota tugs, took off at 0612 hours. In spite of the fearful confusion consequent upon such last-minute changes of decision, including the re-briefing of all pilots and the whole complement of 77 Brigade Officers, they were only seventy-two minutes late.

We of 111 Brigade in our camps near Imphal were ready for them. The watchers and scanners of the sky were out, waiting to wave them forward. It was a moment – mysterious and tantalisingly significant – which was pregnant with incalculable consequences.

It was a calm night. The sky was serene and cloudless. The moon was twenty degrees above the horizon. It rose that evening at twenty past five and was approaching the full. Winds were light to moderate, maximum velocity seven miles per hour at ten thousand feet, varying from north-east to east. At ground level, however, any movement in the air was indistinguishable. Regardless of the fact that the two combatants were reaching for each other's throats, nature seemed sublimely at peace.

We came out of the big marquee where we were writing up plane manifests (I was down to the last three) and stood around, pretending to be casual and indifferent about it. No-one actually spoke. Everything capable of being articulated had already been said.

Away in the distance, it is true, could be heard, from the direction of 30 Column's and 40 Column's *bashas*, the accelerating excitement – drums and singing – of the farewell entertainment which the Gurkhas were mounting for Joe Lentaigne and Jack Masters, both of whom were 4th Gurkha Officers. In our locality, however, all was quiet and still. It was so still that I involuntarily shuddered. Suddenly Doc Whyte cocked his head.

There, from the west-south-west and passing slightly to the south of us, rose the deep-throated roar of the Dakotas. They were cruising at full throttle. The sound quickly intensified, then died. The planes were flying at ten thousand feet. Bang on course for Broadway, they passed impassively away to the east. In response to those engines my skin actually prickled.

It was twenty past six. The telephones in the mess and in Masters's command post started jangling. They summoned Lentaigne and Masters from their entertainment. Masters was ordered immediately back to his typewriter. His Operational Instruction No.1, dealing with the movement of 111 Brigade to Piccadilly, was now out of date. Owing to the change in plan the whole bloody thing had to be rewritten.

111 Brigade was now to fly to Chowringhee. This included 30 and 40 columns (3/4 Gurkhas), 49 and 94 (4/9 Gurkhas), 26 and 90 Columns (Cameronians), and 41 and 46 Columns (King's Own). How such a vast force was going to cross the mile-wide Irrawaddy we had not yet dared to contemplate.

Such, indeed, was the plan. As a matter of history, however, it did not work out quite like that. 111 Brigade's fly-in, it is true, went perfectly. On 9 March, however, when Brigade Headquarters, with 30 and 40 Columns, and 49 and 94 Columns, were already in position at Chowringhee, Brigadier Tulloch, Wingate's Chief of Staff, decided that the Japanese Air Force stationed at Katha could hardly have failed by now to become aware of what was going on so near them – only thirty miles away. He ordered the rest of the Brigade – that is 26 and 90 Columns, and 41 and 46 Columns (our two British Battalions, in fact) – to be diverted to Broadway.

This was accordingly done. They completed their fly-in by 11 March. After that they marched 150 miles in fourteen days to rendezvous with us at a spot just north of Wuntho. That rendezvous was kept on 24 March.

It proved a most effective change of plan. Not only did the Cameronians and the King's Own avoid that dreadful crossing of the Irrawaddy with all the consequent frustrations, disappointments, and loss of morale which it entailed. They also avoided the bombing of Chowringhee. A few hours after the last of us had abandoned the strip and were on our way towards the river, the Japanese came over in considerable strength and bombed the hell out of the empty, crashed planes and derelict gliders we had left there. We all laughed heartily. At the time, it had been exceedingly funny.

It would not have been so funny if we had been present. Owing to the fact of our two British Battalions having been diverted to Broadway, however, we were able to get away from Chowringhee by the early morning of 10 March. This we could not have down under the original plan. Brigadier Tulloch's changed decision proved a most fortunate intervention.

77 Brigade's fly-in, in spite of a somewhat calamitous first night, went smoothly. On that first night casualties were high. Fourteen gliders broke loose from their towing-ropes in full flight. Six crash-landed in Burma in places as far apart as the jungles of the Chindwin on the one hand and the fields of the Irrawaddy on the other – that is, across an expanse of territory extending for more than 150 miles. They created in the Japanese Intelligence Service the most bewildering state of confusion and were infinitely more effective in concealing our intentions than any deliberate attempt at deception. The remaining gliders crashed in Manipur and Assam.

There had been no Japanese ambush on the ground waiting for the invaders, as had been half-expected. Many gliders, however, crashed badly on landing. The clearing was scarred with deep, hard ruts due to timber extraction during the wet weather and this caused serious crack-ups. Towing aircraft had also come in too quickly and closely one behind another so that damaged gliders could not be cleared from the field before the following gliders crashed into them.

It was this factor which prompted the sending of an adverse signal to Lalaghat during the night and caused the cancellation of seven gliders in flight.

Out of a total of five hundred and forty men landed at Broadway on that first night, twenty-four were killed and thirty badly wounded. On the following night nine hundred men were landed. The movement of 77 Brigade's entire quota – a total of some 4,000 men and 1,000 mules, with all their arms and equipment – was completed by 10 March.

Now it was 111 Brigade's turn. I was frantic with excitement. On the night before our departure, Dal Bahadur and I hardly slept a wink.

With trembling diffidence, I had approached his bed. With a touch of inadequacy verging on the insane, I asked him, 'Is this where you sleep?'

He threw back his blanket and blinked. The moonlight seeping between the trees recorded his movements with time-defying clarity. A slightly puzzled expression crossed his face. Then he recovered and grinned mischievously.

'Yes,' he said. 'It's where the sahib told me to put myself. If it please his excellency, pray let him set down his noble presence!'

He was obviously tickled at my sudden appearance beside him, just as I was by his sedulously enunciated classical Urdu phrases. We regarded each other with a sort of grudging enthusiasm. Yet neither knew what to say.

In my eyes he glowed as fresh as a daisy and as bright as a pin. It was as if I had never previously observed him. The first thing I noticed was that he was more youthful than I imagined. The second – that he was incomparably good-looking.

'Why, I never knew,' I began admiringly. 'That is – you never told me. You speak beautiful Urdu!'

He was about five feet four inches in height. For a Gurkha his build was remarkably slender. What made his appearance particularly arresting, however, were his eyes. They were velvety-black in colour, almond-shaped, and so large that they seemed to dominate, almost wholly to occupy, his face. Sometimes, it is true, they could cloud over swiftly with a dimming cataract of inward sorrow, but at other times – and this was when he could be at his most fascinating – they glowed with mischievous duplicity.

He also possessed the most beautiful, ivory-white, milky-opaque, marble-smooth-and-transparent-as-alabaster skin. It reminded you of sleeping fires couched within cloudy opals.

He blushed at my complimentary remark about his Urdu. And no wonder. A few more attempts at conversation along these lines revealed what I ought to have gathered in the first place, namely that it was the only phrase in that language which he knew. Apart from his local dialect, which I was not very good at, he was master of a sort of Gurkha-oriented bastard

Hindi heavily adulterated with Bengali, and this eventually became the *lingua franca* in which we communicated.

For a hill-man, his features were singularly un-Mongolian. They were cast in a Hellenistic mould. But those canons of beauty for portraying god-like facial characteristics in every Hermes or Apollo were conspicuously bought into prominence by the Mongolian aspect of his face: the tightly stretching, typically high cheekbones. They were like shiny satin cushions or polished billiard balls – like mounds of snow heaped over miniature *chortens* – like cumulous clouds interiorly illuminated by lightning – like little offertory cakes moulded out of dedicated rice – or like those peaks of the Himalayas in their perfection, like Kanchenjunga, like Nanda Devi, like Nanga Parbat!

The overall effect was totally arresting. It was even more strikingly emphasized by a high individualistic manner – a mixture of genuine diffidence combined with a wild and irrepressible impetuosity.

Saturated in the beams of the magic moonlight, under the scrutiny of the clandestine examination I was submitting him to, he appeared incomparably far too good for me. Such an incontrovertible masterpiece of the Demiurge's art as he was ought to become the subject only for classic disciplines of contemplation as, for instance, the cow-herd personality of Shri Krishna. To become my lover would surely degrade him.

I had been standing before him, rapt in meditation. With that instinct of courtesy native to him, he had dutifully risen. Having put to rights his blanket, he was now waiting upon my initiative with an innocent expectation untroubled by any qualms of conscience.

There was nothing for me to do but accede to his request and sit down. I therefore did so, indicating that he should follow suit. He lowered himself gracefully to the ground like a dancer. It was equivalent to an elaborate salute.

So there we were, at one o'clock in the morning, on the day before being committed to battle, facing each other from across his bed like a couple of contestants. The space between us might have been the width of continents. For all the contact with each other we had, we might have been separated by centuries.

I had no experience at my disposal for helping me to bridge such an insurmountable gap. I could hardly beg him, in so many words, to come closer. The silence that ensued might have gone on progressively prolonging itself for millennia.

Suddenly, as if performing an act of *legerdemain*, he produced a pair of hands. Rather shyly he extended them towards me. They were peasant's hands and aesthetically quite unbeautiful. They might have looked all right for performing with the pruning hook or manipulating the mattock, but for the tender business of expressing emotions they were quite unsuitable. Yet it was as such that he had undoubtedly intended them. Their palms were fashioned like paws cushioned with pads.

I did not know what he expected me to do with them, but on impulse I took one. It lay within mine, half alert like a cowed bird, yet also with the frightening passivity of a vegetable marrow.

All at once the hand came awake. It fluttered within my grasp with the compulsive panic of a frightened sparrow. I assumed it was trying to escape and let go of it. It flew out of my arms with the abject surrender of total subjection.

The night wore on relentlessly and my position and posture became increasingly cramped. As it grew colder, I ached with rheumatism and creaked with damp. But I maintained myself hour after hour while Dal Bahadur sank blissfully into sleep.

When the last of the night expired and dawn came, I laid him reverently down and covered him over with his blanket. He did not awake. Then I returned to my own bed. It was soaked with dew. But I hoped I had given him a mite of comfort.

# CHAPTER SIX

# Burma

Dear God, I pray we make it. I can hardly believe we are on the wing.

I hadn't felt secure from cancellation or postponement until the last minute. It was only when we were aboard the aircraft that I relaxed. The operation had seemed too complicated, too bizarre to be taken seriously. How could such an undertaking have received approval from professional planners when it was more appropriate to the Arabian Nights?

Yet it happened. Not only did it prove possible to transport 8,000 men and several thousand mules to a spot some 200 miles inside Burma by a sort of magic carpet technique, without the Japanese becoming aware of it – it also proved a poetic experience, as emotionally stirring as it was beautiful. Its danger served superlatively as a sauce – the *frissons* of hazard were important.

I never thought I should take part in history. All the same, Wingate's Order of the Day, published on 11 March when his troops had completed their movement, did emphasize this aspect: 'This is a moment to live in history. It is an enterprise in which every man who takes part may feel proud one day to say, "I was there!"' Naturally, we all affected to think it was all balls. I now think differently.

Our Brigade Headquarters Column was due to fly to Chowringhee on 8 March. It consisted of the Brigadier, his staff with operational command-post under Jack Masters, the two defence platoons under me, all detachments of specialists under their appropriate officers, all the transport. The Brigade advance party composed of a detachment from 4/9 Gurkhas in fourteen gliders – two containing bulldozers – had flown in on the previous night.

I set out from camp with the defence platoons in two gigantic American-style trucks for Tulihal aerodrome at one o'clock. Masters's final instructions had been never to lose sight of them. I was determined to observe his orders to the letter, but it was easier said than done.

Dal Bahadur was seething away like an electric kettle – I could feel him discharging his impulses as from an atomic power-generating station – and all the others were manifesting an equally over-activated state of stimulation.

Excitement flickered about from one to another like liquid lightning, sometimes even alighting on me. I began to doubt my ability to handle such mercurial elements; their volatility was constantly dissolving itself into the atmosphere in clouds of steam.

On arrival, I settled them down in the assembly area just outside the aerodrome's wire-fenced perimeter. It was like a POW cage and would serve my purpose admirably. I felt reasonably secure they would never be able to break out of it.

All our soldiers had been given a bounty of twenty-five silver Burmese rupees. It was meant to buy food or pay for help in the event of their getting separated from the main body. Naturally it was instead being used as stakes for gambling.

'Get out your money,' I encouraged them, artfully. 'Get out the marked decks!'

I was pretty sure that once they had started to gamble with this government subsidy, they would lose all inclination to wander further afield.

Secure in this treacherous assumption, I retired to a discreet distance where I could covertly observe them, lay down, rested my head on my pack, and went to sleep. After spending half the night propping up Dal Bahadur, it is a wonder I ever woke.

But I did so, with a start, at about four o'clock and sat up. The area in front of me was deserted. They had vamoosed – completely vanished! In just one hour's time the whole of the Brigade Headquarters complement were due to be on operational stand-by. I would have been excused if I had panicked.

I was totally unfamiliar with my surroundings and hardly knew in which direction to look. I hurried to the barrier at the emplaning point. A military policeman was on duty and eyed me sternly. I wasn't wearing any pips. All identification and badges of rank had been suppressed. Under his scrutiny, I did not feel any more like a hero poised on the eve of an historic battle; I felt like the malefactor he undoubtedly considered me. My courage completely evaporated. I dared not ask him if he had seen my defence platoons: they were not something you could mislay that easily. Shamefacedly I slunk off.

I ferreted frantically among the Brigade Headquarters remnants instead. There were fragments of detachments without any NCOs, and squads of NCOs without even a fragmented detachment. Everything seethed with a chaos that one hoped was controlled. The lorries were still arriving, moment by moment, from our outlying camps, bringing the Gurkhas who were to follow us and fly in later in the night. They de-trucked and fell-in to muted, rasping orders. A whiffle of tension rippled round their ranks, which quivered with something akin to hysteria. It gave rise to strange urges, like the desire to laugh immoderately, eat a suet pudding, or otherwise yield uncharacteristically to maniacal compulsions.

Some soldiers, no doubt began to long for those they loved. I caught sight of Joe Lentaigne in the distance, his steel spectacles glinting in the sun and his false teeth gritting.

'If only,' I thought inconsequentially 'I could come upon *mine*!'

Young Lawrence hailed me.

'Is anything wrong? You look worried or something! Cheer up! It won't be long!'

No, it bloody won't, I thought, unless I can bloody find them! But all I said was: 'Lovely night for the fly-in. Nothing wrong!' I longed to confide in him that, like Bo-Peep, I had lost my sheep, but my self-respect forbade me.

'See you in Burma,' he shouted back amicably.

Jack Masters stalked past. His brow was furrowed with concentration and his face was livid. He looked absolutely at the end of this tether and near to collapse.

What I did *not* say was: 'Good evening, sir! Please have you seen the defence platoons? Just a little matter of fifty men!' Rather, lest he collar me for some unpalatable duty, I averted my head. He put his hand up. I stopped dead. He was muttering something – something about some unfathomable problem of logistics, no doubt – some problem in depth.

'Well, what is it?' he barked. 'Let's have it!'

'I – I don't know what you're talking about, sir. I didn't catch what you said.'

'A courage never to submit or yield,' he yelled. 'And what is more – not to be overcome. Where's it come from? Where's it from?'

'Training Memorandum No.8,' I replied promptly.

He gave me a sardonic look.

'Well, you're wrong this time. It's not Wingate, it's Milton – *Paradise Lost.*'

This brief exchange completely restored my self-confidence, so much so that, as soon as I got back to the assembly area, I found the defence platoons immediately. There they were, boldly confronting me and decorously playing strip-poker – Bhim Bahadur was down to his underpants – and all wearing the blandest expressions. It was an activity that would not have disgraced the Spartans when combing their long hair before the battle of Thermopylae.

'Where've you been?' I stormed at them.

'We've just been down to the NAAFI, huzoor,' shouted Havildar Tulbir Gurung. He stank strongly of something suspiciously like methylated spirits.

'But what on earth did you use for money?'

'Oh, it was quite easy,' piped up Tej Bahadur ingenuously. 'The soldier-sahibs were getting rid of theirs!'

At that moment, as if by pre-arranged signal, who should stalk past but Sergeant Barker. He was a tough, Cameronian platoon sergeant with whom I had struck up an improbable acquaintanceship. Upon sight of him, I was granted a gleam of enlightenment. He also smelt strongly.

'Look here, Staff!' I upbraided him. 'Wha' d'ya mean by lushing my men up with all the drink! Don't ya know we're emplaning any minute!' He gave me a furtive, guilty look, but rounded it off with a wicked conspiratorial wink.

Now at last the sun descended behind Bishenpur village. On the concrete apron, the first Dakotas were warming up. Lights flashed in cockpits and cabins and from the underbellies of fuselages. Across from me, a radio receiver cracked intermittently with pistol-shot static. Near at hand, an RAF technician poured a torrent of Morse through the key of his transmitter – all indications that a communications network of some sort was in operation, despite the fact of radio silence.

As the last faint glimmer of light faded from the darkening sky, the advance wave of planes took off in a flurry, like a covey of partridges.

'There they go!' chanted Sergeant Franklin, our Cipher Sergeant, a trifle shrilly.

As they hurtled down the runway to disappear in the gathering dusk, they reminded me of game-cocks squaring up to fight, and bristling with erectile feathers. The radio static barked abruptly with a superimposed, monitored voice. The moon rose like an over-ripe fruit and set all the dogs barking in Min Hong *busti*. The frogs in Manipur Lake croaked. A ripple of flute-notes flooded in hauntingly.

For some people, no doubt, these indications stamped upon the evening simply the quality of its ordinariness; but not for me.

'Shoulder your packs!' came the order, passed down from man to man. Already we were talking in whispers.

'Put on your packs, defence platoons,' I repeated. 'Be ready to move any minute!'

'Ready, sahib!'

'Ready, sahib!'

'Ready!'

Three more planes roared down the runway and took off, their lights morseing madly as they merged into the light of the moon.

'Come on,' someone said in a hoarse and scarcely recognisable whisper. 'Let's get going!'

We moved forward fumblingly, cautiously treading on each other's heels. Just before I was led off to the plane with my detachment, Doc Whyte blundered into me.

'Oh, hello!' he said chummily. 'You off?'

'Yes.'

He seemed under the influence of some sort of elation.

'What's up? What's wrong?'

'It's all right,' he responded, in a voice purring with satisfaction.

'Jack's heard from her – youknow – his girl. She's had her baby. He's had a telegram.'

'Are you joking?' I said disgustedly. 'I know nothing of the sort.' I thought the remark was in poor taste, and somewhat coarse.

'Don't you know then?' Doc Whyte demanded incredulously.

'I don't know a thing. I've never heard of Jack Masters's girl. I didn't even know he had one.'

'I'm sorry,' he said, backing away and apologising. 'I thought you knew. Please forget all about it! Forget I spoke!'

Which, of course, I did; it was the one and only occasion I ever conceived of Masters as having a private life.

I did not have much time, however, for trespassing into his personal sphere. The Enplanement Master had got hold of me and was leading me away with my detachment. I could sense Dal Bahadur beside me, panting with controlled excitement like a very loyal but rather frightened puppy. I put out my hand to comfort him. It was intended persuasively, but as an essentially impersonal gesture. Instead he seized on it and returned my pressure convulsively. The whites of his eyes rolled up at me out or the blackness, like china eggs.

We fanned out onto the runway. It was packed with revving machines in ordered lines. They were all Dakotas, all alike, and their sinister similarity rendered them insectival. They were like warrior wasps or swarming ants. The noise was deafening, the tightly scheduled take-offs terrifying, the lights spectacular. Another triad of planes roared past in a flurry of dust and alternating 'bleep-bleep' signals blinking like mythological jewels bleeding from monsters' heads. The one underneath their bellies reminded you of a winking orifice.

In the midst of this flaming confusion it was irritating to notice that our guide still loyally persisted in directing the beam of his modest flashlight meekly to the ground. Could it have been the relic of some outdated ARP technique?

Overhead, sporadically distinguishable between the roaring take-offs and the revving machines, could be heard the drone of our fighter cover.

'Are you all right?' I turned anxiously to my Gurkhas, for it was enough to put the fear of God up anybody.

'Yes, sahib. We're fine!'

'Not feeling too excited?

'No, sahib. It's like *Dussehra* (a Gurkha festival). Who would have thought the Sircar (the Government) had so many planes!'

Weaving in this manner between the sardine-packed transports and the whirling propellers, we arrived at our aircraft and scrambled into it. It was done without any ceremony and even less dignity.

The mules were already in position. They were right forward of the cabin with their noses up against the flight-deck bulkhead. A small space had been reserved there to accommodate a mule-holder. I was comforted to see them stabled so conveniently.

I was not so comforted by the sight of Agam Singh doing duty as the mule-holder detailed to kill them if they showed an inclination to panic. He was carrying a loaded sten-gun with its safety-catch released. As I went up to inspect the arrangements, he pointed it straight at me.

'Here, comrade, give me that gun! I'll give it back to you when you get down on the ground. You're not going to need it, anyway. Look!' I pointed to the mules. 'They're as docile as kittens. Now listen to me! Instead of playing about with lethal weapons, get out the nosebags. Have you got them ready? Good. As soon as the pilot starts up his engine and they begin

**Above:** Major-General Orde Wingate talking with USAF Colonel Phil Cochran. Cochran was the commander of the air operations that ferried the Chindits into Burma, evacuated the wounded and kept the fighting men supplied. Wingate - whom Frank regarded as a myth-maker and magician - was killed shortly after the campaign began.

**Left:** The author, Frank Baines, who saw himself as an amateur among hardened professionals.

Loading mules for the airlift – they carried the heavy armaments and communications equipment and had their vocal chords cut to stop them whinnying.

Two Chindit gunners by a burnt-out glider. The Chindits were airlifted into enemy-occupied Burma by the USAF and RAF in Dakotas and on a fleet of gliders. Some gliders crashed on landing.

A typical jungle bivouac where the Chindits rested during the day's march and harboured for the night.

A column of Chindits advancing with a pack mule on a dusty track in Northern Burma. The Chindits marched up to 20 miles a day with loads of 50 pounds on their backs.

**Left:** Desmond Whyte DSO, known as the Doc. Masters recommended him for a VC, saying he had saved several hundred lives by being calm, efficient and cheerful on the battlefield.

**Below:** Major John Hedley, the Brigade's unflappable and determined Intelligence Officer, who after the war became a housemaster at Bromsgrove School.

**Above:** Frank (in shorts) with Burmese elephants in Mokso Sakan, from where he was despatched with his two defence platoons to hold the pass to Blackpool to the last man.

**Right:** Richard Rhodes James, the Brigade's Cipher Officer, witnessed and survived the hell of the entire campaign. After the war he became a housemaster at Haileybury.

**Above:** Major Jack Masters, the Brigade's brilliant field commander, who became the best-selling author John Masters. Frank said he was ablaze with intelligence and uncompromisingly inelegant.

**Right:** Brigader Joe Lentaigne, who was Brigade Commander until he was flown out to replace General Wingate. Frank described him as a gaunt, belligerent, battered vulture.

**Left:** A Gurkha rifleman in Burma. Many of them, like Frank's orderly Dal Bahadur, were little more than boys, but they were resourceful, hard-working and brave soldiers.

**Below:** A Chindit with one of the mules used for transporting heavy gear and ammunition. The mules also carried the less seriously wounded.

Chindits watering a mule, and taking a well-earned dip.

Communicating by field radio with HQ – a lifeline for organizing supply drops by parachute and for evacuating the wounded from makeshift airstrips. Signals were sent and received in cipher.

to get restless, give them their feed. Watch me. I'll give you the signal. Do you understand?'

'Yes, sahib.'

'Sorry about the gun. I can't have you waving it all over the place, though. Suppose you shot the pilot – that would be a pity!'

'Yes, sahib.'

Everyone giggled at my sally, but it is always a chancy business confiscating a rifleman's weapon. It is like taking a bone away from a bloodhound – they don't like it.

'Now return to your places. You can take off your packs. It will be at least one and a half hours' flight. I suggest you all have a nap.'

The outside doors slammed and we were isolated within the insulated compartment. The pilot opened the communicating door between the flight-deck and the main cabin and peered under the mules' necks.

'Take-off in five minutes! I've had the go-ahead from control. Are you all right? There'll be no problems. Perfect flying conditions.' He apprehended my anxious glance towards the mules. 'Don't worry. I'll take it ever so steady. No steep banking turns.'

'Thanks.'

The communicating door banged. Presently the port, then the starboard engine, coughed and spluttered into life. Agam Singh, feeding bags in hand, looked at me interrogatively.

'No ... er ... not yet.'

The engines increased their tempo and the plane vibrated violently. The mules didn't even twitch. Perhaps they were deaf. Suddenly the brakes were released, the chocks came away from the wheels, and she moved forward. She bumped inelegantly towards the take-off point. Then she turned round and faced down the runway. As the pilot throttled back on the engines and reduced the revs, I could hear him talking laconically to the control tower over his radio in some incomprehensible jargon which might even have been a code.

I managed to find a free window and fastened on to it, but could see nothing but fields. We were at the end of the runway and right out in open country. It looked as blank and drained of subject as a Taoist painting. The soft mist rising from the lake provided a warm background of woven silk.

Suddenly the pilot opened up with full throttle and the plane bucketed.

'Now!' I said to Agam Singh, making soothing movements with my hands. He couldn't hear me but he understood. He began administering the feed as I had told him.

My strategy worked. The mules withdrew their attention from their surroundings and transferred it to the bottom of their nosebags where there were crushed oats.

Now the plane began to inch tentatively forward. We were off! We looked at each other speculatively. Even the normally unimpressionable Gurks relaxed their stolid expressions.

Gathering speed, we ripped down the runway. Landing-beacons whipped by – flick – flick – flick! We roared past the administrative buildings: darkened barracks; assembled aircraft; flashing blips! Out into open country again: pervading moonlight; pearly mist!

Suddenly the nose came up and the mules staggered. They pawed the floor of the compartment, then recovered, but did not interrupt their munching. My stomach jumped into my mouth and Dal Bahadur gulped. I could tell we were almost airborne by the decreased rumble of the wheels. Then it happened. The swimmy feeling which comes of being entirely unsupported by earth is unmistakable.

The engines surged, the propellers bit. The craft swooped smoothly on a swell of buoyancy like a ship. One wing-tip dipped slightly. She soared into the sky under the impulse of her powerful propulsion.

Everybody aboard the plane let out a heartfelt sigh of relief. No matter how *blasé* one might have been, it was impossible to remain indifferent. The only creatures who had shown no sign of emotion during the long build-up were the mules. Now they made an exception. They signalized their appreciation of our being airborne by raising their tails and blowing off two or three whispery farts each, then defecating. It was their only sign of nervousness during the entire flight.

Take a plane-load of young soldiers. Fly them away on a suicide mission, their destination unfamiliar to them. Melt two of them together emotionally. Whip into a froth of expectancy. Add a pinch of pure panic. Such was the memorable mixture. Then serve with full moon at an altitude of ten thousand feet.

Thus much was on the menu. The banquet itself, however, surpassed in excellence every expectation.

The lilac-tinted sky flamed fiercely with an amazing combination of mauves and pinks. The moon had risen and, eclipsing all the stars, shone down on mountain and river. Venus was diamond bright on the western horizon. Our flimsy crate, chugging her way eastwards on her three hundred and thirty-third mission, seemed an impertinent interloper within this sacred purlieu.

Occasionally, the crazy kite surged, skating sideways down the slope of an air-swell and cresting aside some spray of turbulence. At other times she would rise unpremeditatedly several feet, before dropping vertically like a stone for an unpredictable distance. Such lapses, however, were infrequent.

Even the mules were on their best behaviour. Not once did they neglect lifting their tails. The homely stink of stables with which they saturated the place completely neutralized that penetrating smell of hot lubricant and mineral petroleum which permeates the cabins of military aircraft and effectively distinguishes them from the civilian.

Every so often, the co-pilot – an insignificant young man not in keeping with the occasion's dignity – popped his head through the communicating door and explained, above the engines roar, various facts which he thought I ought to become acquainted with, and he continued to keep me informed of our progress.

'We're still over Imphal,' he reported upon his first appearance. 'That's Tulihal aerodrome down there.'

As I turned to get up every time he beckoned me and thrust my head between the mules' rumps in order to hear him, I did not have much chance of seeing what he indicated, for by the time I had got to the windows in the forward part of the compartment the view was blocked by the plane's wing. I have never liked looking downwards anyway, for it gives me attacks of vertigo. I contented myself, therefore, with assuming an intelligent expression and murmuring 'Oh, really!' in an apparently interested voice – although the tone was irrelevant, since he had to read the remark from my lips.

However we had been flying for at least ten minutes and according to my calculations we should already have been halfway to our destination.

My face must have expressed my dissatisfaction. The young man made circling movements with his hands to illustrate his point.

'We climb – we gain altitude – get over mountains.' He indicated a great height.

'Uh huh!' I acknowledged, sullenly.

'Soon start east.'

'You like flyee?' The difficulty of communicating had finally forced him into a sort of verbal shorthand resembling pidgin English.

'Me like flyee velly much!'

Suddenly, from my position in the centre of the aircraft, poised at the mules' rumps, I caught a glimpse of Venus. She was cruising magisterially across a window's aperture. Then, of a truth, I realized we were circling, hence the obviously climbing.

I returned to my place near the tail. Apart from the splashes of moonlight across the sprawling soldiers, it was dark in the cabin. We were flying without lights. I found Dal Bahadur and settled down beside him. I waited until the moonbeam had wheeled past me, then rested my arm on his thigh. My hand I let hang loosely between his legs. Presently he stirred restlessly and I caught the gleam of white teeth within wet lips. The warmth of his body burnt through the stuff in his trousers, kindling likewise my flesh. He lifted up his face to me in the half-light and whispered – I put my ear close to his mouth – 'No, sahib. Not this.'

I snatched away my hand, mortified by his indifference.

Presently he gave me a hefty, un-lover-like dig in the ribs. I bent forward to peer out of the window. He leant back and reclined momentarily on my breast. My hand was within inches of achieving its objective but I did not dare move it that inch. We gazed spellbound below us, my cheek responding ardently to his cheek.

Blue flames were spurting from the exhaust of the starboard motor and discharging themselves through violet to mauve, then finally red. I could see the starboard propeller on the leading wing-edge revolving like a transparent disc. On a surge of turbulence, the craft suddenly tilted. The moon swam out from underneath the wing-tip and hung there like a globule of melting butter. Beneath us in the darkness, the hills and jungles were indistinguishable except as an impression of velvetiness. Away in the distance a huge gash throbbed redly. It was like a banked fire through hot ash. The pilot altered course to bring us over it. It was a gigantic jungle conflagration burning unchecked. It was spanning tens of square miles and devouring hundreds of thousands of acres of forest. Even from this altitude you could see the individual trees going up like torches while their resinous sap exploded and the smell of flaming turpentine invaded the aircraft and even overcame the smell of the mule-dung. Dal Bahadur and I watched it mutely. The plane forged mercilessly ahead.

The insignificant young man appeared and beckoned, and I obeyed his behest. This time I proved completely incapable of comprehending him. Obediently I bobbed and grinned and nodded, and he seemed perfectly satisfied. I returned to place my cheek against Dal Bahadur's.

Quite by chance I glanced casually out of the window. What I saw struck me like an electric shock. We both spotted it at once. There, right below us, clove the mighty Chindwin between mountain and forest.

The flight offered us no sight more majestic. Even the sleepy Gurks seemed instinctively to appreciate it, for they strove somnambulistically against their sluggishness and sat up. Soon they, too, were pressing their face to the window-panes and the young co-pilot, as if he were personally responsible, was bobbing and bowing like a hired conjuror. Not even the mile-wide Irrawaddy was able to compare with it. By the time we sighted her we should have arrived at our destination and would have begun shouldering into our packs.

'There it is!' the co-pilot shouted. 'There it is!'

For some time my consciousness had been informing me of a loss of height. Only a couple of minutes previously we had crossed the Irrawaddy. It looked so big that I was convinced it was only just beneath us, and that I could see waves on it.

'Is that the river we've got to cross?' Dal Bahadur had queried.

'That's it. Yes.'

I knew we must be approaching our objective. Finally the co-pilot shouted a third time. He made it sound breath-catching, evocative, almost exultant. It conjured up in me the same sort of response as those other traditional formulae used to: 'Land ho!', 'There she blows!' or 'Breakers ahead!'

I reacted to it in the traditional fashion. I leapt to my feet. But there was nothing to see. The co-pilot was referring, of course to Chowringhee. Yet when we all rushed to the starboard windows to capture this early glimpse of our landing strip, it had disappeared. Our entire ship's complement rushed to the port side. A buried memory from small-boat-sailing about capsizing a craft by doing just this resurrected itself, but it didn't seem to make any difference to the plane's stability.

And there it was! It was an amazing object to stumble upon amidst blacked-out jungles in enemy territory. It looked like one of the fiery crosses of the Klu Klux Klan.

It blazed forth so decisively from length to length of its meticulously laid out flight-path that its rows of directional flares and marker beacons must have been visible for miles. Yet not a single enemy interceptor interfered with us. Well done the RAF! They had lured the Japanese Air Force in wrong directions to chase after delusive targets.

With more of these pantomime gestures, the co-pilot made me understand we must continue wheeling overhead. I stationed myself, therefore, at a starboard rear window – it was the inner side of the arc which the plane was circling – and prepared to watch the unfoldment below.

At first, my crystal ball was dark and unintelligible. Within my cloudy spy-glass all was chaos. Only the illuminated landing-strip burned twinkingly like a trail-breaker's blaze.

As we in the aircraft turned on a tighter and tighter rein, so the attenuated right-angled parallelogram below us which was the strip – more than 1,300 yards in length – appeared to be gyrating giddily under its own impetus as if it were not we who were turning, but it. It was an example of that curious transposition between here and there – between subject and object – which intervenes at periods of tautened sensibility and heightened tension.

Another huge plane cruised menacingly beneath us. It required a positive effort to realize that it was in fact a machine and not some hitherto unidentified species of icktys. Its projecting, encapsulated perspex nose-cone uncannily resembled both beak of bird and bony-plate-with-premaxillary-toothed edge of fish. I should not have been surprised if it had rolled over, exposing a sort, fat, milky underbelly, and gobbled up a piece of bait. It reflected the moonlight metallically and dully. More of like species cruised overhead.

All at once the young co-pilot reappeared. He seemed to have gone off his rocker.

'This is it! We're going down. We're going in.'

The engines choked several times, cut back severely and coughed and spluttered. The plane dropped vertically hundreds of feet in so many seconds, then the propellers bit again and the wings bore her up. Bhim Bahadur turned a livid shade of green and was unashamedly sick. The engines coughed again persistently and this time cut out altogether.

There became visible for the first time, sticking out above the forest, the tops of individual trees. The pilot banked steeply, completely forgetting his promise. As the floor of the cabin swept up and centrifugal force took over, we were all pushed into it. I felt the blood rush to my feet.

I looked down. There was a splendid view of moonlit tree-tops, as we hung suspended. The plane straightened out with a sort of wriggle and the propellers swished. The sound of wind whistling through the emergency landing flaps was shudderingly audible in the silence.

Dead ahead of us opened the strip. We were one hundred feet up and in perfect alignment. Great trees, like splashes of surf on rocks, reached up greedily to grab at us as we shot the rapids. We soared between them on a whisper of wind whistling through ailerons.

The motors started up again with an ear-shattering clatter. The plane responded jerkily but continued downwards with increased speed. Now the trees were no longer below us – we were below them! An immense bough made an intimidating gesture, its massive forearm bared and its fist clenched. One blow in the perspex from that hand would splinter your spectacles! We slithered past it – the plane positively side-stepping – by the skin of our teeth.

Thirty feet up, dropping rapidly. Landing lights flicking past. Twenty feet, fifteen, ten – but she didn't touch. A band of lights placed across our path raced towards us. They indicated the actual threshold of the strip.

Bump – shock-absorbers telescoping – grind, grind – touch. I could quite clearly hear the pilot applying the brakes. Now the tyres were distinctly rumbling as she settled her weight.

Suddenly the tail came down in a deflating movement and the mules staggered. Dal Bahadur shouldered into his pack and helped me into mine. The landing was complete. I had expected some sensational climax. But everything was so matter-of-fact that we might have been at Croydon Airport in the days of open cockpits and leather flying-helmets.

All the same, there was plenty going on. As we bumped our way off to our deplaning bay, I continued to stare out of the window.

Dakotas were moving about clumsily, manipulating their awkward appendages with elaborate artifice in order not to bump into each other – which, notwithstanding, some of them did. Their motors and propellers were buzzing as angrily as a disturbed hornet's nest.

Our plane moved with such force over the rough ground that its wings flapped up and down quite visibly. Finally it arrived at its parking place, feathered its propellers, and stopped.

The silence which ensued was quite off-putting. I unlocked the plane doors and we jumped out. In our excitement, we forgot the mules. A little wheezy squeak from within the aircraft attracted my attention. I looked back. It was Agam Singh. At the prospect of being left behind, he had lost his voice.

A guide appeared and demanded to know who we were and directed us to Brigade Headquarters. He said he would bring some planks to disembark the mules; but he failed to return.

In the meantime, we had unhitched them. We backed them out of our stalls and waited patiently for his reappearance. Full of oats, they were in no mood to remain passive. They tore themselves free and leapt to the ground. Heads and tails erect, they cantered away. The last I saw of them was racing across the landing strip with a flash of heels in a split-arse gallop.

Aeroplanes were landing and taking off, one every ninety seconds, the beams of their landing lights cutting swathes through the darkness. At any moment I expected to see one of them collide with my mules, sparking off that much-to-be-dreaded pile-up which could put stop to the whole op. Would they ever come back?

'Oh, yes sahib,' insisted Tej Bahadur. 'They'll come back just for the companionship.'

Secure in Tej Bahadur's assurance, I led my little detachment off. I found the other components of Brigade Headquarters Column and reported my arrival. Then I made a tour of inspection to satisfy myself that my small command was operating effectively.

Everything was in apple-pie order. The two havildars, Thaman Bahadur in charge of animal transport and Tuibit Gurung in charge of 3/4 Riflemen, had arrived before me. There wanted only Ganga Bahadur in charge of 4/9 Riflemen. He arrived while I was making my rounds. They got everything going with as much precision as if we were on the parade-ground.

The mules were dispersed and tethered to their picket-spikes – I had to confess shamefacedly to Thaman Bahadur about mine – and the saddles were neatly disposed at the side, while each animal had his nose deep in a feed bag.

The riflemen had scraped out their slit trenches and some were lying beside them already asleep. Two sentries together were on watch in their respective sectors: they were in possession of the password and well practised about when to challenge. They knew whom to arouse as their relief, at what time and where to find him.

Everyone was conversant with the drill in case a general alarm sounded; section fields of fire were laid down properly; the Bren guns were in position; each man was loaded with spare ammunition, six days K-rations (eighteen packs), half a dozen grenades, change of socks, and sleeping blanket and groundsheet.

I congratulated the havildars, told them that stand-to the following morning would be at six, and retired to my bivouac. Dal Bahadur had placed my pack handily and laid out my groundsheet. My blanket was neatly folded at its foot. It looked cleanly – virtuously – inviting. His own bed he had placed a couple of arm-lengths away. I lay down and stretched luxuriously. It seemed the right moment for an exchange of intimacies.

The trees rose up all round us in solemn witness, their boles innocent of branches and beautifully polished. Away on the strip the operation was still going forward under full steam with all the anguish and anxiety which it entailed, but here, in our little enclave, we seemed momentarily withdrawn from it. The sparse leaves on the teak trees under which we encamped received the full impact of the moonlight, then scattered it, like fairy gold, at our feet.

I lay on my back and gazed though them. One or two stars twinkled – stars that I should come to know intimately, during the months ahead, at every aspect of their rising and setting.

A mosquito droned near me, then disappeared into my ear with a high-pitched shriek. That, too, would become familiar.

I turned over on my side and glanced longingly at Dal Bahadur. He had turned in my direction but I could not distinguish in the darkness whether he was glancing at me. It seemed too blissful a possibility to contemplate. I stretched out my arm towards him coaxingly, my fingers fully extended; but he was beyond my reach.

He did not reciprocate. Probably he had fallen asleep. I, on the other hand, wanted someone to share my enthusiasm with. My heart was dilated with joy and a supreme peace flooded my body. I had achieved my objective. Now the reality was proving more perfect that I could have imagined.

Fireflies were flitting between the tree, pulsing incandescently with their airy impulses. A band of warrior ants discovered a crumb of K-ration I had eaten – it was chopped-pork-and-egg-yolks – and were carrying it off, regardless of the threatening motions of hand and foot.

This was an ecology where nothing would be wasted. Dear, dead body, here you too may return peaceably to your earth! It will receive friend and enemy, native and alien, indiscriminately. It will be a fitting receptacle wherein to deposit this mortal cabinet of nature's marvels.

Musing thus, I turned restlessly on my back; I threw out a hand. It came warmly in contact with a bunch of fingers. Our fingers crooked compulsively, then intertwined and clutched.

# CHAPTER SEVEN

# Across the Irrawaddy

We left Chowringhee at eight o'clock on the morning of 10 March. Tej Bahadur's prediction proved accurate; my runaway mules had returned to me. Brigade Headquarters, together with 30 Column and 40 Column (3/4 Gurkhas), and 94 Column and 49 Column (4/9), all landed safely. Apart from some crashed gliders on the first night, and a few wrecked Dakotas, there had not been a single casualty.

94 Column and 49 Column (called Morrisforce after their Commander, Jumbo Morris) now left us to go east. The rest of us headed towards the Irrawaddy.

In our position immediately to the east of the river we were in the dry zone. At this season of year it was devoid of springs. We did not expect to get a drink. Ambling with patient endurance knee-deep through the layer of fallen leaves which carpeted the area, our mules looked a bit jaded. Their last watering had been on the afternoon of 8 March. As for us humans, our water-bottles and *chagals* containing extra water were full, but we had been given orders not to drink. The assumption was that something might happen, and we might get trapped here and have to hole-up for an indeterminate period.

It was a strangely cautious attitude to take. In a situation where the more natural reaction would have been to throw caution to the wind, I should have expected a more dashing approach. Indeed we all felt triumphant. Here we were in Burma – after months of training and preparation we had finally made it! This should have resulted in a sense of certitude; and in most of us it did.

The solitary exception was Joe Lentaigne. Marching through the sparse jungle on that first day, with the dry leaves crunching under foot and cicadas trilling, he should have been in his element. But he didn't look right. His was a mildly pathetic, slightly dispirited figure. You felt sorry for him because he seemed lonely. Gone was the caustic wit, the sardonic comment and the commanding personality. He had become an old man.

At about ten o'clock, as we marched in extended formation through very open jungle, the Japanese planes came over. They passed by at about five thousand feet without giving us a look. They went direct to the strip we had vacated and bombed some of the abandoned gliders. These still contained a few cans of petrol intended as bulldozer fuel, and this the Jap tracer bullets ignited.

Huge columns of black smoke arose and no doubt, from the air, the attack appeared highly successful. It certainly looked realistic to us on the ground.

This incident ought to have proved extremely useful. To a commander in Joe's position, bent on crossing the Irrawaddy, it should have been a distinct advantage to have the Japanese discover and destroy our landing place. No general in his senses would land a force east of the Irrawaddy when his intention was to operate to the west of it. The Japanese, on this assumption, were bound to expect that our force would be proceeding in the opposite direction, with Morrisforce to the east. This should leave us free to cross the Irrawaddy at our leisure, without molestation; and indeed it did.

Lentaigne, however, did not take this view – or if he did, it failed to modify his prudence. He proceeded in his approach to the river with the old-maidish caution of one who expected something in the nature of the opposition encountered at the Normandy beach-head. As a matter of fact, nothing happened.

Naturally, if simple facts are translated into military jargon and detailed in the style of a *sitrep*, they inevitably appear rather impressive. You seize this, take possession of that, and consolidate t'other. You send scouts to reconnoitre here, and you push out probing patrols to put pressure on there. In the last analysis, however, all you need do is to march straight to the bloody river and cross it.

It was a mile wide, but so what? Did anybody imagine that the tiny bands of armed Burmans who were reported to be holding Inywa, two miles upstream, and Ma-ugon, two miles downstream, were going to fire off the flintlock fowling pieces they were armed with, in the face of the mighty force confronting them, which had arrived as if by magic from the skies (for they must have heard the Dakotas flying overhead and drawn their own conclusions) – a force with its bombers in close support and its fighter cover, its gliders, its supply drops, and its dozens of powered life-rafts buzzing back and forth? Of course not!

They would have thrown down their arms at once and gone racing off to the nearest Japanese post with the news that the whole British Army was crossing the river, accompanied by squadrons of tanks, armadas of planes, and fleets of river gunboats.

But in spite of anxieties on the part of our commander, some of which filtered through to us, the predominant atmosphere was sanguine. I myself was convinced that our crossing was bound to confound the gloomy prognostications of the pundits.

In the event, the Irrawaddy crossing proved a severe set-back. It was a disappointingly muted beginning in place of bold and aggressive tactics, particularly at the outset of the campaign when we were in real need of success.I put the fault squarely on Lentaigne. Of course I am aware that there were difficulties. I am simply saying that he should have surmounted them.

What we were all waiting for was the opportunity to indulge in some razzmatazz. We were waiting for inspired leadership. We failed to get it. Lentaigne's decisions turned out to be models of their kind: they were eminently sensible, but they were so insipid that they inspired no-one. The flamboyant gesture was lacking.

We arrived at the river in the late afternoon of 11 March. None of us had drunk any water for thirty hours.

A crackle of musketry from the north indicated that the patrol sent to secure the village of Inywa was in action, but on the bank immediately opposite us all was quiet.

I, personally, was only released from my duties to go and have a drink at half-past six. The defence platoons had been holed up in a warren of sand-dunes and pampas-grass since four o'clock. We were one mile from the river, in open country; the teak jungle had ended one mile further back.

When I gave the word, my Gurkhas went racing down the track to the water like a bunch of children. Dal Bahadur and I followed more sedately, strolling towards the shore like friends walking on a beach. I only just prevented myself holding his hand.

When we arrived within sight of the river, dusk was falling. The air was balmy with those scents of evening which are intensified by expanses of water, and a pearly light illuminated the sand-dunes and was reflected back from them to the sky.

As we descended the path between the clumps of esparto grass and the sounds of gravel, we entered a layer of cooler air which was perceptibly different. Then we sensed the presence of the great river.

'Come on!' I said to Dal Bahadur. We started running.

'There it is,' he said, arresting his steps and putting his hands to his lips.

It was like the sea. The opposite bank was indistinguishable, for twilight had given place to darkness, and the moon had not yet risen. The river appeared as just a triangle of steely grey between dark dunes opening onto a wide expanse of sandy beach.

Dal Bahadur ran towards it, leaving me behind. Suddenly he disappeared from sight. When I caught up with him, he had reached the water's edge and fallen on his face to drink. I, too, saw the water, transparent as crystal, rippling enticingly at my feet.

We lapped it up like animals, and drank and rested. The water of that beautiful, pellucid river slipped down my gullet as suavely as syrup. It was so innocuous that I felt I could have waded out into the depths of it and let it flow smoothly over my head.

It had got quite dark. Irradiating the eastern horizon, however, and just tinting the ragged edge of the earth-mass which represented the distant jungle, the moon's nimbus was faintly discernible.

Groups of Gurkhas were labouring like mad. They were collecting firewood for bonfires to guide in the gliders which were due to touch down that night – in fact, in an hour's time! They would bring inflatable rubber boats and rafts, outboard motors, fuel oil, mae-west life preservers, ropes, block-and-tackles, and other assorted equipment necessary for making the crossing on the following day.

Warm airs tantalized my heightened sensibility, like hot hands stroking sensitive skin with tormenting caresses. They carried wafts of scent from anonymous villages – at one moment patchouli, at another pig. The intoxicating fragrance of frangipane flowers hung in the air, maddening the sense with irresponsible suggestions.

The moon rose. It hung low in the east-south-east, bisected by an ominous zeppelin-shaped cloud like flying saucer. A gigantic oyster-coloured halo surrounded it, illuminating the southern hemisphere right up to the zenith. It promised sultry conditions and high humidity for the next day.

A flicker of summer lightning played far to the west of us, over the range of mountains beyond which flows the Chindwin and where stand the frontiers of India. It was strange to think that over there a huge storm was raging, just as ferocious in its intensity as the Japanese offensive then being launched against Imphal; whereas here, which ought to have been the centre, things seemed rather quiet. As yet, however, we were not aware of that action.

This was the night of 11 to 12 March. All I was aware of was that the air hummed intoxicatingly like a drunken bee in the bell of a flower. The planes turned up overhead punctually at eight.

Lentaigne was down at the spit discussing with Frankie Turner the probabilities of the mules swimming the river. Chesty Jennings was on the spit talking down the Dakota tugs before they released the gliders. Briggo was on the spit talking to Air Base, and his Signals Sergeant was talking to Rear Headquarters on another radio. The air hummed with radio signals.

Jack Masters was on the spit handing out messages for Briggo to dispatch, and Rhodes Jones was on the spit coding-up the radio messages which Masters was handing out. Doc Whyte was on the spit, attending to the evacuation of some sick Gurkhas who were going to be sent out later that night by snatch-glider. Dal Bahadur and I were on the spit, watching.

The fires were lit. They blazed up instantly. Surrounded by groups of soldiers looking like Walpurgis Night celebrants, they might have been honouring some archaic god – indeed the god of our own far-flung battle-line.

Pile on more palm and pine, Ghan Bahadur! The conflagration must not die down! More timber – more tinder!

The conjuration succeeded. We were granted a manifestation of eagles. A glider wooshed out of the sky like a great bird, and swished low overhead with a rush of wind through wings. We all ducked as if it were coming specifically at us.

A second glider followed a few seconds later. They coasted down-river together unconcernedly, with all the condescension of superior creatures, and ended up two thousand yards downstream, and well beyond the terminus of our signal fires demarcating the landing area. This was the first of those difficulties which I mentioned earlier. The second was, of course, that the mules refused to swim.

The failure of the gliders to touch down in the target area was due to a layer of warm air created by the bonfires. The fires attracted a contrary current of inward flowing air from the opposite direction which, contrary to all aerodynamic predications, kept the gliders airborne.

It was an example of how chance can confound the most expert planning. It was an absolute disaster. It meant that all the heavy equipment which the gliders carried would have to be dragged manually or by mules up-river to the point chosen for the crossing.

Everybody was dumbfounded. Presently, however, I heard Jack Masters. He was speaking in hushed tones, but matter-of-factly and in a way which injected confidence.

'You'll have to harness up the mules – mumble, mumble – and that's all there is to it – mumble, mumble – muster all the men and let's start dragging the equipment to the crossing point – mumble, mumble – of course it can be done – mumble, mumble – anyway, it'll have to be!'

'Come on!' I said to Dal Bahadur, taking his arm and twisting it playfully behind him. 'You've done enough for tonight. You're off duty. Go back and tell Thaman Bahadur and Ganga Bahadur and Tulbir Gurung to bed the men down. We'll have a hard day tomorrow. I am going to help the cipher-sahib decode signals. You can find me at the signals bivouac.'

All ranks laboured back-breakingly through the rest of that night. By dawn the work was nearly completed.

During those long, tedious hours of travail, I had consoled myself with the thought that the defence platoons were enjoying a reposeful and refreshing sleep. Wrong again!

They were too excited, and too frightened of missing something good, to take any rest. They had refused to obey me. Without my knowledge they had trooped down to the river and laboured with 30 Column and 40 Column in dragging the equipment from the overshot gliders and back up to the crossing point. It hadn't been work to you, had it, you naughty deceitful little boys? You don't mislead me – you are only masquerading! You aren't soldiers at all! You are only here for the fun of it! It is just a game!

At two o'clock in the morning the Dakotas returned to snatch off the gliders. It was the most extraordinary sight. A stationary glider at rest on the ground was snatched into the air by a Dakota flying immediately above it by means of a sort of clothes-line contraption erected over the glider and a boom-and-hook lowered from the tug. The glider reached a velocity of eighty miles per hour from zero in one and a half seconds.

I perfectly appreciated that the defence platoons would never have forgiven me if my orders had caused them to miss such a marvel, for it certainly verged on the miraculous.

And verging on the miraculous, too, was the voyage of the first two assault boats. Finally assembled and driven by huge outboard motors, they chugged from the comparative calm of the moon-drenched beaches into the middle of the stream. Each boat was towing two others. They were crammed with soldiers, bristling with weapons, and armed to the teeth. We watched while they were caught, and momentarily arrested, by a temporary whirlpool. The high cliff of the opposite bank began to announce itself as a prominent feature. In the uncertain light of morning it did not look scaleable, even with ladders.

Three fighter-bombers swooped over and attempted to sever the telephone line running along it. It was imperative to get this link cut early in the proceedings before the enemy could receive precise information about what we were doing.

When the bombs failed to achieve an effect, the leader lowered his undercarriage. Flying at zero feet, he severed it with his wheels.

Soon a red Very light floated into the turquoise sky with the slow trajectory of a Roman candle. It signified that the assault boats had landed. They had deposited the soldiers, who had taken up position. There had been no opposition.

It was all done according to the best traditions of Camberley and Quetta syndicates. It would have been awarded high marks by any Staff College examiner. It also got high marks for aesthetics, for it was singularly beautiful.

The only thing wrong with it was that, if you are a good commander, you know automatically where the enemy is – that is, if your reflexes and intuitions are working correctly. If you don't know where the enemy is, then your reflexes and intuitions are not working correctly and you remain stuck within some conventional Staff College conception, which is where Joe Lentaigne found himself.

The fact that very few people make good commanders or use that intuition – being apparently unaware that such a faculty exists – does not invalidate my criticism.

Lentaigne could have gone straight ahead with his river crossing without the fiddle-faddle of the Very lights. And, instead of consenting to the fighter-pilots endangering their Mustangs and their lives by cutting the telephone wire on the further bank in that dramatic manner (for all that it was a spectacular sight), he could have allowed our advance party in the assault boats to do it with a step-ladder and a pair of rose-clippers!

I made my own crossing in the company of Jack Masters and Doc Whyte at about mid-day. By that time it was evident that our crossing was a failure. Apart from the fact that initially several of our outboard motors failed to start, owing to some mechanical defect or other, what really put paid to the thing was that our mules would not start either. We could get the men across by one means or another. The mules we completely failed to persuade. They would not follow the boats and we could not get them across in sufficient numbers to justify calling the operation a success. Many of them did get as far as mid-stream but at that point they lost courage and turned back.

The immediate prospect was bleak. A column without its transport was inoperable. It meant it would be without its three inch mortars, its heavy machine guns, its reserves of ammunition, its explosives, its demolition set, its medical supplies and its radio transmitters, all of which depended on mules.

By one o'clock of that day (12 March) the entire crossing should have been complete. In actual fact, although most of 30 Column were over with the men and equipment, less than one fifth of the mules had made it. 40 Column had not even started to cross and was still holed up on the other side.

A decision had to be arrived at and was accordingly made: 30 Column's crossing was to be completed by 1500 hrs, and that of Brigade Headquarters Column with as many mules as could be managed. After that, no further movement across the river was to be initiated. 40 Column would be abandoned on the eastern bank. They would return the way they had come and join Morrisforce, now a good two days march east of Chowringhee, or four days march east of our present position – in other words, eighty miles away.

I personally have always thought this decision was a mistake. Lentaigne should have been prepared to accept the risks involved (which were of being discovered, pin-pointed and followed), and should have made a further attempt to get 40 Column across on the following day. But, the decision having been made, it was implemented. 40 Column slipped away.

Mercifully we of Brigade Headquarters and 30 Column had managed to get enough mules across the river to carry our essential equipment and radio sets. We were able to ask for a supply drop and replenish. But it would never have been accomplished without Mike MacGillicuddy.

All during that forenoon I had been watching with mounting admiration the antics of this fascinating young officer of 30 Column. His behaviour, as morning wore on into noon and it got hotter and hotter became more outrageous and more extravagant.

He was an excellent horseman and, riding now a pony, now a mule, he drove his mounts at the water and swam them across the river, at this point flowing at more than six miles per hour and covered with heaps of water-hyacinth which the mules mistook for islands and frequently, and with disastrous results, tried to mount.

His example soon encouraged others. Presently he was heading a group of Gurkhas, all good horsemen and excellent swimmers. Riding a very trustworthy female mule of Brigade Headquarters complement who later became a general favourite, he plunged into the stream. His Gurkhas plunged in after him. They seemed to trust MacGillicuddy's leadership. There is no doubt that their instinct was correct.

The Gurkhas leapt onto their mounts and, riding them recklessly bareback, pressed relentlessly towards deeper water. Suddenly there would be a strangled gulp (all the animals had been devocalised), and they would be swept off their feet. MacGillicuddy and his men would slip soundlessly form their backs into the water and, clinging to a mane or a tail and fearlessly indifferent to the flailing hooves and flashing teeth, would swim in the water alongside them. The current then bore them downstream.

Assault boats laden with equipment chugged past like dirty British coasters. Others, more impudent, would skate past MacGillicuddy, their helmsmen running rings round him, while some of them offered him a carrot.

MacGillicuddy did not take offence. Gradually everyone shed more and more clothing. It wasn't long before MacGillicuddy's boys rode their mounts entirely naked. In their excitement, they completely abandoned their traditional modesty. They tossed away their *langotis* (loincloths) and strutted in front of all ranks in unabashed splendour.

I could never have imagined such an exception to the generally prevailing Gurkha prudery as being possible. It was quite a tribute to MacGillicuddy's remarkable influence. Mother naked as they were born, their cock-and-balls crumbled sideways by the withers of the horses and looking like a fragment of Praxitelean sculpture from the pediment of the Parthenon, they rode their mules at the river. Their shouts and cries of enthusiasm rang echoingly across the water.

'Why are you showing off like this?' I ungenerously upbraided MacGillicuddy, when we briefly encountered each other in an interval of the action. I had never previously met him and didn't know him from Adam. It was genuine diabolical envy, therefore, which prompted such a spontaneous outburst of professional jealousy.

He looked rather surprised.

'Well, someone's got to do it. You're not a fool. You can see for yourself what it's like.' He nodded cursorily towards the river.

I gazed at it with new eyes. I had been regarding the scene from the point of view of an amateur – as something amusing and piquant for my personal gratification. Now I looked at it militarily.

MacGillicuddy was right. Mules and men who had unsuccessfully essayed the crossing and been driven back by the current were crawling out of the water all down the eastern bank. They were the passengers of those boats which had broken down in mid-stream. They made the shore look like a sea-beach after the catastrophe of some gigantic shipwreck.

Deserted life-rafts and abandoned radio transmitters proliferated for five miles down-river, beside which some hapless study of a forlorn signaller sat, mourning the drifting boats and coils of rope, the bobbing mae-wests and spinning Gurkha hats. I looked out over the sparkling waves and downstream at the scene which had seemed so animated, and was overcome with a sense of hopelessness.

'Why don't you come in too?' MacGillicuddy said, not unkindly.

'I can't swim at all well,' I replied, while tears of mortification welled into my eyes at my inadequacy.

'All, well,' he said, slipping away like an eel, 'another time!'

I felt cross and fractious from loss of sleep, and as for MacGillicuddy – I decided that I hated him.

When it was over and we sat, huddled and despondent, on the western bank, the cold tropical evening descended on us and cooled the sweat trickling down our backs and chests. I felt giddy from weariness, self-disgust, disease and a sense of deprivation. Dal Bahadur crouched at my side. His head loosely lolled against my shoulder. He was sleeping on his feet.

When Jack Masters gave the sign to advance, we started. In the fast fading twilight, we moved from the river. We harboured in a dense re-entrant running down from the Gangaw Hills. It was over them and to the westward that lay our theatres of operations and our concentration point – our rendezvous on 24 March with the Cameronians and King's own.

Jack Masters was the only one who remained awake that night. He was at work composing the signal which called for our first supply drop two days later. Everyone else dropped insensibly to sleep.

But, if things looked unduly depressing to my jaundiced eye, prejudiced by fatigue and blunted by over-facile enthusiasms, it is well to remember that the preceding day was the occasion of Wingate's jubilant Order of the Day dated 11 March.

Moreover on 12 March – the particular day on which we had crossed the Irrawaddy – Wingate availed himself of his right to communicate with Churchill and sent him a *sitrep*. It informed the Prime Minister that twelve thousand Chindits were within fifty miles of Indaw.

The precise details, when broken down into their components, were something like this: 77 Brigade had landed at Broadway and established a stronghold and airship sufficiently well organized to accommodate a squadron of Spitfires. These were successful in beating off a heavy Japanese air attack by thirty planes the following day (13 March).

Brigadier Calvert of 77 Brigade was marching with a force of five columns to establish a subsidiary stronghold near the railway station of Mawlu. It would permanently hold up all railway traffic from Katha and Indaw through to Myitkyina. The stronghold later came to be called White City on account of the thousands of supply parachutes caught in the trees which made it visible from the air for miles.

111 Brigade was crossing the Irrawaddy and moving to cut Wuntho-Indaw communications – something which they achieved by blowing up a large railway bridge on 24 March.

Morrisforce were moving east to cut Bhamo-Mandalay communications. And 16 Brigade, Wingate informed Churchill, was entering the Meza Valley where they would establish a stronghold and fully operational airstrip near a place on the map called Taungle (later to be known as Aberdeen), before continuing on their way to attack Indaw.

Wingate concluded: 'Enemy completely surprised. Situation most promising if exploited.'

It was true. Moreover, these dispositions made it possible for us to make up our deficiencies and to receive reinforcements with total facility. Those most valuable of all our necessities which (unlike three-inch mortars, reserve ammunition, or radio sets) could not be dropped to us by parachute – namely, mules – could be flown by powered transport planes straight to Stronghold Aberdeen and marched to us. Seven hundred Dakota sorties were flown in and out of Aberdeen in eight weeks.

# CHAPTER EIGHT

# The Gangaw Hills

Youth is so sanguine – all its cares are put to rights by a good rest!

On the following morning, the Brigade awoke like a giant refreshed. Joe Lentaigne, I regret to say, did not show the same resilience. During our march across the Gangaw Hills his health had deteriorated quite considerably.

The ostensible cause of this illness could be diagnosed with exactitude. He drank some contaminated water and 'got the shits'. The deterioration of his morale, however, was of a more complicated and psychological nature. The process whereby a human being loses his vitality, and hence his hold on life, is not explicit. It seems to spring from depths beyond superficial observation and beyond control by the intellect.

Lentaigne's slide had started immediately after we landed in Burma. I had earlier had suspicions about him – he seemed just a little bit too larger-than-life to be entirely authentic – but the reason for his failure at this particular juncture remains unclear.

I can only speculate that it had something to do with the responsibilities of commanding troops in battle – an occupation at which he had reputedly proved extremely successful during the 1941-42 retreat from Burma but which now he did not seem quite capable of.

I watched him day by day, during the course of that march, become weaker physically, more vacillating in character, and more indecisive in command. I thus began to wonder what on earth was going to happen to the rest of us.

But if Lentaigne was finding the march taxing, I was finding it revitalising and stimulating. I was bubbling over with vigour. Until we came to that mountain torrent which gave us all dysentery, where Lentaigne met his Waterloo, I was even under the impression that the terrain was healthy.

I suppose it was a natural enough misconception. It was hard to imagine that the clear water contained deadly elements of contamination. It was just another example of our total inexperience.

From the military point of view also we were comically ineffectual. We were inclined to expect a Jap to be hiding behind every bush. Lentaigne plunged us into an unnecessary night-alarm on one occasion and the defence platoons had to perform, in deepest darkness and under the most spooky conditions, an unnerving search through some small, mysterious huts discovered in the jungle. Mercifully they proved empty, but that didn't prevent my men and I from becoming extremely frightened. We were afraid not of encountering some rage-intoxicated samurai, which seemed unlikely under the circumstances, but rather that, as we plunged our bayonets about recklessly in the heaps of straw lying piled on the floors, we might puncture a human body. Luckily, however, the only casualty from these operations turned out to be Agam Singh – thank God it missed his bloody eye – lightly japed in the forehead by my bayonet!

In actual fact the Japs were rather thin on the ground. I imagine that at this point in the campaign they were far too busy defending themselves from 77 Brigade around Mawlu (White City). In the battle for the group of small hills which made up that Stronghold, Calvert himself led the opening bayonet charge on 18 March. According to all the histories, the fighting was characterized by almost medieval hand-to-hand ferocity. Lieutenant Cairns, of the South Staffordshires, was attacked by a Japanese office wielding a two-handled feudal sword. The officer hacked off his arm. Lieutenant Cairns shot him. He then seized the sword and continued to lead his men until he dropped dying to the ground.

While this sort of engagement was going on within a hundred and twenty miles of us, we were being over-cautious. Yet from the point of view of natural hazards and obstacles we had become over-confident. We refused to believe in the presence of debilitating diseases. However, in the long run the climate and terrain were to prove even more destructive than the Japs.

The ubiquitous little men we had expected to discover everywhere were notably absent, but bloodsucking leeches, the disgust-evoking propensities of which we had considerably underestimated, lurked beneath every leaf.

The graceful fronds of the pampas grasses, supposedly elegant enough for the most refined flower arrangement, had blades on them as sharp as knives and as serrated as saw-edges which would cut your army-issue denims to ribbons with a single slash.

The elephant grass clumps and the romantic cane-brakes harboured blood-sucking ticks which carried typhus. They bored into your skin within minutes, leaving their blood-inflating bags of bodies like black bubbles on the surface of your skin. When you pulled them out, you invariably severed their rear parts – which were composed all of stomach – from their heads which contained the boring mechanism. The heads remained deep in your skin to suppurate, forming ulcers full of purulent matter which the flies fed on.

At night, the deadly anopheles mosquito brought its fearful doses of malaria, heralding its attack by a burning puncture and a scalding itch.

Several forms of bacillary and amoebic dysentery flourished, and naturally we all suffered from jaundice. From the face and eyes of the sufferer, however, this was difficult to diagnose, because we were all so heavily dyed by the yellow-coloured anti-malarial drug called *mepacrine*, which imparts a bright, brassy tinge to the skin, that jaundice is difficult to distinguish. But we knew all right when we had it, because it makes your shit turn white!

The ground round the villages teemed with hook-worm on account of the rooting pigs.

In the bamboo forests through which we were often forced to march uphill for mile after mile, the half-rotten stems fallen beneath the clumps were so thickly strewn that walking over them elevated you two to three feet above the ground. They were so slippery that it was almost impossible to retain your balance. In such a situation, our clothes drenched and discoloured with sweat, we had to struggle desperately to navigate the mules along the best possible line of advance. Often enough they could find no sure footing either and similarly got stuck. Then you would have a nervy, jumpy animal on your hands whose load had probably wedged in the low, overarching stems ahead.

When you fell flat you were presented with the frightful hazard of the sharp bamboo spikes which projected from their joints. Their purple, blackberry-coloured thorns were livid with poison, and were so sharp and punctured you so easily that you were not even aware of a prick.

At night, the air droned with mosquitoes; during the day it buzzed with flies of gnats. I sometimes saw Dal Bahadur's hat, shoulders and pack black with them. We used to stagger along in single-file, dead-beat from exhaustion, every man holding in his hand a switch of greenery with which to beat the flies from the back and shoulders of the man in front of him.

Every so often a tiger-striped or panther-spotted horsefly would alight on your neck and make straight for your jugular. Before you could put your hand up, it would have drawn blood and flown off, leaving a swollen contusion.

The heat was intense. The plants in the jungle grew with fearsome vitality. I always felt they could hardly wait for one of us to fall dead. When that happened, they would barely bother to restrain their impatience. They just pounced. They laid hold of the corpse at once. In a matter of minutes the process had started which would reduce it to tilth.

I remember a particular occasion during one of our mid-day halts – it lasted about an hour – when Dal Bahadur sliced through the trunk of a plantain tree and laid out the leaves for us to sit on. When the time arrived for us to depart, Dal Bahadur pointed out that the centre of the trunk projected beyond the outward skin by the length of two feet. It had grown that much during the space of sixty minutes.

We harboured one night in a thicket of brambles. Where they sprang out of the ground they were as thick as your arm. They had transparent, ruby-red thorns on them as big as mussel shells and as sharp as scimitars, and where they arched over and trailed back to the ground would have covered a house.

I established Dal Bahadur to lay out our kits as comfortably as possible inside this hideous cage and then went off to attend Brigade Major's conference. When I got back, he wasn't there. Instead, Briggo had pinched the place and laid out his blanket. Dal Bahadur was skulking some distance away, looking rather hurt.

My own equipment was still in the place where he had put it, and all that was required was for me to make up my bed, stretch out beside Briggo, and go to sleep.

Instead, I decided to make a scene. After all, I had promised Dal Bahadur that I would look after him, and the occasion now seemed to have arisen where it was necessary to fulfil it.

'Where's Dal Bahadur?' I demanded shortly.

'He's over there. I told him to go and make his bed somewhere else. It's difficult to get a decent kip in private. He'll be all right. Don't worry.'

I saw red.

'Get fuckin' out! Get fuckin' out and go back to where you came from. Don't dare talk about privacy as if you were too good for a sepoy, or I'll rip out your gizzard.'

I paused, panting with fury, to take a breath. Briggo looked shattered.

'I will!' I reiterated with murderous intensity. 'I'll rip out your gizzard. You know perfectly well that we're supposed to go round in pairs and officers must not make a pair with each other but must pair with their orderlies. Well, Dal Bahadur's my orderly and I want him here!'

I pointed at Briggo's bed like an avenging demon. My voice had risen several semi-tones in pitch and was verging on hysteria, and it looked as if I might do something silly. Dal Bahadur came slithering on his belly under the bramble branches to calm me down, but Briggo had already decided that discretion was the better part of valour. He capitulated and went away.

'It's a very funny sort of relationship you have with your orderly,' he flung over his shoulder as his Parthian shot. 'I don't profess to understand it.'

'And what precisely do you mean by that? Are you implying that there's something improper in it? Is that what you mean?'

My sheer boldness startled me as much as it must have shaken him. If he had said 'yes', it would have set in train a whole string of incalculable consequences – and we had enough on our plate already.

'Well,' he prevaricated, hardly knowing what to say.

'I'm waiting for you to explain yourself.'

Waves of righteous indignation radiated from me, not on account of my innocence, which was non-existent, but on account of the fact that I intended to make an issue of it.

It did the trick.

'Of course I don't mean any such thing. You're making a mountain out of a molehill.'

The concession did him great credit, and proved, moreover, that he was a wise and tolerant man. My behaviour had been perfectly outrageous.

There the incident ended. It does not redound to my credit, but I was in love! Thereafter nobody ventured to say a thing.

But if it was a pyrrhic victory, the encounter was still one I could not have avoided. I had pledged myself to Dal Bahadur. I could not permit anyone to kick him around. I would have felt dishonoured. It is, after all, precisely on its adherence to such droll concepts that the quasi-feudal, hierarchical structure of an army is founded.

What a sublime period that was! How full of moving experience and tender impressions!

I used to awaken every morning before dawn, then watch and wait for the light. One or two stars would be shining, wanly emphasising the ephemeral darkness. Sometimes they twinkled, but mostly they just stared at you and it was the leaves on the trees that winked. Then gradually the stars would lose their intensity and sink exhaustedly into day. Slowly the surroundings would assume shapes, yet remain empty of colour.

A dawn mist might flit between the towering trees, low down among the undergrowth. It would be so diaphanous – so removed from any suggestion of bodiliness – that you thought you might have seen a wraith, a genuine tree-sprite. Yet the leaves would be wet. A faint wind would stir tiredly the trembling tree-tops and the condensation would fall in drops. It would patter down in great plops. The dead leaves on the ground would respond with a positive clatter.

No matter how exhausting the previous day might have been or how late to sleep the night before, such awakening became my invariable pattern. I would find myself drawn outwards and upwards without any conscious volition. Imperceptibly such a state would expand to embrace a relationship with the world outside and with others. But the process was slow. It was so natural, however, that it appealed to me as having something elemental about it. Indeed, I felt myself to be indistinguishable from the subterranean life of gnomes and undines and sylphs and salamanders and plants and flowers.

I awake refreshed. As daylight increases and colour floods once more into the earth, it is like the flowing back through long disused channels, of rejuvenating blood to a corpse. Nothing is moving. Dal Bahadur lies beside me on his back, his blanket thrown carelessly aside.

Down the slope to my left, a valley plunges precipitately into shadow. Down there something is lurking indistinguishably – maybe a monkey, maybe panther, maybe Jap. Whatever it is, it is untouched as yet by any redemption of daylight.

But look! Beyond the tree-tops in the bleaching sky the sun is already tinting some wisps of cirrus.One early riser stalks past, hawking throatily. It is Shiv Jung. He has in his hand the entrenching tool with which to bury the tell-tale spoor – not out of concern for hygiene but for concealment. He will shortly be followed by others.

Some of the mules are eating; there is a crisp, crunching sound of cut-bamboo leaves being munched like breakfast cereal. The soldiers are beginning to get about and to light their fires.

Dal Bahadur sits up and contemplates his surroundings as if he does not believe in them. Evidently he is half asleep. He looks doubtfully towards me. I shut tight my eyes and pretend to snore gently but he is not deceived.

He leans lightly across my stomach in such a way that I cannot possibly ignore him. I gave him a light punch and he slumps back swiftly on his hunches. He regards me quizzically just at the moment when I decide to embrace him. He must have read my intention from my face.

Throughout most of the march we were accompanied by troops of monkeys. Exceedingly beautiful to look at and bubbling over with fun and vitality, their movements were correspondingly graceful.

Breathing the cooler air of the higher plateaux, we would break cover from the thickly afforested lower slopes to crest over the crown of some park-like expanse of hill. Here the trees would be growing extraordinarily tall and placed independently, like specimens in a botanical garden. In the tops of them, browsing languidly off the tips of the best, we would come upon a family troop.

They would not, however, on that account always take off prematurely. If we did not too obviously interfere with them, they would stay with us, eventually developing an almost child-like capacity to attract attention. They had to be liked.

Then suddenly on receipt of some preconcerted signal they would be away. Racing through the tree-tops at incredible speed, they used to remind me in their herd personality of a beautiful sailing ship. Each individual would represent one unit of her sails, but all drawing furiously to thrust that corporate personality onwards. They were bowling over the other side of the ridge, lolloping lazily from branch to branch in a movement that was almost slow motion, so suspended it was in its suspicion of speed withheld.

Most wonderful, though, in all their breathtaking performances, were their mellow and mellifluous voices – so high and pure in key and of such a carrying quality as could be heard for miles. Disappearing into the distance and getting fainter and fainter, their cries had a certain sort of sadness which never failed to tear at your heart.

They seemed somehow special. They did not indulge in the senseless pastimes and foolish chatter of others of their kind, but retained their dignity in front of humans. There was a sort of nobility in their demeanour – something priest-like – which made me understand why certain breeds of monkey have been worshipped. During the dry season, however, these monkeys were seldom encountered at lower levels.

Here, in the flat-lands through which ran the roads and railways – for example, in the paddy-cultivation and bamboo-jungle on either side of the Meza River – everything took on a completely different configuration and complexion.

Tramping through this sort of country in the height of the hot weather, you had to be quite an exceptional person to resist the manifold temptations which assailed you – temptations to succumb to panic.

Noon, after all, is the hour of Pan! At noon, then, this whole basking paddy-cultivation, with its carefully contrived bunds and levels shimmering and shivering under the blaze of the noontide sun, would don its special mask of equivocation and indifference. It would half-raise its saurian eyelids and assume a smooth, semi-sphinx-like smile as it simmered in the quaking silence of the sinister heat.

Across the flat, parched clearings where the earth gaped in cracks and fissures, the wall of the opposite jungle would be dancing and quivering. Inside it, the shadows would be black as ink.

A flock of snow-white egrets might take off swoopingly from a nearby mud-hole where the tepid water still harboured a few gasping fish. They would rise triumphantly upon a lifting thermal, to circle centripetally like pieces of flapping paper. The piled-up concentration of interiorly boiling cumulus provided a stunning background of hot-weather, blue-blacked thunderheads.

All plant and animal life was suspended – dazed or dumbfounded by the heat. Teak jungles are the same. The trees shed their leaves at the onset of the hot weather and didn't regain them till the rains. They exerted a peculiar, illusionist effect upon the onlooker. The columns of men trampling through them seemed strangely unreal. First you thought you saw a section shuffling through the leaf-carpet; then you didn't see them; then you did again.

During our hourly halts, when we dumped our packs to the ground and stretched ourselves out to suck at cigarettes, the silence was palpably present. After the susurration of countless footfalls shuffling through dead leaves, you strained after some sound which would exorcize the numbing stillness. Yet words, if formed, failed you; they died on your lips for want of the will to articulate them. The sun, vertically overhead, beat down on the top of your skull.

It was at such moments, when the whole of Brigade Headquarters Column had been bulldozed into a stunned insensibility by the sheer weight of heat, and the quality of the silence induced by high temperatures was at its most torrid, that I used to try and detect, as a sort of private pastime, first the detachment, then the fall downwards, of every leaf.

As soon as the column had come to rest, unhitched its packs, dropped to the ground, and lit its cigarettes, I would unleash my antennae and obtrude them. Yes – I have a reaction – I can feel a leaf detaching itself – I can hear that crack!

Tracked with mathematical precision as it knocks – tock, tock, tock, tock – against various obstructions, it hits the ground with a crash.

Another leaf from a different direction detaches itself and strikes the ground – tock … tock, tock, tock, tock (not quite so regular this one). It has been blown off course by a slight wind. Rather a serious deviation actually. It nearly hit me!

Here is a rarity; this one spins! Listen! All around you, dry leaves the size of dinner plates and as brittle as biscuit are falling nervelessly. Can't you hear them – eternal shedding of waste tissue, perpetual autumn in high summer, interminable fall of dead leaf from skeletal trees? They drift down all round you as determinedly as if dominated by a motivating intelligence.

A tiny breath of air starts circulating stubbornly. All the crisping leaves on the near-naked trees throw up their little flippers and turn over vulnerably. For a moment the jungle comes alive with their movement.

Now, as if in culmination to such climatic effort, they collapse. You can hear them pattering down all round you like the rattle of buckshot. Do you think our Father in heaven is aware of the fall of every leaf as he is aware of the fall of every sparrow?

Now at last we came to that mountain stream. We had all been sternly forbidden, during our year of training, to drink any water that was remotely suspect. That was all very well, of course, in Lalitpur and the Central Provinces, where a refreshing water-truck was never far distant. Here, however, in the Gangaw Hills, I think we realized that the time had come to modify such precepts.

We were all dying of thirst; our water bottles and *chagals* were empty; and here was this delicious freshet coursing happily over the rocks.

'Well, what shall we do then? Shall we drink it?'

Everyone looked at Doc Whyte. A little bit of conversation ensued – to make things look as if we were deliberating rationally and hadn't simply come to a decision unilaterally out of an inability to endure thirst – but it was plain what we intended. We were merely talking ourselves round the situation before talking ourselves into it.

Doc Whyte summarized the orthodox position most efficiently. This was to the effect that the water would almost certainly be contaminated in spite of its sparkling aspect and the fact that we were quite high in altitude. He pointed out that it was a big stream and thus must have already travelled a considerable distance from its rising and that the only way to ensure absolute purity was to drink from a spring at its source. It only needed, he said, one herdsman, hunter, or high-level cultivator to squat down beside it and have a crap and the natural systems of dew and drainage would do the rest.

Having said this, and fulfilled his obligations satisfactorily, he got down on his knees with evident satisfaction and had a long drink. We all followed suit enthusiastically.

Within twenty-four hours we had the 'shits'.

Yet Doc Whyte undoubtedly did the right thing. You can't keep your body immaculate while wallowing in a mud bath, and it was pretty evident that sooner or later we should have to abandon all those clinical customs which are admirable for inculcating habits of cleanliness and discipline in recruits, but which in action are tedious. This was one of them.

Drinking contaminated water was a circumstance we had to go through and get inoculated against in order to put ourselves in a similar position to the locals. It would mean that we would all have dysentery more or less permanently, for it is very difficult to eradicate, but it ought not to incapacitate us. However, it did incapacitate Joe Lentaigne.

At first it was a bit of a joke, but gradually we were forced to admit that it was a serious problem. Yet such is the nature of the military establishment and its etiquette that, although all officers of the Brigade Headquarters were painfully conscious that Lentaigne was sick, they forbore communicating a single word about it to anybody, even among themselves. However he was forced to ride a horse.

Eventually he became so ill that he stopped wearing his false teeth. Such a circumstance always indicates that a man has plummeted to his lowest. In my experience, old and sick people seldom surrender like this except when they are near death. Lentaigne however, was only forty-six. Yet it soon became plain to me that unless he could be got out, he was going to die.

At that time the nature of what was affecting him was quite incomprehensible to me. It could not, however, remain a mystery much longer. After our first enthusiasms had worn off and the hardships of the campaign really began to bite, such illnesses became a comparatively accepted phenomenon. Lentaigne was simply the first and the most illustrious of our number to take that loose slippery slide down the long hill slope, the nadir of which was a surrender to inanition. Later in the campaign, in exactly the same manner but under more adverse conditions, I would witness hundreds of other soldiers similarly approaching death – namely, by inches – unless reprieved by being taken out of the front line and away from the demanding responsibilities of putting their own lives and those of their comrades at hazard.

I watched and waited, therefore, with frantic curiosity to see how Jack Masters would respond to this crisis. I wondered whether he would resolve the delicate problem by initiating a palace revolution.

On 21 March we crossed the Wuntho-Indaw railway. It ran, in that place, through the dense jungle. I don't think there was the slightest chance of meeting a live Jap. All the same, it was frightfully weird stepping out of the dark woods onto a track of rails and sleepers. By now the furtiveness and secrecy of our progress had penetrated deep into our souls and contact with any of civilisation's mechanisms seemed positively peculiar – even a bit creepy.

Masters and Lentaigne were busy sending scouts reconnoitring here and pushing probing patrols out there, and everything hummed with the promise of battle. As a prelude, Geoffrey Birt went off and demolished a railway bridge.

The Cameronians and King's Own arrived and, while their column commanders were reporting to Lentaigne, I managed to wangle a chin-wag with some of my mates. Sergeant Barker described an engagement near Banmauk in which we had killed a score of Japs for three or four of our own, and in the evening Geoffrey Birt returned and reported that one whole span of the bridge, about one hundred feet long, had been demolished.

The initial, preparatory phase of the undertaking was over.

# CHAPTER NINE

# A Change of Plan

I was on duty with the ciphers late one afternoon. We were crouched together, huddled away from Brigade Headquarters command-post down a tiny back-alley, far away from the splendour of the principal administrative offices and the Presidential Palace. We were Rhodes James, Sergeant Franklin, a cipher corporal whose name I cannot remember, and I.

Briggo's radio receivers and transmitters were set up for convenience not very far away. Their antennae, aligned upon a correctly calculated compass-bearing to trap signals from Rear Headquarters two hundred miles distant, were strung between two trees. The little generator-motor for recharging the batteries was discreetly chugging and Dal Bahadur had just considerately brought me a brimming mess-tin filled with delicious hot sweet tea.

Every so often the signal orderlies – riflemen from the defence platoons who had to perform this fatigue in rotation just as I had to work at a session de-coding or encoding ciphers – trotted obediently back and forth between radio sets and us, or between us and Brigade Headquarters command-post, bearing the flimsies – bits of the appropriate message-pad, Army Form K-2L0/4536-DJ (for yes, bureaucracy reached as far as the interior of Burma and even the ranks of the Chindits were not exempt) upon which the signals were written. It was a scene of perfect domestic peace.

Quite a lot of messages were coming in – acknowledgements of our sendings, *sitreps*, weather reports, intelligence details of Jap dispositions. They were all graded according to a certain priority and those with the highest priority were naturally decoded first. Sergeant Franklin was sorting through them and putting them in their appropriate order. Now he uttered an encoded grunt – and began feverishly thumbing through his code-book.

'What is it?'

'It's unusual. We don't often get this priority.' He licked the stump of his pencil.

'Well go on!' I said, exasperated by his reticence. 'Embroider on it! You don't ordinarily miss such an opportunity!'

He pursed his lips. 'I've never seen it used except for A1 information.'

'Let me see it, please, Sergeant!' ordered Rhodes James.

Franklin handed over the slip for Rhodes James to scrutinize. 'He's right,' he said, giving me a funny look.

Sergeant Franklin got to work with his code-books. Suddenly, out of the blue, he displayed the most remarkable example of intuition.

'General Wingate's dead,' he announced in a sepulchral voice. 'You don't need to tell me. I don't need to de-code it. I know. Wingate's dead! We'll never get out of here. Never. Who's going to look after us? We're done for!'

It must have been one of the most remarkable tributes Wingate ever had. Rhodes James snatched the flimsy from Franklin's nerveless fingers and began to work on it, writing down the words as they came. I shall never forget watching as the critical message unfolded: 'General Wingate killed in air-crash – Lentaigne fly out immediately – assume command force.'

Lentaigne was reprieved after all. With the message announcing Wingate's death came another, announcing a change of plan.

Our present operations had been designed to assist Stilwell's penetration from the north by destroying Jap road and rail communications in the neighbourhood of Indaw. Now, however, with the Japanese offensive against Imphal in full swing, it was intended that we transfer from assisting Stilwell on the northern front, to assisting Fourteenth Army's Corps on the Manipur front. We were ordered to abandon our harassment of north-south communications and to concentrate on harassing east-west communications.

The area chosen for our new location was in and around Pinlebu. This was a small town, about forty-five miles north-west of our present position, occupying an important place in the Japanese lines of communication to the Manipur front at Imphal and Kohima. It was ideally suited to our purpose, being packed with supplies which would burn beautifully, yet manned by second-grade line-of-communications troops such as pay-clerks and quarter-masters who could be easily terrorized by surprise attacks.

We recalled our columns, cancelled their planned ambushes and demolitions and marched to a flat bit of paddy where we flew out Lentaigne.

Whew! What a relief! Now we could expect a bit of action.

Intensely curious about the succession, I approached Jack Masters to find out what was the position. Without prevarication, he told me. Lieutenant Colonel 'Jumbo' Morris, our most senior man with the best right to the position, was to command 111 Brigade with the rank of Brigadier. As he was now one hundred and forty miles to the east of the Irrawaddy commanding three independent columns operating in the Sinlumkaba Hill Tracts, he was obviously not going to do much commanding of 111 Brigade to the west of the river. But, just in case he should commandeer a light plane and come hurrying back to take over our forces, he was expressly ordered to stay put. In fact, he was offered the rank of Commander but was positively forbidden to exercise command – in other words, his promotion was an empty gesture.

That part of 111 Brigade operating to the west of Irrawaddy was to be commanded by Masters. No doubt Lentaigne – for he had originated the orders – thought he was being extremely clever. To me, on the contrary, they appeared to be nothing but a typical piece of old-fashioned military window-dressing – something which we young officers who were not members of the traditional hierarchy were trying desperately to get away from.

Why the hell Lentaigne didn't just give the bloody thing over into Masters's keeping together with the Cardinal's Hat? It was because Lentaigne feared to trespass too openly on the sacred ground of seniority.

As Masters was in no position to complain, I did it for him. I expressed my disgust. But he was far too well trained to allow a comment to escape him.

So we began that series of ambushes and attacks which developed round the large group of villages, fifteen miles to the north of Pinlebu, called Kyaungle. I wish I could remember more about them.

First, one column goes off into the unknown and has a bash, and another comes back; then a second column goes off into the night and there are machine-gun bursts accompanied by sporadic small-arms fire, while the first column is licking its wounds, flying out its injured form a light-plane strip, or taking a supply drop. This was the general pattern of operations, hence this much I can take for granted. What is difficult to distinguish is which column did which, in what direction, and when. And was it now, or later, that Geoffrey Birt first developed that hideous brazen colour which is the initial symptom of amoebic hepatitis?

I recall that I was very aggressive in my outlook towards the Japanese during this period. Like the soccer enthusiast, however, I did all my fighting by proxy. It was a vicarious aggression, nurtured in, and launched from, the security of the spectators' terraces. At this stage, I never actually went out into the field.

30 Column was sent to engage the enemy before the others. Theirs was the first, deliberately sought, face-to-face confrontation of our campaign. Naturally I was wild with excitement. I expected a resounding victory and, as the estimated time of their attack drew nearer, I found myself in imagination eagerly projecting myself into their shoes at the place of engagement.

We were holed up as usual in dense jungle, but strung out along a well-demarcated although apparently unused track which cut across a steep, sharp slope. It was so steep that we had little option but to use the track for picketing the mules and other household arrangements, and there, as it got dark, we bedded down.

Dal Bahadur and I chose a place as far removed from Brigade Headquarters command post as possible. I might have been eager to engage the Jap, but I certainly didn't want another confrontation with Briggo.

As daylight faded and night drew on, we indulged our imaginations by visualising the Gurkhas of 30 Column creeping towards the enemy with blacked faces, their kukris in their teeth. In this manner, and according to the best traditions of Errol Flynn, we fell asleep.

I was awakened by the distant stutter of machine guns. I looked at my watch. It was ten o'clock. I could see Dal Bahadur's eyes gleaming beside me out of the darkness. I was glad he was awake. We sat up.

A hell of a hullabaloo was coming from the direction of the main road about two miles distant and it was difficult not to hug oneself with delight in contemplating what 30 Column were doing. It was possible to distinguish in addition to the stammer of their machine-guns, a crackle of controlled small arms fire, volley after volley, and the detonation of grenades.

Then all was quiet. Dal Bahadur and I were much too excited to go to sleep. The moon, which was just past its first quarter, sat behind trees.

Suddenly, from the direction of the road, there was the most frightful, deep-throated boom, which was followed by others. What could they be?

'30 column is certainly giving it to them,' I said to Dal Bahadur, doubtfully.

'Yes, it is,' he replied, equally doubtfully.

Finally I could stand the uncertainty no longer. I had to get up and find out.

'I'm going off to Brigade Headquarters,' I told Dal Bahadur. 'Be back in a couple of minutes.'

At the other end of the track, in Brigade Headquarters command post, they were all awake too. A glint of torch-light was gleaming through a blanket where Rhodes James was encoding the last of the cipher-messages. At the radio transmitter the operators were impatiently waiting for the signal before they closed down.

Jack Masters and John Hedley were in a sort of conference, and I went straight up to them. '30 column are certainly giving it to them. Those sound like heavy mortars!'

'They are,' replied John Hedley grimly. 'Only 30 column don't have any. It's the Jap. He's counterattacking.'

I returned to Dal Bahadur, feeling utterly dejected and hardly able to speak. The cannonade went on all night. I pulled my blanket over my ears to try and keep out the sound, but it penetrated. I wondered how it felt.

When 30 Column returned, I had the opportunity to find out. They had suffered several casualties and I asked Ray Hulme, a Company Commander of 3/4 Gurkhas and a farmer of Earls Colne, hence a neighbour of Coggeshall.

'What was it like?'

'Fuckin' awful.'

After that it was the turn of the King's Own. They put down an ambush on the same road on a similar silent night – the only difference being that the moon was a little later in setting – a little fuller. But it gazed down on the scene of carnage just as indifferently.

The opening bars of the action crashed into full orchestration exactly at the same time – ten o'clock. This fact must have had something to do with the way the Jap assembled his convoys. Probably the convoys of troop reinforcements travelling to the Assam front stopped at the staging barracks of Pinlebu all day, in order to avoid our air attacks. The lorries would move out from Pinlebu at nine – long strings of them, some twenty at a time, each containing twenty men.

As the leading lorry, its headlights almost blacked out and its sidelights dimmed, reached that bend in the road where our ambush was waiting for them, it looked in the moonlight like one of those unwieldy covered-wagons lumbering down the Oregon Trail to Nevada – or wherever – which we were all familiar with from our childhood trips to the cinema.

It was such a powerful image that it was almost impossible to stop yourself identifying with them – poor benighted bastards, indistinguishable facially from our Gurkhas and with just the same endearing qualities of simplicity and loyalty as we loved in our own men.

The King's Own very cleverly let it go. And the next one – and the next one. The trucks lurched past the crouching ambush-party unsuspectingly. They would be engaged by another hidden trap further down the road, specially selected for the purpose.

When the convoy was neatly divided in half, the King's Own let fly. They opened up with their bazookas. They hit the initial targets flat in the radiator-mouth at thirty yards' range. The projectiles travelled through the steel engine-casings until they reached the petrol tanks, which exploded. The vehicles burst open, scattering dead bodies in every direction. The detonation was heard at Brigade.

Lurid flames lit the sky. Then the carnage began. This is always the most antipathetic part of it. Unhappily, when dealing with the Japs, who can seldom be persuaded to run away, you have to go systematically through their ranks exterminating them.

The total bag at the end of the day's shoot, according to the gillie (although I have a distinct impression there were more) was forty-eight.

A little later, in a more formal set piece, the Cameronians mowed down over two hundred.

My friend young Lawrence who all during this period was performing the duties of a Platoon Commander with 30 Column told me some strange things about how the Jap reacted.

'You know, they're quite young – almost boys. They're certainly different to our own fellows. When we hit their leading truck, of course it went up and there were no survivors. The other trucks stopped and naturally we expected they would de-truck and deploy. There was plenty of cover and they could easily have disappeared into the jungle, regrouped and counter-attacked within fifteen minutes. But, instead of disappearing into the jungle, they simply jumped down and started digging. It was most methodical. They were in full view and made not the slightest attempt to take cover. They must have been given this order, you see, that when in doubt, you dig a foxhole. Of course, it's good advice all right, but they applied it without the faintest indication of intelligence. I can tell you, to stand there and watch them behave like that was spooky. I walked down the side of the road with my Bren gunner and he picked them off like rabbits.

They made not the least attempt at resistance. They didn't even look at you. I think if one of them had looked me in the eyes, I couldn't have done it.'

It was in such a manner and according to such a pattern that Jack Masters softened up the Japanese around Kyaungle. Finally he decided to take the village.

Needless to say, I didn't participate in the attack, but I did get as far as the edge of the paddy and watched the King's Own go in.

For twenty minutes they had been lobbing three inch mortar bombs at the place (the heavy mortars were man-handled from mule-back in the jungle up to the front especially for that purpose). One or two huts on the edge of the village were already burning. It looked dirty and deserted and so unkempt as not to be worth the life of a single man. In the haze kicked up by the mortar bombs, the site gradually subsided under clouds of dust, but I could clearly see the panic-stricken pigs and the petrified pie-dogs running crazily about the debris and backing away from the bursts.

We had called for a close-support bombing attack, but the bombers failed to materialize and Masters decided he couldn't wait. The King's Own went in. It is wonderful to watch an infantry attack trotting into action, rifles at the ready, pouches bulging with grenades and Bren guns hung sideways and waist-high, ready for firing from the hip. Imagine the anxiety while the men are in the open paddy and uncovered. Will they make it?

They did.

Emboldened by such successes, Masters decided to attack and capture Pinlebu town itself. Our morale was high; everyone was enjoying the battle; the Jap had proved anything but invincible. There is no doubt that, had we been allowed to, we should have taken it.

Impelled by the intrigue of Stilwell in the north, however, acquiesced in by Slim, acceded to by Joe Lentaigne, we were ordered north again to complete our previous assignment: to relieve pressure on Stilwell's five Chinese divisions facing towards Mogaung and Myitkyina at Kamaning. This implied being thrust into the thick of a battle along the sector occupied by the Japanese crack front-line 18th Division, a very different proposition from the mediocre line-of-communications troops who had fled from us, or been massacred, at Kyaungle, for they would have all their divisional artillery intact. We were to lay down a block just south of Mogaung, athwart the enemy's lines-of-communication to that city and immediately to the rear of his font line facing Stilwell, in a position which was bound to activate his most sensitive reaction. The block was to be called Blackpool.

But before we started north, up the Meza River and past Aberdeen towards our new operational area, something happened to me of importance. Masters sent for me and told me to prepare for going over to the attack.

I thought he meant in a general kind of way – a matter of readjusting my attitude – although, God knows, I should have thought I was aggressive enough in my outlook to have satisfied the most bellicose. However, he meant real action right away.

It was half-past seven in the morning. Obeying his summons, I turned up at Brigade Headquarters command post without having had any tea. I found him sitting between Macpherson, the Burma Rifles bloke, and an unknown villager. This Burman had come into camp very early with a few facts and an unusual request. Macpherson was translating for him.

The facts were: that about twenty Japs had descended several weeks before on his sister-in-law's village fifteen miles distant, where they had assembled large stores of clothing, petrol, rice and other commodities and from where they were terrorising the neighbourhood. The request: would we come and drive them away?

'Certainly,' said Masters, although I cannot imagine what could suddenly have given him such confidence in me. 'We'll send Baines.'

In a few sparse phrases he gave me my orders. It was all over in minutes. 'And,' he finished, 'I want you to take a prisoner.'

I was so excited I could scarcely breathe.

We were to leave immediately. Macpherson and his section of Burma Rifles were to accompany us as liaison with villagers and as interpreters. The Burman was to act as guide. The whole thing was settled so quickly that I hardly had time to comment on the orders, let alone turn them over in my mind. I was just able, while Masters was finalising them, to send Dal Bahadur off to alert havildars Tulbir Gurung and Ganga Bahadur and to tell them to prime the grenades. Thaman Bahadur, I regretfully decided, I would have to leave behind.

'Remember,' Masters persisted, 'that I want you to take a prisoner!'

Minutes later I was racing through the jungle at Macpherson's elbow at the head of my fifty men – that Burman trotting along enthusiastically.

Thirty miles there and back is quite a lot of mileage to traverse in eight hours (which was what Masters had allocated for the exercise). I calculated on getting to the objective in three hours, spending two hours on the attack and destruction of the depot, and taking three hours to get back. It meant whipping along at five miles an hour; but of course we had our heavy packs.

Luckily the jungle proved less formidable than I had anticipated, but doubtless our Burman led us by the most easily negotiable tracks.

A good many reflections occurred to me while we were on the march, now that I had some moments to give attention to them. Principal among these were some unwelcome thoughts about the process of taking a prisoner. This was a matter about which I had distinct reservations. It would mean edging up close to a Japanese and actually touching one. I visualized it as like trying to snare a snake.

Some extremely unpleasant stories were current about how beaten Japanese soldiers avoided being taken. They generally involved some beastly attempt at suicide and included taking their captor with them. The more I thought about the subject, the more daunting it became. How on earth did one go about it? I hadn't liked to ask Masters in case I should appear ignorant.

With such thoughts preoccupying me, we arrived within striking distance of our objective. Time and miles seemed to have flashed by too quickly. I had kept on repeating to myself that I was bound to be visited by some sort of inspiration. Now it was too late.

We had emerged from thick jungle, which offered us plenty of protection, onto the open platform of a much used and well beaten track. Our Burman guide stopped dead. He pointed diagonally to another part of the wood where dense scrub grew in a sort of saucer beneath tall, stately trees, and said simply: 'There it is.'

We all peered myopically in the direction indicated as if expecting to see Japan's warlord Tojo himself appearing in a sort of vision, but absolutely nothing was visible. All the same, I felt the blood slowly draining from my face while my feet turned to lead.

'Are you sure that's it?' I turned to Macpherson suspiciously. 'In that direction?

He repeated my question to the guide who nodded vigorously and added a few phrases of his own.

'He says the house is about three hundred yards in that direction. After you've gone a short distance, you'll see the roof. It will be sticking out above the bushes. The village is in this direction. You can also reach the house this way, but it's a bit longer and means traversing the village street. Now he wants to go. He doesn't want to be mixed up in the business. He's asking for money. Shall I give it to him?'

'I suppose so. There's nothing else we can do. You don't think he's leading us on a wild goose chase?'

Macpherson turned to the guide and evidently voiced this suspicion. His protestations were so obvious that there was no need to translate. I believed him. I nodded. Macpherson transferred this huge sum in silver from the pouches where he ought to have been keeping his grenades, and the detestable transaction was completed. I don't think, in fact, that the sum involved was more than thirty silver rupees – the traditional price for a betrayal – but it seemed to my tingling senses and sharpened perceptions to represent a king's ransom.

The guide smiled broadly on receiving it, and the flat face that had formerly seemed to be homely and trustworthy suddenly appeared hateful. I was deeply shocked at such a dubious exchange.

I was eager to go. Every minute that we spent in this exposed position might spell disaster, and I fully expected a Japanese patrol to come trotting round the corner. In spite of it, our guide insisted on counting every shekel. When he had finished, he vanished into the shadows.

Macpherson and I were left alone. We gazed blankly into each other's faces. Brief but bleak, that exchange of looks revealed everything. It told me that I would be wasting my time expecting help from that quarter. I would have to rely on myself.

Accordingly I propounded my plan. It was not particularly creative, but it was the only one available if we didn't want to rush headlong up to that Jap occupied house as an undisciplined mob and end up shooting each other in the back.

'Look here, Mac,' I said, assuming the tone of a master strategist. 'If you'll take the 4/9 defence platoon the long way round and up the village street I'll take the 3/4 platoon straight through this hollow. I'll probably get there first but I'll try and hang back in order to give you a chance to get into position. If I meet a lot of opposition and get pinned down, you'll be able to come in from the flank and sweep all before you.'

Well, that's how they talk, isn't it? Infantry Commanders? Note that bit about being pinned down – there speaks a real pro. Masters would have been proud of me.

I am glad to say that Macpherson responded to my plan without demur and assented eagerly. We accordingly divided the platoons and I told Ganga Bahadur to go with Macpherson.

'Tulbir, you stay with me. Get your grenades out of the pouches and hang 'em on your belt. Don't take the fuckin' pin out, you pubic hair. Not yet. Wait till you throw 'em. Have your spare clips available. Now put one up the spout and put the safety-catch on. Keep your safety-catch on until you're well in sight of the house. I don't want you alerting the Japs before we're ready, or shooting me in the back of the neck.'

The crash of twenty rifle bolts withdrawing, engaging, then driving a live round into the chamber was deafeningly loud. I imagined it might have been heard in Rangoon, but not a leaf stirred.

'Are there any questions?'

'No, huzoor.'

'No, huzoor.'

'No, huzoor.'

'Then does anybody want a shit or a piss?'

At first there was an uncomfortable silence in response to this challenge. Finally a little squeaky voice from the rear piped up: 'Yes please, I do!' It was Agam Singh. Everyone collapsed into uncontrollable giggles. So we all responded to a call of nature.

Then we started out. Underneath my bravado I was as pale as a ghost.

We advanced in open formation, strung out in a long line – twenty-five of us. I was in the centre. Tej Bahadur, the Bren gunner, was the right of me. Dal Bahadur was to the left of me. I glanced at him anxiously, wondering how he was taking it. I was horrified to notice how he had changed. His eyes were popping, his mouth was grinning, and his short bristly hair was standing on end. His normally gentle personality had undergone a complete transformation. At the prospect of battle, he had become quite frenzied.

The last thing I wanted to see was my little friend running amok and getting himself killed in his enthusiasm. I didn't have any personal weapon other than a small .38 pistol. I am one of those who have never felt it part of their business to rush into the thick of the melee and lay about them. I belong to the school who believes that an officer should not only not be armed with a sword, a Bren-gun, a bayonet, a rifle or any other of the selection of military hardware available – I believe that he should be armed with nothing more aggressive than a stick. I consider, moreover, that in an attack he should be guilty of no more offensive action than occasionally flipping the head off a dandelion.

You can only behave like this with very highly disciplined and sophisticated troops. I could not stand idly aside and flick the heads off dandelions while there was the slightest possibility of my little friend rushing about and flicking the heads off Japs. Accordingly I had to think up a stratagem to keep him near me – and out of mischief.

'Would the honourable rifleman,' I whispered, 'consent to lend the humble officer his personal arms? In the heat of the moment this stupid person has come away without providing himself with the appropriate weapons. I'll let you have a pistol in exchange.' This was artful, for I knew he secretly fancied firing a revolver.

'Will you really?' he replied with heart-warming simplicity.

'Yes.'

The exchange of rifle-and-bayonet for .38 pistol was effected in less than a second.

'I want you to guard my back. Be a good boy and don't leave me. I need you to protect me while I'm occupied with other things, so please don't go running about after the enemy.'

'Huzoor, I promise.'

'Good. Thanks.'

In this manner, then, creeping forward with excessive caution and taking extreme pains not to tread on any broken twigs, we finally came in sight of that house, just as the Burman had predicted.

It was an ordinary Burmese village house of modest proportions, probably belonging to a well-to-do person who had been able to spend a certain amount of money on it. It was built of wood and roofed with shingles. The walls were of boards. There were one or two refinements, however, which made it outstanding, notably the carved gable-ends, the decorative shutters and, particularly, the massive teak timbers like stilts which raised it several feet above ground-level and kept it dry. It must have been this feature which prompted the Japanese to choose it for their store in the first place.

I now had quickly to formulate in my mind some sort of scheme about what to do when we got there. It was still several hundred yards away – in fact, its roof was only just visible over the bushes. All the same, if we continued to creep forward even at the stealthy pace we had adopted, there was the distinct possibility of our creeping right up underneath its walls without being detected. This was a circumstance I definitely wanted to avoid.

There are, of course, several cinematographic sources available to draw upon in such an emergency. They are mostly, however, based on aggressive and masculine American techniques with which I was totally out of sympathy. I honestly couldn't see myself shouldering through a door into a roomful of seated Japs – probably all playing cards – and picking them off unerringly. My hands are far too unsteady.

The only other alternative, namely of lobbing half-a-dozen grenades through an open window, seemed vaguely unsporting. It did not appeal to me – more particularly as the board walls might prove so thin that they would be no protection to oneself against splinters.

In that case then, the only solution would be to get the Japs out into the open where they could run away. How to do that, however, was the problem. As I was cogitating, we drew implacably nearer. Not all my caution was able to keep us away.

Blast! Neither sight nor sound of a sentry! Such negligence seemed positively criminal.

I was saved by an intervention of providence. Which god is it, I wonder, whose symbol is the cock? He was the one who did the trick! Suddenly from the grass at my feet there rose up a *jungli murga* (wild cock) with the most frightful screams of alarm. He flapped away over the roof of the house, his wings beating loudly. He was followed immediately by his hen. We were about two hundred yards distant and we had the house clearly within our sights.

A man – he might have been a villager (and this was an unforeseen development) – appeared. He was bare-chested and wearing a *longyi*. I had not expected that the Japs would be in civvies and that there would be a problem of identification. This fellow looked exactly like a Burman. The only thing that provided a clue to his identity was his posture. He took up exactly that distinguishing stance which you see all Samurai do in Japanese prints. It is absolutely unmistakable and, once seen, can never be forgotten.

I therefore raised Dal Bahadur's rifle-and-bayonet to my shoulder and tried a winged shot. Thereupon all hell broke loose. Lots of little men with bare chests and wearing *longyis* poured out of the house and took up similar postures, with the additional refinement of putting one hand up to the brow to shade the eyes.

My men greeted them with a volley. There was nothing for it but to cover the remaining two hundred yards to the house as quickly as possible.

'Raise a shout, Tulbir,' I yelled at him. 'Raise a shout, Tej Bahadur.'

I had heard about the blood-curdling quality of the Gurkha battle-cry, so I anticipated something really chilling.

I was rather disappointed, therefore, at the weak quality of their response. We were all so breathless with excitement that it sounded like a deflating organ-bellows. However, my tactics resulted in the desired effect.

The Japs abandoned the house and retreated slowly down the village street. I followed them fearlessly. When we were within striking distance, I said simply, 'Grenades!' Twenty-five grenades went bowling gracefully over.

'Down!' Everyone flattened themselves.

The explosions were terrific. They were the last thing I remember.

Everything was confusion. It always is. You go into action with a consecutive plan settled in your head but you soon lose all sense of cohesion. You wake up to find that you've won, although totally undeservedly, or that you've lost, equally through no fault of your own. So it was in the present instance. Smoke was everywhere. Through it, I recall seeing Tej Bahadur firing his Bren gun from the hip. The spurts of the bullets kicking up the dust were just like those machine-gun bursts I had experienced from the dive-bombing JU-87s on Martlesham Heath.

All of a sudden I was confronted with this towering Jap. He was very young, very tall, and very fair in complexion – he had a delicious apricot-and-cream skin – and he was dauntingly handsome. I went weak at the joints; how absolutely typical of me to have conjured up something so beautiful. He was wearing the same type of Burmese garment around his lower limbs as his companions wore, and was also bare-chested; but in addition he sported the cloth headband or *hachimaki* of the traditional feudal warrior around his forehead. He stood facing me about ten yards distant.

I sensed at once that he was an officer. We immediately locked ourselves in mortal combat. I don't mean to say that we actually touched or anything like that. There was nothing filthy about it like physical contact. Rather, we squared up to each other with aggressive intent.

Grenades were exploding all round us and smoke was billowing about in clouds. The smell of cordite was acrid in the nostrils and bitter on the tongue. The rat-tat-tat-tat of Tej Bahadur's Bren gun punctured the strife every so often with its reminder of battle. In addition, that extraordinary machine-gun from the Japanese armoury of bizarre weapons known to us as the woodpecker was tapping out its deadly message. Yet my adversary and I seemed totally isolated. We might have been two antagonists facing each other from the feudal period and the Gempei Wars.

I was astonished to observe how completely I had regressed. My middle-class background and pseudo-educated manners had vanished. In their place I felt uneasy to feel a cool, wary character taking over inside me – someone who confronted his adversary with detachment and an indifference to committing violent acts.

We watched each other for what seemed an eternity. We had withdrawn from contact with our fellows, each holding the other's glance as duellists lean upon and engage each other's swords.

Finally I could bear the tension no longer, and fired.

I raised my rifle to my shoulder, took careful aim at the middle of the man's torso – it was quite hairless – and pressed the trigger. The action was entirely spontaneous. It did not spring from military training and was certainly divorced from any feelings of hate. It was more nearly associated with early rabbit shooting and the sporting instinct. I can remember the emotions with perfect clarity. They were precisely those with which I had tried to bag my first sparrow with the miniature 410 sporting gun given to me by my grandfather at the age of ten.

The results were also similar. Nothing happened. I reloaded at shoulder as you are taught to do when firing rapid and tried again. No effect.

All round me the fight was raging; people were crying: 'Have at you!', 'On guard!', and 'Attack!'. Yet where I was, the most flawless abstraction persisted. Completely withdrawn from external preoccupation, I was devoting all my energies to steadying my hand and to keeping my head.

Eventually, without touching my man, I emptied the magazine. I lowered the rifle in order to recharge it and in so doing stole a glance at the target. It had taken up the most peculiar position which I was hard put to explain. What on earth was it doing?

Imagine my rage and consternation when I interpreted its attitude – it was firing at me! That confounded Jap was taking aim. I slammed the clip down into the magazine and redoubled my efforts. Now, as I gazed along the sights and took aim, I could see quite clearly that the Jap also had his rifle to his shoulder and moreover – something that was quite sobering when you come to think of it – little spurts of steam were fuming from the hole at the end of his barrel. It required quite an effort of imagination to realize that they were bullets.

Luckily that Japanese officer's aim was as ineffectual as mine was. Gradually our tensions relaxed. I finished my second magazine and lowered my rifle. He also seemed to have come to the end of his cartridges. We had time to look around us. I realized with a sort of shamefaced surprise that I would win.

Suddenly with a gesture of despair he threw away his gun and stood before me defenceless. He squared his chest. With a horrified feeling of revulsion I realized that he was waiting for me to go in with the bayonet. I looked at the end of the blasted thing speculatively and wondered whether

I had the guts to do it. Why the hell didn't he run away? This was the perfect opportunity for taking that prisoner which Jack Masters wanted, but I couldn't see my doing it without wounding him. I didn't want to do that. We continued to stare at each other almost obsessively.

My Gurkhas began to return from various parts of the front. If he kept standing there much longer, one of them would shoot him. I did not want that. With a gesture of excessive irritability I waved him back. His scowl cleared and his face lightened slightly, but he still looked surprised. I gestured again. 'Do go away. Bugger off. Vamoose or whatever they say. I mean it!'

He came smartly to attention. Then he bowed courteously and saluted me.

At that minute one of his men from behind him threw a grenade. It was one of those plastic things – and made out of Bakelite – and it landed right at my feet. By this time there was quite a concentration of my own men behind me. I turned round to see Dal Bahadur blazing away with my pistol. I decided that discretion was the better part of valour and yelled 'Down!', at the same time pointing at it and miming the movements which indicated that everyone should fall flat.

It was smoking away like a saturnine seed, disseminating its baleful influence, and although I had heard that these things were no good, going off indeed with loud bangs but doing comparatively little damage, I still thought it better to follow suit, seeing that it was only several inches from me. Accordingly I fell flat too.

After it had exploded and I got to my feet, I was glad to see that the Jap had taken the opportunity to escape. So had all the others.

I glanced around to see if any of my men had been wounded. We had sustained not a single casualty. I was astonished to notice Macpherson. In the excitement of action I had forgotten all about him.

After a short interval to allow me to regain my composure, we burnt that small, pretty house to the ground. We distributed tons of rice and quantities of clothing and blankets to the villagers and allowed them to take as much loot as they wanted. My last memory was of seeing them struggling down the village street burdened back-breakingly with booty.

When we got back to Brigade Headquarters, I duly reported to Jack Masters that my mission was completed, and asked his permission to have a kip. For several hours I slept the sleep of complete exhaustion.

When I awoke, Masters sent for me and congratulated me.

'I've had an opportunity to speak to Macpherson. He gives you a good report. He says you were well out in front.'

So he had sent Macpherson to spy on me! What cheek!

# CHAPTER TEN

# The March North

That march up the Meza River and across the Kachin hills to Indawgyi Lake was the last we did that had any joy in it. The weather was flawless. There was no sign of rain.

Day followed burnished day with the radiant newness of childhood days of summer. Butterflies flitted about floppily, alighting indifferently on faeces or flower. In bramble brakes the wild roses abounded. In the deep woods, and beneath the overarching canopy of shade, lilac-tinted slipper-orchids nodded down at us from the moss-encrusted branches – but always just out of reach – like elfin countenances from a child's picture book. Everything seemed geared to drive home the lesson, not only of man's hatefulness – which by now had made itself fully apparent – but of his unloveliness in comparison with the world he inhabited.

In spite of the heat and the psychological burden imposed by marching to war through so idyllic a landscape, the troops were in good spirits. They had been sufficiently successful around Kyaungle to feel thoroughly at home here in Burma, yet were not spoiled enough by victory to have become sated. Even the defence platoons had been blooded and had acquitted themselves with comparative credit. In these circumstances Jack Masters suddenly came up with one of his most inspired ideas.

He ordered the whole Brigade – two columns of King's Own, two columns of Cameronians and one column of 3/4 Gurkhas, plus Brigade Headquarters – into a remote and inaccessible fastness. He called for a supply drop and a double ration of rum. Then, with a defensive perimeter pushed far out to secure a wide zone safe from attack, he issued instructions for a Saturnalia. Strictly for one night only we were to light huge bonfires, talk and shout openly, and get as drunk as the extra rum-ration allowed. Never were the parachute loads from a supply drop handled more carefully. Never did the soldiers of my defence platoons go to more trouble in collecting them.

'Rum, sahib,' Tej Bahadur and Shiv Jung would announce libidinously, beaming all over their faces, as they manipulated the massive packages, square like crates of soap, and deposited them respectfully at my feet like a favourite cat depositing a murdered mouse.

I watched while the precious cargo of priceless liquid was stacked. Then, under my directions, it was issued. Not one case was broken open, not one bottle cracked. The fatigue-parties from the columns carried off their allocation reverently. As a special mark of favour, Masters gave me an extra half-bottle for myself.

When the sun had sunk below the horizon and blissful darkness descended, the bonfires which we had prepared for the occasion sprang into blazing life. They lit up the underside of the great tree-canopy with uncanny light. Presently a faint murmur arose. It was as if the columns were only just getting used to speaking above a whisper. Then, a little later, individual tones became distinguishable. Finally, halloos and shouts. The hillsides and mountains gave us back their echoes. The stars in their course looked down. The monkeys and parakeets and all the wild animals assembled, amazed at such irreverent behaviour. But we weren't laughing at you, beautiful creatures! We were laughing at ourselves.

At last the hullabaloo and the fires died down. Exhausted by the day's march and the unfamiliar extra tot of rum, our soldiers fell asleep, if not actually in each other's arms, then nearly.

I glanced at Dal Bahadur with a questioning look. Ought we to? He gazed back at me, his eyes limpid.

'I've got an extra tot of rum stowed away in my pack,' I whispered to him. 'Slip back to our bivouac, and I'll join you in a minute. I'm just going off to have a piss.'

For all the eavesdroppers there were, I could have shouted my intentions at the top of my voice. Everyone was asleep. As he got up to go and act on my suggestion, the big fire around which we were sitting flared up briefly, then collapsed into simmering ash. It revealed my soldiers around me locked into various suggestive poses exactly as they had drifted off to sleep.

Bal Bahadur and I surveyed them in astonishment. It was as if our companions had been fortuitously transformed into blocks of wood. The opportunity was too good to miss. He turned about and went, but not without casting a sizzling look back at me. Quite giddy from so much rum and drenched to the skin with libidinous suggestion, I wandered away. I wanted to savour my concupiscent sensations alone.

So it was here, in the heart of this ancient wood and illuminated by the flares streaming forth from a natural stage-lighting, that it was destined to come to pass – and indeed this was our best opportunity to get it over with in dignified silence and under cover of a decent seclusion.

The time was temptingly ripe and the place was prepared. It was as if they had both been specifically put aside to enable me to assuage my passion for Dal Bahadur with propriety.

The place, in particular, possessed a sort of poisonous appropriateness, the hour a sort of opportune privacy, which neither of them could conceivably be expected to retain simultaneously in like measure for very much longer. Nor was it likely that such propitious circumstance and suitable conditions would ever recur.

In the velvety shadows, then, under the trees, and sheltered by the violent darkness from any possibility of contagion (such as Briggo's defiling presence), was where I hoped to perform the act.

I was in the grip of an overwhelming desire to fuck Dal Bahadur.

It sounds bald and unlovely, I know, and I have to admit that it was a cheeky thing to expect. It passes belief, I suppose, to imagine that a respectable Gurkha rifleman would have consented to such an approach at one o'clock in the morning – or, for that matter, at any other time.

However – not to prolong the agony – he didn't!

When I returned to our bivouac, I found that Dal Bahadur was asleep.

*** 

On our way northwards, we holed up for twenty-four hours in the vicinity of 16 Brigade's stronghold of Aberdeen. It was St George's Day. Jack Masters picked a wild rose. He also took the opportunity to fly off to White City. He wanted to have a look at the defensive and administrative arrangements.

The orders awaiting us at Aberdeen fully confirmed our previous instructions. All the Chindit Brigades were to move north. Their new role was to act entirely as support to Stilwell. 16 Brigade, however, on account of the hardships they had suffered during their march into Burma and depleted by their unsuccessful attempts to capture Indaw, were to be flown out. Strangely enough, however, 16 Brigade succeeded in seizing Indaw on 27 April. Finding the airstrip there to be only a fine weather field and not the important military installation they had expected, they did not exploit their success, and withdrew. They were flown out from Aberdeen at the beginning of May.

They were replaced by 14 Brigade, with orders to wait until we had laid down our block at Blackpool and then abandon Aberdeen and follow us. They were to support us in Blackpool by roaming the countryside outside our perimeter and locating and attacking the Jap artillery who would be shelling us. In accordance with this plan, they duly abandoned Aberdeen about 5 May, which was roughly the date we got into position. In spite of it, they did not succeed in covering the less than one hundred miles to Blackpool before we were expelled from it on 24 May.

77 Brigade, in the light of these new depositions, was also ordered to move north. They were to capture Mogaung. Our own block at Blackpool, twenty miles south of that city, was designed to help them. They marched to their objective on a course parallel to our own, but about forty miles to the east of us.

A West African Brigade, which had flown into Aberdeen at the same time as 14 Brigade and then marched to White City, was to garrison that latter stronghold after 77 Brigade had evacuated it. They were to continue in occupation of it until we had laid down Blackpool, whereupon they also were to march north to support us. They abandoned White City on 3 May – one day before the Japs launched an annihilating attack against it. They did not, however, succeed in reaching Blackpool any quicker than 14 Brigade. But they did arrive in sufficient time to provide sterling service as porters and stretcher-bearers. Undoubtedly it is to the Nigerian Regiment's efficient performance at that time that many of our soldiers owed their lives.

Broadway – 77 Brigade's original fly-in strip – was to be abandoned. The garrison troops were to rejoin 77 Brigade and march with them to Mogaung.

So that was the general picture. All the Chindit Brigades were moving out of the lines-of-communication area. They were moving into a sector – heavily supplemented by artillery and with plenty of ammunition – just behind the enemy's crack 18th and 33rd Divisions' fronts facing Stilwell at Mogaung. It would be into an area under the immediate personal control of some of the best Japanese Generals. They were likely to react very violently to the threat of a Chindit attack on them.

111 Brigade were to start first. The other Brigades were to follow. 77 Brigade, of course, whizzed up north to Mogaung comparatively quickly. They actually passed Blackpool at the height of our crisis, but they were on

the opposite side of the valley. They could not give us as much help as they desired. They did, however, send two battalions across to reinforce us. In the event, their objective, Mogaung, only fell after a protracted battle.

We left the vicinity of Aberdeen on 25 April and followed the Meza River. We struck out early in the morning along the west bank. The scenery was magnificent, the weather – at that time of day – delicious, and as we were in no danger from the enemy, being temporarily under the shield of the stronghold of Aberdeen, we advanced widely strung out. One or two of us even whistled.

But quite soon the park-like scenery round Aberdeen, some aspects of which fairly successfully duplicated the feeling of an English meadow, changed to something more craggy. The shallow declivity through which ran the smooth river turned into a gorge. The placid waters became a torrent. The undulating landscape gave place to mountains. And the track, instead of following now one bank, now another, proceeded – between high, precipitous cliffs – along the actual bed of the stream itself.

After spending two whole days trapped on the river bed, hemmed in by rocks, we all at once came in sight of this marvellous cleft. It opened in the rock wall to our right almost miraculously, like an hieratic gesture – visualize the expansive movement of the celebrating priest upon extending his hands.

At one moment there was simply the uninterrupted face of this towering cliff with one or two sinewy saplings clinging to it; at the next there appeared this momentous fracture. The two sides of it were leaning slantingly apart as if conveniently tilted. They exposed cleanly shaven surfaces.

The floor of the fissure was finely sanded. Down the centre trickled an artless watercourse, from the bed of which gleamed back at us the deep flash of gold – or more likely, of iron pyrites.

Without a word – silently – but nevertheless with a brief glance backward to indicate that we were expected to follow her, the trail disappeared up this cleft like a flighty goddess. Dutifully – for by this time we were all suffering from a sort of obsessive follow-my-leader compulsion – we followed, and were led out into the uplands, into the Kachin hills.

Finally, one evening, after cutting our way through impenetrable bamboo thickets for the whole of a day, we breasted a rise and saw below us Indawgyi Lake.

Already Jack Masters had abandoned his temporarily assumed relaxed personality. It was plain that our brief holiday was over. Dimly glimpsed indications of forthcoming attractions also began to make themselves apparent. The reverberative crumps and thumps of a distant artillery barrage gnawed at our perceptions.

Indawgyi Lake glowed. I gazed upon this impeccably disposed landscape with its scattered islands, its tree-clad promontories, and its elegant pagodas filched from a milken screen, an enamelled porcelain plate, or an embroidered picture, with eyes distorted by distemper. Already, I suppose, disease was laying its hands on me. The lake seemed somehow leprous, disfigured for me by a sinister Mona Lisa grin.

Far away over the mountains lay Mogaung. From that direction, faint on the windless air but sickeningly familiar, came the boom of gunfire. It beat against the eardrums and broke there, then withdrew like a wave – heavy artillery of over one hundred millimetres in calibre – a fugitive, almost casual sound, soberly reminding me of what waited.

In some of us, no doubt, that sound still had the capacity to activate martial impulses. In me it inspired nothing but dread. But we picked up and shouldered our packs, and marched methodically towards it.

Pushing our way across the low ground on the following day, we came upon a collection of lake-side huts dignified by the name of Mokso Sakan. It was a village, if you could call it such, which for several weeks was to serve us as a sort of temporary headquarters while the majority of the brigade went over the hills and put down the block of Blackpool.

The flat ground nearest the lake was covered with clumps of swamp grass. It was nearly ten feet high, had leaves like saws, and stems as stout as walking sticks. Meanwhile, the low spurs from the foothills running out into the swamp were clad in thickets of *lantana* scrub. This shrub, which is occasionally cultivated in England in greenhouses on account of its pretty orange and sometimes pink flowers, was in its turn furnished with thorns as murderous as fish hooks. Both species of plant made progress supremely difficult.

It was while I was laboriously hacking my way across one of these spurs that I was brought up short by a hideous smell. It was the first time in my life that I had ever come across the smell from putrescent human carrion, yet now that I was close to it, there could be no mistake.

I halted the work of the advance guard by raising my hand. In the ensuing silence I looked at Thaman Bahadur questioningly. I always did this when I was in the slightest degree doubtful about my competence, for I had come to rely on him unhesitatingly. Briefly he confirmed my suspicions by nodding his head.

The corpse proved more difficult to locate than expected. On account of the airless conditions, the area of dissemination over which the smell persisted turned out to be greater than we had allowed for.

'Found anything yet?'

'No, nothing.'

The little windless hollow in the dense undergrowth got hotter and hotter. The shimmering heat rose from the damp ground in quaking flakes. The impression which this phenomenon created of unstable undulations in the atmosphere was intensified by hosts of butterflies. Flexing their yellow wings, they perched not only on leaf and flower, but also on the ground at our feet. Their trembling antennae and probing tongues struck me as having a veiledly obscene aspect.

'Have you noticed them?' I remarked to Thaman Bahadur chattily. I indicated the wave upon wave of butterflies that seemed to be rising from the space immediately between us in fluttering flight. He did not reply, but paused and regarded them curiously.

As he did, I followed his gaze. There could be no doubt that they were ascending and descending through a small aperture which opened upwards in the ubiquitous greenery like a sort of funnel. With a sudden insight I gingerly parted the undergrowth and revealed a spectacle that was both grotesque and strangely beautiful. It wasn't a Jap, it was one of ours – an anonymous British corpse in an advanced state of decomposition, which was providing the butterflies with sustenance.

# CHAPTER ELEVEN

# The Build-Up to Blackpool

In spite of all I had learned, while pursuing my career as an Army Officer, about the unpredictability of human nature, and in spite of the gloomy forebodings which broke in on me when contemplating Indawgyi Lake, I still retained my military innocence.

I retained this innocence in the sense that I did not believe the Brigade would be committed to an impossible operation. That is to say, I did not believe we would be compelled to commit suicide. This was my way of affirming that I still had faith in our commanders.

We had no reason to distrust Joe Lentaigne – he was, after all, our very own. And little, if anything, was known about Stilwell under whose command we had now come in order to support his Chinese Army's approach to Mogaung. His sobriquet of Vinegar Joe was rather inclined to endear him to us than otherwise.

Consequently it was with no sense of forthcoming evil whatsoever that I answered Jack Masters's call to report to his command post when I arrived early one afternoon (this time at the tail end of a column) at a small village. I reported to him rather in the mood of one who expects to be allotted to some unspectacular task on the perimeter. What was my surprise, therefore, to find myself destined instead to play a part upon which the future of the Brigade, for several weeks ahead, depended.

A small digression into matters of tactics is necessary here in order briefly to explain the implications.

I have already mentioned that at Aberdeen, Masters's orders to put down a block south of Mogaung to disrupt Jap road-rail communications and prevent reinforcements from arriving in that city from the south were confirmed. That was the reason for our undertaking this march northwards in the first place.

The rough area for this block had already been determined upon by the General Staff, namely near Hopin. But it was left to Masters to choose the precise location. Aerial reconnaissance photographs and detailed maps had already been dropped to him by light plane several days previously, soon after we left the Kachin hills. He had, therefore, had a certain amount of time to study. The place he decided on was near the village of Namkwin.

One of the most elementary necessities of the future block-site would be that we should be able to get to it, swiftly and unobserved, across the mountains to the east of our present position on the shore of Indawgyi Lake. Also that we should be able to get back.

There were several pretty well demarcated passes across these hills marked on the map. There were others which we received information about from villagers. At least one of them, however, was reliably reported to be in enemy control. Probably some of the others were as well. One tiny detachment of soldiers placed in a defile and enfilading the pathway could hold up an army more or less indefinitely with just a light machine gun.

For this reason Jack Masters deliberately ignored the more obvious places such as the Kyusanlai Pass and slipped the Brigade along the shores of Indawgyi Lake to Mokso Sakan. The maps and reconnaissance photos informed us – and local sources confirmed – that from here a tiny, unfrequented footpath led to the summit at Nawku, about 3,500 feet, and then down to the plain, where it came out at the required place.

It was essential that this pass over the mountains from Mokso Sakan to the block-site be denied to the enemy. Someone (some unattached officer without too many commitments) and some small body of troops (troops who could be disengaged from their main body without leaving too large a gap) would have to be detached immediately and sent to seize the summit where the path from Mokso Sakan crossed the mountains.

It was obvious that the choice could have fallen only on me. My two defence platoons were too plainly cut out for it. It was to give me my orders on this account that Masters sent for me. When I heard what my assignment was – it was so important – I went glossy with pleasure. It was that ideal sort of command to which every young subaltern aspires: detached, independent, self-sufficient, and so completely cut off from headquarters that it would be impossible to receive contravening orders.

I did not stop even for a moment to consider the dangers and difficulties of the Brigade's position nor how, or on what terms, the Brigade was going to carry out its mission. It certainly never occurred to me that Stilwell and Lentaigne were committing the Brigade to a type of operation totally unsuited to it. I simply reacted like any young soldier who hears he is being sent on an adventure training course.

Masters told me to get my platoons together immediately and assemble them in marching order without taking a rest. He outlined the tactical situation to me just as I have presented it. We were completely out of rations, having been for the period of five days without a supply-drop, but I think one had been arranged for that or the following night. My sojourn in the hills was expected to last up to one month. It was essential for us to scrounge around and pick up something to eat. Masters had some reserve K-rations stashed away on mule-back especially for emergencies such as this, and these he turned over to me. Since he was most persistent that we depart on our mission immediately – for he wanted the pass at Nawku to be in our hands by noon the following day – it was not possible for us to wait and stock up from the supply drop. He gave us two mules to carry these rations, cadged from the King's Own column, with two King's Own riflemen called Jim and Jack as mule-drivers.

As I was about to leave him after receiving my orders, he called out, 'You are to hold the pass at Nawku against all odds.'

'Oh, yes,' I replied, not quite catching his meaning.

'Don't you understand?' he said irritably. 'You are not to withdraw on any account until I give you the order.'

'I see. What happens if the enemy attacks so strongly that I get driven out?'

'That's just the point. You are not to be driven out.'

'You mean to say that I have to allow myself to be slaughtered rather than to retreat or surrender?'

'Exactly. Those are precisely your orders. I hope you understand them.'

'I do. So I am to go down with the ship?'

'Yes.'

As I gathered together my little flock and told them of our mission, I found it difficult to hide my excitement. This is what I had joined the Chindits for. To have received an assignment like this was to have achieved independence.

'Where are you off to?' demanded young Lawrence as he caught sight of my detachment passing through the perimeter on its way forward. My two mules, with Jim and Jack in attendance, were bringing up the rear, and everything was in splendid shape.

'Buggered if I know,' I answered promptly. 'Into the unknown.' I wanted to be mysterious and stimulate his curiosity. 'Actually, I'm going to the top of the hill to hold the pass until the brigade goes over there.'

'Bully for you. Wish I could see a bit of action.'

We harboured that night along the way, about ten miles from Brigade. We had made splendid progress. It was on the banks of a little *chaung* that we settled, about one hundred yards from the path and in a tiny grove under some diminutive thorn trees. We had come upon the place by accident, after dark, but it suited our purposes admirably.

Jim and Jack bedded down their mules. They cut fodder for them from the plentiful supplies of bamboo that were available. There was abundant water, too, in a little stream. We proceeded to organise our little camp and make ourselves comfortable. At a point near an angle in the path, where it divided, I posted a picket of two sentries – two in order to keep each other awake and for company. Their orders were to observe who, if anybody, passed, but to take no offensive action and on no account to give their position away. In the event, however, not even a wild cat stirred during the whole of the night.

I did not think it necessary to take absurd and obsessive precautions about the remainder of our perimeter. I am pretty sensitive to danger and I always let this instinct guide me. In the present instance it told me that all was clear. The dense nature of the jungle would in any case have been adequate protection – particularly on this murky evening without a glimpse of moon or the glimmer of a star.

The rest of us snuggled up together in close contiguity, to gain the reassurance of companionship against the darkness and dangers of the night. It was rather spooky being for the first time without the encompassment and sense of security imparted by large, supportive bodies of troops. This was something, however, that we should have to get used to. All the same, feelings of loneliness and isolation were present. It was practically impossible to banish them.

When the sun had gone down that evening and it had got dark, I could not help observing how a gloomy cloud hung over the top of the mountain like that pall of smoke upon the Holy Mount. It was nearly the end of April and therefore not far from the monsoon, with its attendant electric disturbances and thunderstorms. My heart trembled at such possibilities, exposed as we would be to the full fury of the elements. It had been difficult enough to ensure our survival during the hot weather, when our regular supply drops weren't in doubt. How, I asked myself, should we survive in the rain when the monsoon storms would make it doubly difficult for the dropping aircraft to locate us? It was better not to dwell on it! We supped our tea.

The last of our fires twinkled for a few minutes and then went out, each rifleman firmly extinguishing them with the heel of his boot or a rifle-butt. Black darkness descended, broken only by the glowing cigarettes of my soldiers signalling to each other in whirls and spirals.

It had grown quite quiet. Gradually the last mutters of conversation subsided and were extinguished like the glow of the cigarettes and the ashes of the fires. Within me, too, all my fires seemed to have subsided. I was beginning to have serious doubts about my capacity to complete this operation. I assume that such feelings must have assailed all of us during the course of the campaign, at one time or another, but in those days I was neither sufficiently experienced nor self-confident enough to realize this. I felt guilty and tried to summon up a few shreds of better morale from the depths of my being. They refused to come. Almost panic-stricken in case I was in danger of moral collapse, I turned for help to Dal Bahadur. He was close beside me but blissfully asleep. I didn't know what to do, and I certainly didn't want to wake him. I thrashed restlessly about.

It got colder and colder. An icy chill started to creep up my legs from my feet. 'When it reaches your heart,' I told myself, 'you're going to snuff it. You'll be dead.'

Suddenly, without being in the least bit aware of how it got there, I felt the deliciously warming touch of a beguiling hand caress my crepitating skin. I was quaking with ague. 'Sahib! Sahib!' a tiny voice implored, breathless with agitation. 'Are you all right?' But by now my teeth were chattering so fiercely I could not reply. It was Dal Bahadur. I did not even possess the strength to pull him towards me but he seemed to know what to do.

It was what I wanted. Gradually my motor reflexes began to generate some current. I recovered. That beguiling hand had persuaded the strength to flow back into the extremities with surges of energy which quite surprised me. We were lying breast to breast. Our shirts were open and our trousers unbuttoned. I honestly believe he had intended nothing more than to warm me with the fusion of his body, but it had quite a different effect. Now that he had succeeded, he did not withdraw. All at once he kissed me several times on my mouth, and he yielded to my silent importunity without a demur.

\*\*\*

142

On the following day, at exactly noon, we broke clear from the hillside jungle into the open space which crowned the top of the pass. It was just as Jack Masters had predicted. The last few miles before we reached the summit were very taxing. I had taken the morning's march at a tremendous gallop and we were all completely out of breath. Even the mules were panting heavily.

I saw before me a roughly tilled open space of *taung-ya* cultivation from which had been harvested a crop of rudimentary tomatoes. It consisted of about two acres. One or two sere and depleted vines still clung to it like the derelict specimens of husbandry you sometimes stumble on in abandoned gardens, but there was nothing derelict about this lot, small as they were, hard as marbles, and tiny like unripened persimmon fruits – this was a cultivator's main crop, and he would have been lucky indeed to have secured anything larger in such unfavourable conditions.

The path ran straight across the field and dipped out of sight down the other side. It was the path to the Blackpool block-site and the opposite plain – the path which the Brigade would have to take on its way to battle. It presented a scene of unprecedented peacefulness and, at this moment, inspired great confidence.

A couple of young girls, accompanied by a very old crone bent double as in fairy-story books, were plucking the remnants of the unripened tomatoes and gathering them into baskets, while, in the further corner of the plot most distant from us, two fat babies and a pile of bundles were being guarded by a lean dog. The two young women wore huge, pagoda-shaped woven-straw hats on their heads, and the old crone wore a twisted cloth. The babies were naked.

Considering that we were soldiers and strangers, they looked at us dispassionately. We might have expected hostility. But nothing was said. They simply packed up their bundles and baskets with some despatch and disappeared over the brow of the hill without ceremony. It was positively insulting. Their evasive action, performed in front of my very eyes and thrown, as it were, in my teeth, made me feel like a monster. I was responsible for bringing war to this peaceful environment. I felt like one of the famous scourges of history – Tamerlane, Genghis Khan, Attila. I did not bother to follow them, however, nor to explore the path down which they had fled, for I smelled Jap.

Another path crossed that on which I found myself, bisecting it at right angles and running along the top of the ridge. It was heavily trodden. Plainly it was used very extensively. Whether it had been thus worn by the enemy or was so clearly demarcated by the regular movements of the locals, was a matter for conjecture. I examined its surface carefully to see if I could detect the characteristically split-toed sign of a Japanese footprint, but the earth had been stamped too hard to retain any mark. All the same, my instinct warned me that it was used as a patrol route. It seemed right to assume that it would have been a necessary precaution for the Jap to have patrolled the top of the ridge.

There was a thick piece of cover growing out of a shallow declivity immediately to my right. I told Jim and Jack to take their mules down there and hide them, but not to unsaddle. Then, dropping off a section to protect them and to rake the open space in front, I installed a second section a couple of hundred yards to the left. Having thus, according to the text-books, secured my front and flank, I raced with the rest of the platoon along the path that led to the right. It was from this direction, my senses told me, that there emanated that smell of danger which had activated my instincts.

I was feeling particularly well. What had been wrong with me was only too apparent. Now that I had fulfilled my function as lover, I had merely to fulfil it as soldier. This I felt superlatively able to do. I was so full of fire and fine spirit that it never occurred to me that the role of soldier, so similar to the role of lover, can be distasteful. Of course, I know that such moods vary considerably. At that moment, however, I am sure I would have bayoneted an enemy without compunction, and certainly would not have connived at his escape, as I had done with that Jap officer.

I raced, therefore, along the path to the right, maintaining no sort of formation and even less discipline – concerned simply to put as much distance as possible between the track junction where the Brigade would pass and any possible position from which the enemy would be able to mortar it. Rounding a corner, I was astonished to stumble into the arms of another villager. I imagined that my radar screen ought to have alerted me in advance to the possibilities of such an encounter, but it didn't. Our mutual surprise was great and both of us were equally discomfited.

A situation such as this, keyed up as we all were, and with everything cocked, contains extraordinary hazards for the military. In the present instance it immediately aroused in me the suspicion that the villager was either a spy or a Jap in disguise, and that I ought to shoot him. This inclination – a product of the sheerest nervous instability – I am glad to say I resisted.

Our meeting was so sudden that at least this villager did not have the opportunity of running back and giving away our position, as usually happens. Instead, he gave away the Japs.

'Are there any Japs? Are they there? Are there any Japs?' I gabbled in English, quite impervious of the fact that he could not communicate in my language. I emphasized my meaning, however, by making mime-gestures of attack.

My movements evidently succeeded in impressing the villager with my seriousness. His face paled and he grinned at me with ghastly servility. I was slightly shocked at having made him so frightened. He nodded in reply to my queries and gesticulated wildly behind him. I patted him gratefully on the back and he disappeared into the jungle beside the path like a shadow. I raced on.

Just at this spot, to the left of the path, there was a little knoll the size of a large tumulus, about fifteen feet high. It was encircled by some magnificent pine trees. It was a splendid place to put a picket, for it looked out on both sides of the mountain on account of the fact that ridge here narrowed somewhat. I remember looking through the boles of some trees to my right and seeing stretched out below me, at several removes, the whole of Indawgyi Lake with its boats, its pagodas, and its islands. I shouted to Thaman Bahadur, 'Here! Put a section here! Hold this sector!'

I had only the haziest notion of what I wanted them to do, but they at least covered my front. The path now descended down a steep hill and left us exposed on its forward slopes.

Suddenly, from away ahead, there rang out a shot. In that serene environment it sounded stark and solitary. It pulled me up short so suddenly that Dal Bahadur asked in alarm, 'Are you hit, huzoor? Are you wounded?'

I brushed away a tear which had started to my eye – it must have been an autonomous nervous reaction – and pushed him over-protectively behind me.

'No, of course not. Keep behind me! Watch!'

As if transfixed, I continued standing there and staring. Under the same sort of compulsion to delay the action as long as possible, my men did likewise. I could hear the wild creatures of the wood reacting to our intrusion. Nature was tensing herself. 'Get out of the way quickly,' ran the message. 'Man has arrived. You are in danger!'

A covey of crows dropped heavily from the gnarled branches of the pine trees and flew away, cawing. A couple of wood pigeons took off from a nearby *kanyin* tree like rockets and hurtled overhead, their wing-flaps loud as handclaps.

Just before we opened up, a panic-stricken jackal came racing down the track towards us. It had the peculiar bounding gait which terrified dogs adopt when they can't run properly on account of having their tails clamped tight between their legs. This one was so fear-crazy that he ran right through us. It prompted me to wonder what on earth the Japs could be doing, and again my pathological distrust made me suspect some trap.

'Gerrout!' yelled Tej Bahadur, aiming a well directed kick at his ribs. It caught him on the side, and the pathetic creature let out a piteous howl.

'Look to your front, Tej Bahadur,' I upbraided him irritably, 'and attend to your business. Now let 'em have it!'

Dimly, figures could be seen running and dodging between the trees. I had hardly given Tej Bahadur the order when Thaman Bahadur opened up from behind me with everything he'd got. My own party at the bottom of the hill followed almost simultaneously. Our fire was delivered from the whole of our armament: two Bren guns (Tej Bahadur was firing his from the hip) plus a fine selection of small arms. It had the requisite effect.

The enemy disengaged promptly. He brought into action his grenade launcher (always the sign of a withdrawal) and under the cover of its bombardment, retired to a cautionary distance, leaving me technically in possession. I had fulfilled my orders. I had not only seized the head of the pass; I had also seized the initiative. It now merely remained to see whether I could keep it.

The overall situation presented considerable difficulties. It was a problem position. It was the first time in my life that I had been called on to make tactical decisions. It will not require much imagination for you to appreciate the nature of my anxieties, namely:

I was on top of this thundering mountain – an inexperienced junior officer in command of a lot of endearing but unpredictable young puppies who were quite as capable in their unpremeditated fashion of bringing disaster upon all of us as they were of precipitating victory. I was separated by over twenty miles from my main body, with no proper means of communication with it, in an entirely unfamiliar environment, without sufficient food to last for more than a week, and with no water. I was confronting a cunning foe, doubtless of vastly superior numbers, and, if not, then at least a foe who was able to summon up reinforcements when he wanted them, and one who was well acquainted with the ground – which I wasn't.

I could only hope to survive under these circumstances and to cope with them if the enemy proved more inadequate than I was – which seemed unlikely. So much for my tactical 'appreciation'. In addition, I had domestic worries; but more about these later.

The obvious and immediate thing to do was to dig in with maximum expedition. This I did. I am no Prince Rupert, no inspired leader of cavalry charges. I though the best thing would be to remain where I was, in the positions I had 'occupied', and 'consolidate' them. These are the words from the technical vocabulary which applied to the situation. I felt a good deal happier for having used them. These terms from the pages of the Army Training Memoranda helped to justify what was fast becoming an untenable position.

Just before dusk, when most of the slit trenches had been completed, I sent out a patrol to prospect for water. It was successful. After half-an-hour of poking about in unlikely places, they found a sort of spring – but much trampled about with muddy footprints – which dribbled into a shallow pool. It was about a quarter of a mile away.

Without fires, rum or a hot drink, we sat down to eat an unappetising K-ration. I could see that I was not far from having to cope with a mutiny. Dal Bahadur was tired and fractious. So were the rest, including me – but the soldiers did not have the buoyancy of command to sustain them over dull places, as I did. I realized that I would have to make allowances for them. All the same, I dared not risk giving away our positions to the enemy just in order to provide them with hot tea and help them get over a difficult moment. But my restrictions undoubtedly bore heavily.

Night fell. We stood to. Nothing happened. We stood down. A dark cloud came down and sat on our position, and desultorily and distantly it thundered. Then a light rain descended which succeeded in further dampening our enthusiasm. We were at a low ebb. Also I was convinced that during the hours of darkness we could expect an attack. Thaman Bahadur thought the same. I had only recently promoted him to jemadar (platoon commander) and not unnaturally the other two havildars, Ganga Bahadur and Tulbir Gurung, were jealous. Ganga Bahadur and Tulbir Gurung had already started intriguing among their adherents to undermine Thaman Bahadur's position, to such an extent that I could visualize our situation degenerating into becoming intolerable. It was under these unpropitious domestic circumstances that I settled down to a blustery night.

Bleakly I surveyed our future prospects. An attack which had not come at dusk could now be expected at first light. I made sure that every man knew his business – when to roll out the grenades; how to hold his fire until the last minute; and, finally, out of the slit-trenches and in with the bayonet. They had practised it so many times that they were boringly familiar with it; and in whatever other respects I might lack confidence in them, I had complete confidence in this: that they could hold their fire until the ultimate second. My expectations were fulfilled and my precautions rewarded at exactly four o'clock. I remember consulting my watch.

I had dropped off into an uneasy and dream-haunted slumber. I was awakened by one of Shiv Jung's sentries. Shiv Jung was now a full corporal and I had given him the charge of the most forward section. My own headquarters I had established on the pine-clad knoll with Thaman Bahadur because it had such a marvellous view. I had established Ganga Bahadur with a section to defend the declivity where the mules were harboured. Tulbir had originally been allocated what was now the most rearward position – the one I have described as being 'a couple of hundred yards to the left'. In the evening, however, on account of this position seeming less important in view of recent developments, and because I wanted to keep an eye on him, I had withdrawn him and kept him in reserve. He now occupied a place roughly midway between my own position on the knoll and the declivity which contained the mules, commanded by Ganga Bahadur.

'What's the matter?' I demanded, jumping up and clamping my hands professionally over my carbine as if the boy were attempting to steal it. 'Are they coming?'

'Yes, sahib, they're coming. We can hear them.'

'Rouse Thaman Bahadur. Tell him to have the section stand to. Go and repeat the same orders to Tulbir Gurang and Ganga Bahadur. Then return to your section. Report to me in the forward position in ten minutes.'

'*Bahut accha, huzoor! Acchi bat!*' [Very good Sir! Right on!]

He clicked his heels, saluted, swivelled round smartly, and trotted off. I hadn't experienced such a manifestation of military precision from my soldiers for months. Evidently the prospect of action was having a salutary effect. I moved forward shakily, trying to master the hollow sensation in my stomach and tuning my ears to each sound.

Shiv Jung's section was absolutely palpitating with excitement: the atmosphere there was so tense that I feared for a moment that their sense of preparedness might communicate itself to the Jap. It was impossible not to react to it with heightened sensibility. Shiv Jung and I settled down in the forwardest slit trench – the Bren gun already in his shoulder – and listened intently. I was already beginning to respond to my stirring surroundings with similar martial impulses, when I heard a clink.

It was absolutely unmistakable and so exciting that my skin rippled with prickly horripilation; I was invaded by an unnatural feeling of exultation which was quite foreign to me. I had difficulty in restraining myself from getting up and charging the enemy, regardless of consequence.

'So this is the berserk madness of Nordic Vikings – famous in history!' I thought sententiously to myself. I never knew I was capable of it. It imparted a feeling of intensity – a tingling with vitality – out of all proportion to the circumstances, and it somehow confirmed my military integrity.

Now that the adrenalin was pumping itself into my veins in great spurts, I needed no longer have such reservations. All around me the trees dripped despondently; a mist suddenly descended, blanketing everything so effectively that it was impossible to see or hear a thing; and the drops from the branches reverberated as loudly as footsteps. There it was again – dead ahead and perfectly unmistakable: a rustling, unlike anything else we had experienced, followed by this clink.

'They are being absurdly clumsy,' I whispered to Shiv Jung, complacently. 'They are giving themselves away. We've got 'em! Hark at the clink of that rifle-bolt!'

He smiled back triumphantly in reply. I was beginning with a certain pleasure to anticipate the blood-letting that must ensue. I turned around, attempting to see in the darkness how the rest of the section was taking it. In the gloom, their eyes were glowing like fog-lamps. I wet my lips. Shiv Jung began methodically arranging his grenades along the parapet. Imperceptibly the darkness began to thin.

The noises to our front increased in volume and intensity and the clinks became quite undisguised. A whole enemy section was approaching. Shiv Jung released the safety-catch on his Bren gun and I did the same with my carbine.

'I'll roll the grenades out,' I whispered, 'while you concentrate on the shooting.'

'Very good, sahib.'

Behind me, I could distinguish similar silent preparations going on among the men. Quite suddenly a cloud must have lifted from the mountain, for unexpectedly it was light. The sight that met our eyes beggared description.

A huge, half-wild elephant was browsing placidly about a hundred yards away. On his rear leg he still wore the shackle and fetter of domestic servitude, to which were attached two or three links of chain. He was one of those working elephants who were released at the time of the Japanese invasion in order to deny them to the enemy. Clumsily, he passed through us. Of Jap, there was no sign.

***

The next morning – actually the same morning – I had to reassess my position. All sorts of unsavoury things had begun to happen. Also, we were obviously in for a long siege. The patrol which I had sent out to fill the platoons *chagals* and water-bottles at first light – immediately after our false alarm – had returned empty handed with the most unsatisfactory information. They had encountered the Jap. He was calming filling his own pannikins and water-skins as of pre-emptive rights, as if we – his enemy – did not exist. What impudence!

The only mollifying circumstance to arise from this encounter was that my patrol very sensibly remained in hiding and neglected to strike. This in itself was such a gratifying omission that I could only congratulate them. They looked slightly dazed. They naturally wanted a confrontation with the enemy as little as I did, yet were probably feeling rather guilty about it.

But in all seriousness, it was best. I didn't want to call down on my defenceless head any revengeful reprisals – the sort of thing which must have happened if my patrol had insisted on denying the enemy the spring. In the event, my tacit acceptance of the fact that he also had to live – the realisation, namely, that we both needed each other for us to continue to fight – formed the basis of a most constructive compromise. The enemy and I succeeded in working out, wordlessly and entirely by instinct, an extremely acceptable agreement.

I allowed him to draw his water at dawn unmolested on condition that he extended a similar courtesy to my own party at dusk. Such were the terms of the pact. Neither side, obviously, was prepared for a show-down.

A second unpleasant factor which I had to consider was the matter of Tulbir Gurung and his obsessive insistence on his – as he quaintly called them – rights. He seemed to have developed an *idée fixe* on the matter. He was at such pains to air his sense of grievance at not being made up to jemadar that I began to appreciate the danger to myself of becoming an object of odium. The common soldiers were increasingly beginning to interest themselves in the outcome. The situation was developing, in fact, into just such a contest or trial of strength as I must never allow.

It was early in the morning of the second day, consequently, when everyone had settled down and the lineaments of this subterranean conflict began to make themselves more clearly visible, that I privately sought out my havildar. It was during our ensuing conversation that he unknowingly revealed to me that he was an unacceptable risk. Regretfully I accepted the fact that I would have to put into operation my contingency planning.

In order to get to the root of the matter I feigned sympathy, deliberately drawing him out, acting as an *agent provocateur*. It was all the easier for me to do this because we actually liked each other and he trusted me, and because I was hanging on his words deceitfully with a simulated care for his well-being. It was true, what I had intuited – he was a strong and determined character far in excess of the defence platoons' trifling requirements.

As a matter of fact, I was rather frightened of him. He was a man whom, on account of his independence of mind, the other soldiers respected. He could very easily have led them into courses of action we might later all have had the occasion to regret. I decided I would have to get rid of him.

I wrote Jack Masters a letter. I described my situation as precarious. I assured him, however, of my confidence in being able to retain control of the pass on condition that certain obstructions to my success were removed and certain deviations from discipline were rectified – for instance, the bearer of this letter. I then told Masters what had been going on and asked him to keep Tulbir Gurung away from me.

'Tulbir!'

'Huzoor!'

'Come here! I have a very important commission for you.'

'Huzoor!'

'I want you to deliver this *chitti* to the Brigadier. I can't send anyone of lesser rank with it because I don't trust them to get through. You are a man of resource. I want you to go alone. I can't afford to send anyone with you. It's twenty-five miles of rough country. Do you think you can remember the path? Can you find it?'

'Is it about me?' he asked suspiciously.

For a terrible moment I feared he was going to refuse. There would then be the difficult situation of confrontation, close arrest, court-martial and probably mutiny as well.

'Yes.'

'Does it concern my promotion?'

'Well, in a sort of way it does, and in a sort of way, it doesn't. I can assure you that your whole future may depend on it. Take the letter. Deliver it personally to the Brigadier. Go with God!'

I saw disbelief and distrust battling in his face for mastery against his personal regard for me and respect for an officer. It was a titanic struggle. Regard and respect won.

'Very well, sahib.' His sternness broke disarmingly. 'Do you want me to go at once?'

'Yes, got at once. If you push hard, you may still get there before night-fall. It's all downhill.'

Having successfully deceived him, I could not now bear that he should linger for a moment. So Tulbir Gurung went. The upshot was that the men conceived a new respect and admiration for me, as being incontestably more cunning and crafty than others. It was inconceivably disconcerting.

Tulbir's career had come to an end. He was returned to unit and went down into Blackpool. But because of his unsatisfactory record – the result of my adverse report and counter-recommendation – he was exposed in the most dangerous positions and sent out on the most difficult assignments. During one of these – on 17 May, to be exact, and while gallantly fulfilling his duty – he was shot in the chest. He died instantly. They did not recover his body. He was remarkable, so one of his companions told me, for never opening his mouth. During the whole of the two weeks he was with them, he never answered more than 'no' or 'yes'.

# CHAPTER TWELVE

# Blackpool

The Brigade came over the pass and descended towards the Blackpool block-site on 5 May. The first I heard of it was from one of Ganga Bahadur's sentries. He came running up to the forward section where I was, and reported that strange soldiers were coming over the ridge. I rushed back to the path intersection, not quite having fully understood him. It was with considerable relief that I discovered that the *taung-ya* cultivation had merely been occupied by a British battalion. It was a platoon of the King's Own acting as advance guard who had squatted down there to enjoy their ten-minute smoke. They were followed, after a short interval, by Jack Masters himself.

I received him with all the ceremonial formality expected of a minor, feuding vassal in welcoming his king. He completely failed, however, to respond to the honour. He was very preoccupied. He listened to my excited account of adventures courteously enough, but he couldn't conceal from me that he hadn't absorbed a word of my explanations. Compared to his responsibilities, of course, my trifling affairs were insignificant, but I had hoped that he would break a K-ration with me. He shook his head.

It was rather a solemn moment. I stood at the side of the path and watched the long column of men and animals pass down towards the block. I was waiting for young Lawrence. I wanted his advice about my practical problems.

In this he was very accommodating. He delayed his departure while together we inspected all my weapon-pits, slit-trenches and prepared positions. He was able to point out one or two ways in which I could improve them.

We ended up in Shiv Jung's forward section-post. It was strange that I should have picked on this particular morning to send out a patrol, but so it was. Feeling secure enough now in my dug-in positions and a little more familiar with my environment, I felt capable of showing some initiative. I had sent out Shiv Jung with orders to proceed cautiously along the path ahead and discover where the Japs were located.

I had already established by further interrogation of some villagers – not nearly so nervous, these, as the earlier ones, for they had come and volunteered the information quite spontaneously – that there was a village, now deserted, about half a mile along the ridge. It was abundantly clear to me, from the enemy presence every morning at the water-point, that the Japs were occupying it. I told Shiv Jung, therefore, to creep along with his section and, if he should get an opportunity, put in a good, long burst with his Bren. After that, he was to skedaddle back without paying undue attention to heroics.

Now young Lawrence and I were standing in his section-post, staring speculatively out into no-man's-land and waiting impatiently for his return.

'Come on,' he said. 'Let's take a walk along the path to the village and have a look.'

It led slightly downhill. At the bottom of the incline, screened by some ferns and bushes, it turned a corner. Just around the bend the Japs had started to construct a block. They must have been interrupted by my earlier arrival. It could only have been from here, or from a point just a little further to their rear, that they had fired their opening shot. The obstacle was quite rudimentary and consisted simply of some felled thorn trees and a tangle of brambles.

All the same, it might have been booby-trapped; consequently it was impossible not to admire young Lawrence's bravado in negotiating it. He simply brushed through it. I was most impressed by his calm professionalism and coolness.

We were in the process of peeking about like a couple of broody hens newly released from the hen-coop when, from way ahead, just what I had been waiting for happened. It was a long – long – incredibly long – burst of light-machine-gun fire, succeeded by a shorter one. It was followed by complete, sustained silence. In the suspension of noise which ensued, I thought I detected pounding footsteps.

Yes – along the path ahead whence came that burst, Shiv Jung and his section were legging it towards us with all the speed at their disposal. They were making no pretence about conducting an ordered withdrawal and were panting heavily. On their face I noticed the most extraordinary expressions.

They wore that pleased, lolling-tongued look of hounds returning after a successful hunting trip. Young Lawrence was slightly scandalized.

But there could be no doubt of their success. The patrol reached me and crumpled at my feet, collapsing in laughter.

'Right in the middle of 'em!' shouted Shiv Jung. 'It must have killed or wounded ten – right in the middle of 'em!'

Suddenly, as if the enemy had only just recovered from his shock, all hell broke loose. Light machine guns started rat-tat-tat-tatting form the Japanese positions and grenades and mortar-bombs went a-popping. Then there began an indiscriminate bombardment from two inch mortars, some of whose shells came uncomfortably near.

'Come on,' I said to young Lawrence. 'Let's take cover.'

He had the grace to look impressed. It was fortunate that the Jap should have emphasized his position by this spirited display of his presence. It made my contribution look almost convincing, and Shiv Jung got the military medal.

To the accompaniment of this tiny bombardment, the Brigade descended to the block. Their story, for the next few weeks, is part of history. As I was not present during that phase of fighting, I can say nothing about it. I can only affirm one thing. Despite the obvious difficulties and dangers which menaced the enterprise, none of us expected failure or defeat. I bade goodbye to young Lawrence, therefore without any scruples of conscience.

The day was oppressive and clammy. The weather menaced thunder. A sort of brooding calm hung over the pass; we were not far from the monsoon. Nothing, however, of this sombre atmosphere marred my parting with young Lawrence. We stood at the path intersection conversing for a few minutes before he left. He was rather late. His platoon (30 Column's explosive platoon, the same to which Tulbir Gurung was attached, and the only one of 30 Column's contingent to accompany the Brigade to Blackpool) had gone on before him.

He was loaded with pack, groundsheet, blanket, a new pair of boots dangling by their laces, all his guns, ammunition and grenades – to say nothing of his K-rations, his haversack stuffed with spare socks, his pouches bursting with fresh clips, his water-bottle, his map case. Despite this heavy equipment he ran comparatively lightly along the path across the *taung-ya* cultivation, holding his flapping map case and water-bottle with his hands while his slung carbine jogged over his shoulder. He stopped when he got to the other side where the path started to descend, grimaced absurdly, then laughed and waved. His wave was of such grace and elegance and he looked, too, so young and handsome that my mind immediately filled with all the things which I had wanted to say to him but had either never found the opportunity to or had forgotten. My heart felt heavy as lead.

'See you,' I shouted confidently, 'when you come back.'

Silently he nodded, and then disappeared below the crest. He left me feeling lonely and empty, and so forlorn that I could have wept.

Thereafter, the long slow days passed so leadenly that they seemed to seal us on that mountain top in a sort of self-closed, hermetic limbo. I was completely cut off and out of communication with both parties. On the west side, on the shore of Indawgyi Lake, 30 Column Gurkhas were maintaining a sort of rear headquarters in the village of Mokso Sakan. On the other side of the mountains to the east, Jack Masters was established in his unassailable fortress, which was to defy the might of Jap 18th and 53rd Divisions with two depleted battalions of British infantry until 14 Brigade and the West African Brigade arrived to reinforce him. There was no reason to be pessimistic. As I look back now, however, it seems an incredibly foolhardy venture.

In the event, echoes of the fearful battle that had begun to be joined at the foot of the mountain at Blackpool reached me only furtively. By some quirk of ground configuration I noticed hardly any sounds that might indicate a desperate fight. Sometimes at night Dal Bahadur and I would lie awake listening to the rattle of the heavy machine guns, but generally we heard little.

All at once, without warning, the wind might change. We would become aware of the fearful, sinister thunder of the guns' heavy shelling. Under such circumstances, we could not help – all of us – becoming very jumpy.

Meanwhile storm-clouds, more tangible than war-clouds, started discharging. It poured with rain for days on end. Sometimes, when the storms lifted momentarily, the planes would come. They would fly close to and parallel with our ridge – DC-3s laden with supplies and provisions for Blackpool – then dip through the cloud layer that blanketed the block and its strip. We would hear them going round in circles against the chatter of the Japanese 'woodpecker' and the rumble of the exploding mortar bombs.

My own situation was also becoming increasingly unhappy. By this time we had completely run out of food. The Gurkhas, moreover, were displaying a degree of psychological instability which had me extremely worried. One night I was awakened by a strange sound, only to find

Thaman Bahadur's headquarters section barking and yapping in their sleep like dogs. When I complained, however, it became apparent that Thaman Bahadur regarded such a demonstration very philosophically. He muttered something about *bhutas* (spirits) and then dismissed the matter, going on to discuss something else. I found I was not myself able to adopt such an uninvolved attitude. I could no longer conceal from myself that we were haunted. I was dreadfully uneasy and deeply perplexed, particularly as Dal Bahadur became a principal sufferer. I had been watching him narrowly for several weeks.

The manifestation generally occurred after he had had several hours of undisturbed sleep. I would find myself called out of my own dream-troubled slumber as by a sort of mysterious affinity and an obligation to support him. I would lie there, unaccountably awake. The moon would be rising, late and exhausted. In its ghastly illumination, Dal Bahadur stretched out beside me like a corpse – long since dead but still beautiful and, of course, perfectly preserved.

'Perish the thought!' I muttered superstitiously, looking round for something to neutralize it.

Suddenly his body shuddered as if activated by a hideous, larval infestation from another world. He sat up stiffly like an automaton and let out a single, wolf-like howl. Coming from someone I loved, it was absolutely spine-chilling.

I made a movement of embrace. A voice – it was Dal Bahadur's – speaking from away behind my right shoulder said sepulchrally, 'Don't touch me!'

*Noli me tangere!*

I recoiled. He proceeded to disengage himself from his blanket with clumsy fingers. Then he threw himself upon me with a hungry sort of vampirism. His limbs clamped themselves to mine like a vine. Thank God, I had enough good sense or love or compassion or something – anyway, I did not reject this terrifying manifestation (and terrifying it was, for I felt I was being devoured) – but accepted it. I did all in my power to let pass from me to him whatever psychic substance it was which he wanted.

He had been taut as a tensed spring when he first threw himself on me. Gradually I felt him relax. The fit passed, leaving his limbs cold and lead-like. I waited until my arms had warmed him affectionately. Then I gently displaced that breathing, trembling, clinging, palpitating creature – for it was not a person – from on top of me and disposed it, as gently as I could, under its proper blanket, on its proper bed. He did not wake up, nor did he ever know anything about it.

But, notwithstanding these disturbing psychic proclivities during the night-time, he was still absolutely indispensible to me during the day. His was a temperament of tremendous resource and resilience. He now proved to possess a perfect flair for wandering about and searching for spoils in the jungle; also for cooking little meals in mess-tins out of the spoils he had procured.

All the Gurkhas, in fact, possessed this remarkable facility for foraging. In our present circumstances it was just as well. This talent was the indispensable prerequisite for survival. We depended on what we could grub out of the ground by way of roots and tubers. The first aliment on which we descended was naturally the crop of tomatoes. We stripped these plants bare. Inevitably we were in due course forced to search further and further afield.

The men's physical and psychological deterioration inexorably moved us all nearer to the point where we would crack and crumple. Under such circumstances it was not in any degree convenient to be told that Ganga Bahadur was ill. I had had just about enough of this Brahmin havildar's over-weening pretensions and assumption of arrogant superiority. I felt almost venomous towards him.

'What's wrong with him?' I asked the man of Ganga Bahadur's section who had come to report the matter to me. 'Can't he get about his business even a bit?'

'He's sick.' The man went through the motions of vomiting. 'And he's got pains in his belly.'

I looked at him with such hostility and with such lack of concern for the sufferer that it must have been that which did the trick. In view of my obvious disbelief in such symptoms, the man feared to show the slightest signs of sympathy. At any rate, his stolid expression, probably caused by my own ill temper, was an exact reflection of my own scepticism. I wrongly concluded that the messenger himself did not believe in Ganga Bahadur's condition. I therefore nodded cursorily in dismissal, and equally I dismissed the man and his matter from my mind. I simply assumed that it would be some entirely temporary malaise.

Completely immersed in other activities, I forgot all about it. At the onset of the rains, all sorts of herbs and shoots were sprouting. They provided excellent opportunities for food gathering. I was very concerned that we take advantage of them. Every day patrols went out to collect mushrooms and fungi, sweet yams, unfolding fern-shoots and tender bamboos.

What was my surprise, therefore, on the following day, to receive another plea from Ganga Bahadur – only this time couched in the form of a summons: 'Will his excellency please come and examine the patient. The Havildar has taken a turn for the worse.'

I could not very well refuse. I went along, although with bad grace. Ganga Bahadur was lying, well cared for by his section, in a hollow of earth. It was scraped out to form a sort of nest into which he could lodge his hip and lined with leaves and dry grass over which had been spread his groundsheet. He was lying on this and covered on top with his blanket. He looked a damn sight too clean and comfortable for my liking, curled up like a hare in its form, and this fact by itself predisposed me in his disfavour. We were all as scruffy as scarecrows, as dingy as gypsies and as screwed up as hell. I found it insupportable that this man alone of all my Gurkhas should somehow have escaped the general dirtiness.

When he saw me, he made an inadequate attempt to struggle free from his surroundings. It was not a success. He fell back, feigning exhaustion and weakness. All this was simply what I had led myself to expect. There was only one circumstance which caused me surprise. This was that his face had unmistakably become illuminated with hope and expectation as soon as he saw me. It ought not to have done if he was, as I surmised, swinging the lead. It was this fact alone which made me wonder whether he was indeed malingering. Otherwise he looked, I thought, extremely well.

'Well, havildar-ji,' I said with forced courtesy – it sounded as painful and unconvincing as it was insincere. 'What is it?'

He launched into a detailed description of his symptoms. I could make nothing of them. His manner betrayed a sort of superstitious confidence in me which, however, I was afraid I was going to disappoint. I recalled to mind that Tulbir had been encouraged by this same Ganga Bahadur's connivance and support to convert himself into an intriguer. Now Tulbir was disgraced, and I did not feel disposed to extend my clemency towards his coadjutor.

'Is it a cold?'

'No, huzoor,' answered several voices, eager to get into the act. 'It's a chew – sheu – cheou.'

My medical vocabulary was not up to these terms. I imagined his malady to be one of those absurd oriental superstitions like the supposed weakening effects of nocturnal emissions. Hindus make such a fuss about them. If I refused to be impressed, then Ganga Bahadur would come to his senses and get better. I should then forgive him, and he would return to his allegiance.

'Get up!' I said brutally. 'And get on with your job of helping me to run this platoon. That is where your duty lies and I will thank you to do it. Be on your feet tomorrow and no more will be said.'

At my harsh words, his features underwent an extraordinary change of expression – from confident to disfigured.

'Won't you even send for a doctor?' he whimpered despondently, all his bounce and bluster gone.

I had been about to go. Now I turned back.

'My dear Ganga Bahadur,' I enunciated patronisingly and unctuously. 'The nearest doctor is twenty-five miles away. It will take a messenger one day to get down to Indawgyi and the doctor another day to get back. I am certainly not going to send for him on the slender supposition of your illness. Quite frankly, I don't believe in it. There must be persons among the men who have experience of Ayurvedic medicine. Well, use them! By all means try herbs and simples. All I am asking you is not to rely on me.'

He had managed to raise himself on one elbow while I was saying all this and to incline himself hungrily forward. Now he threw himself back.

'Then I am finished. I had some hope. You have taken it from me. I resign myself to die.' His face became quite composed under this impact of this realisation – his posture almost dignified.

'Stuff and nonsense,' I declared, still quite convinced he was bluffing.

'It's a *chew – sheu – scheou*,' he muttered.

'It's a *chew*. If only his excellency could understand.' Suddenly he screamed at the top of his voice in torment of anguish, '*Chew – sheu – scheou!*'

But I left. The next morning Dal Bahadur said to me, quite chattily, 'Ganga Bahadur is dead!'

Correctly interpreting my terrible look of consternation, he continued, 'You couldn't have helped him. You see, he'd eaten this! *Chew – sheu – scheou!*' He held up a small specimen of *amanita muscaria*. Ganga Bahadur had eaten a poisonous mushroom.

As is the way with Gurkhas, nobody seemed to take Ganga Bahadur's death very much to heart except me. He passed from this world and was buried in an anonymous grave, rolled up in his groundsheet, without a sigh of regret. I, on the contrary, was very much troubled by it. It was the first time in my life that I had perpetrated such a disreputable act. I had not even felt his pulse. It was genuine deed of wickedness.

I returned deeply upset from viewing the corpse and certifying the death. Try as I might, I found myself incapable of escaping liability for it. Ganga Bahadur fastened himself like a leech on the tender stuff of my susceptibilities and proved far more tormenting dead than alive.

I sat on top of the pine-clad tumulus where Thaman Bahadur had established the headquarters section, and gazed out over Indawgyi Lake. The clouds, momentarily, had lifted, but the dazzling landscape for once afforded me no sense of spiritual refreshment. It was dimmed by my personal shadows.

It rained and rained. Huddled in our sopping slit-trenches or under the leaking grass roofs of our diminutive *bashas*, the defence platoons and I no longer put up any pretence other than of clinging desperately to survival. Crushed into close and constrictive confinement in an effort to escape the pitiless rain, dry our soaking clothes, or warm our icy limbs (for the temperature between rain storms fluctuated wildly), we were all unavoidably forced either into wallowing contact or wallowing conflict.

The feculent, foetid smells exhaling from our sweaty bodies luckily failed to repel us. They exerted an exactly contrary effect. A veritable furnace of sensuality seemed to take possession of us. Nor were Dal Bahadur and myself exempt. With torn and tattered clothes whose rents sometimes appeared to me to have been contrived deliberately, the Gurkhas seemed to be under the influence of a permanent excitation.

The rain continued to pour down.

Suddenly this private domain, cut off entirely from communication with the rest of the world and inhabited exclusively by lustfulness and secret indulgence in forbidden pleasures, became once more a centre of activity. The West African Brigade's 6th Battalion of the Nigeria Regiment arrived – huge, black, intensely grinning negroes. I have never to this day been able to discover which direction they came from. They simply appeared, their officers bringing with them all sorts of terrible rumours: 111 Brigade had been defeated – Jack Masters was dead, kicked by a mule, shot by a bullet or exploded by a shell – or he had simply vanished into the terminal shadows – there were hundreds of casualties – 111 Brigade had ceased to exist – we were disbanded, finished, kaput!

They descended to the plain, scarcely bothering to conceal their satisfaction. It was evidently their intention to take over.

They were closely followed by 30 Column Gurkhas from Mokso Sakan. In the van was Mike MacGillicuddy in charge of all the mules. Jack Masters had wisely sent the animals transport back to Mokso Sakan from Blackpool, consequently all the brigade mules were now available for evacuating the wounded. It was these mules, together with 30 Columns's own transport, that MacGillicuddy was hastening to take down to the block.

I wasn't able to have many words with him nor did he know very much, merely having received a brief signal, but he confirmed my worst suspicions.

'Is Jack Masters all right?'

'Yes, he's OK. Unwounded. I don't know who else is gone. Oh, yes. M (he mentioned a mutual acquaintance) is dead.'

'Anybody else?' I was thinking of young Lawrence.

He shook his head. 'Tommy Thompson (the Colonel of the King's Own) is wounded. He got his in his neck. I don't know anything else at the moment. Look here, I've got to go. The rear of the column is bunching up.'

'Do you want me to come?'

'No, we've already got the West Africans. Anyway, the path is too narrow. There's no room to manoeuvre.' With this depressing information he left.

My worst forebodings were fulfilled two days later. One of my sentries came running to me and announced, 'The Brigadier is coming.'

I hastened, therefore, along the path across the *taung-ya* cultivation, now become a perfect quagmire, and down the opposite hill. Parties of wounded men, in twos and threes, were struggling up it, their eyes glazed with exhaustion, while the leaden hue of their faces, dull like some lustreless metal and as blue as cobalt, betokened many hours of wakeful nights. They exemplified the frightful effects which a decisive defeat can have on an army, for these stricken wretches, reeling from fatigue, shock and humiliation, belonged to no recognisable unit and owed allegiance – temporarily – to nobody. They were intent solely upon saving themselves and their mates, and if any attempt had been made to rally them with the familiar slogans, they would have turned on the individual attempting it and torn him to shreds.

They did not even look at me as they passed, but avoided my glance. They knew me for an officer and feared I might give them an order which they would refuse to obey. Eyes riveted to the ground, they chattered incessantly to themselves like very old, or mad, people who are completely cut off from their fellows by their obsession with their private sorrows.

But this was merely the advance party – a faintly adumbrated foreshadowing of what was to follow. There were simply the walking wounded, those who could fend for themselves. Some of them had uniforms hanging in tatters, ripped from their backs by shell-splinters and exposing ghastly, shrapnel-shredded wounds. Others, except for the parachute-cloth or segment of torn blanket which covered their genitals, were naked. Their unresilient flesh was mercilessly exposed to the teeming rain.

I was overwhelmed with compassion and longed desperately to help. For the moment, however, they were beyond contact. I felt myself, on account of my association with (at however far a removal) those who had submitted them to this ordeal, rejected without benefit of appeal. I belonged, you see, to the military establishment, and on that account was not to be trusted.

A little further down the path I came upon my friend Sergeant Barker. He was always a loner and, even under these circumstances, except for the comrade he bore on his back, was unaccompanied.

'My God, but I'm glad to see you,' he said unashamedly. 'I never thought I'd make it.'

'Are you all right? Are you wounded?'

'I'm all right. It's me mate! I can't turn me 'ead. What's 'e look like? Is 'e dead? I can't bear to have carried 'im all this way an' 'e be a gonner!'

The man, indeed, looked moribund. His survival, I suspected, must be very much in doubt. I did not, however, like to say so. His eyes were closed, his head was lolling and he was quite obviously unconscious.

As if aware of what I was thinking, Sergeant Barker interpolated in extenuation, 'Of course, 'e's full of morphia. It makes 'em ever so dopey!'

Every so often, however, the man opened his mouth quite automatically and let forth a gobbet of blood. It stained his teeth with a hideously macabre effect as if he had been chewing *pan* (a confection of areca nut and betel leaf used as a masticatory by the inhabitants of South East Asia, which causes a flow of brilliant, brick-red saliva); but his face remained studiously passive. I did not think there was the slightest hope for him.

'It's only quarter of a mile to the summit,' I assured Sergeant Barker, encouragingly. 'Do you want me to take over?'

'No thank you, sir. I can manage.'

'Before you go – er – have you seen my friend, Mr Lawrence?'

'No sir, He'll be further back. I'm almost certain he's with the Brigadier's party.'

'Yes, that would make sense. Good luck with your friend, and thank you.'

Next came a party of mules. They had managed to get some of the more seriously wounded men astride them bareback, and to support them there with some success. The men walked, one either side, to prop them up. At just the place on the path, however, where I had encountered them, some jutting rocks and a sharp, precipitous ascent made a successful negotiation very problematical. The leading mule gathered her legs together for a jump, thought better of it, stumbled, and in striving to regain her balance, struck her rump against a rock. She lurched drunkenly off the path and, in recovering herself, threw the man off her back. He fell in the mud with a sickening thump. The expressions on the faces of people who are old, sick or injured, and on account of their disability are subjected to galling indignities, are often strikingly pathetic. I remember particularly the expression on this man's face of outraged innocence. He looked like a very old baby who has been rudely precipitated from his pram. We all rushed to pick him up, but it was plain that he was dead.

I did not want to witness the look of baffled fury, mortification and perplexity which invaded the face of his friend – who had been supporting him – but I could not avoid it. He simply sat down on the edge of the path and surrendered helplessly to a fit of sobbing and to a wringing of his hands.

I moved on down the hill into the thick of it – where the hundred and fifty or so casualties the doctors had managed to evacuate were being borne on improvised stretchers by the West Africans.

Here, the sheer carnage caused by intensive shelling was painfully apparent. It was particularly evident, too, how the fog of war had confused the combatants. Whenever I came on anyone I knew, I persisted in enquiring after young Lawrence. All I got were contradictions.

'Oh, yes. He's up at the front. I saw him an hour ago. He gave me a drink from his water-bottle.'

'Oh, no. He's with the rear guard. I passed by him this morning.'

But despite the horror of the situation, the withdrawal was in fact an astonishing success.

Here a tiny Gurkha trudges through the wet, on his face that perennial look of surprise which never seems to leave a Gurkha, no matter under what circumstances. He leads his devoted mule, head nodding, ears bobbing, and also wearing a persistently perplexed expression. Man and mule are further indistinguishable by being covered in mud. On the mule's back there rides a battered soldier of the King's Own, rocking backwards and forwards at every lurch of his mount. His head is swathed in bandages because he has been blinded by a shell. He is covered in mud too, and is in addition entirely naked. He looks like an earthen image.

He is closely followed by a file of earth-grey soldiers, each with his carefully preserved personal weapon intact. The last group in the file staggers under the weight of a three-inch mortar-barrel and base-plate while every other man in the platoon is loaded down with a ten-pound mortar bomb in addition to his own equipment. They plod past methodically, eyes blazing out of mud-plastered faces and their breaths inhaling and exhaling in short, stertorous gasps.

Now comes a group of West African *sipahis* volunteering as stretcher bearers. They tower over the rest of us like picturesque Nubians taking part in Cleopatra's procession. They are so strong that, if need be, two of them can raise above their heads at full arm's length a stretcher with a wounded man on it. On the stretchers the wounded lie, lulled by morphia, like flat little piles of old clothes – quite unidentifiable as human beings. Everyone's uniform – if you can so dignify the rags which hang from their backs – is black with wet or sweat.

Suddenly I rounded a bend and came on the Brigade Headquarters command party led by Jack Masters. I don't know what I expected, but I was surprised that they all looked the same. After so many gruesome sights, I was half-afraid that I would be unable to recognize them: Geoffrey Birt; Doc Whyte; Briggo, looking supercilious as ever; Smithy, black as a boot. John Hedley, I knew, was not there for he had been wounded and flown out. But where – my eyes scanned the group and penetrated into it deeply – was young Lawrence!

Masters was devouring a hot, cooked chicken! His orderly was standing nearby with the savoury, grease-glistening carcase in his hands and tearing pieces off it. At the moment I came upon them he was in the act of passing Masters a leg. The scene was such a domestic contrast to the frenzy of battle that I halted self-consciously. I feared to rush in and spoil their interlude.

Masters glared at me over the top of the drumstick he was gnawing and greeted me with an unemotional 'hello'. Then he wiped some grease from his mouth. Although I felt I ought to be profoundly grateful that he had been spared to us, I was unable not to feel envious of him on account of what he was eating. This must have taken a certain amount of sincerity out of my greeting. However, I said 'How are you, sir?' with as much solicitousness as I could manage.

'Seething with rage and frustration, he responded without an instant's hesitation. He said it with such venom, and so ferociously, that I felt ashamed.

'Why?'

He followed up the remark with so many reasons for rage and frustration that I realized his emotion was deeply felt: because he had been defeated; because he had been driven out of his position; because he was tormented with hunger, fatigue and sleeplessness; because he yearned – and here he expressed himself self-deprecatingly – for some nameless good which he could only guess at. For these reasons he seethed with rage and frustration, and his gaze challenged me so directly to deny their validity that I averted my eyes. I feared lest inadvertently I should trespass upon his privacy and deface it. I withdrew. In the presence of such noble despair I felt unworthy and humble.

I buttonholed Doc Whyte instead. 'Where's young Lawrence?'

I asked this so accusingly that Doc Whyte must have felt I thought him personally responsible. Of course, by this time I had guessed the truth. Doc Whyte betrayed it by allowing his eyelids to flicker.

'Well?'

Doc Whyte cleared his throat. I raised my eyes and saw that he was looking at me helplessly.

'How did it happen?'

Doc Whyte's voice was so hoarse and throaty that I hardly recognized it. 'He was killed by a shell.'

***

Leaving another platoon from 30 Column to relieve me and hold the top of the pass in my place, I withdrew with the rest of the Brigade to Mokso Sakan. Here I was able to relax on the shores of Indawgyi Lake, where everybody enjoyed a respite of blissful recuperation.

The Brigade certainly needed it. I too, my twenty-eight days of solitary duty having been accomplished on the top of that hill, found that my reserves of energy needed recharging and that I was sorely depleted. The period had certainly proved an eventful one. It turned out to have required an expenditure of effort on my part over and above what I was really capable of. It already seemed months ago that I had first climbed those mountains and come face to face with the Japanese beyond the *taung-ya* cultivation and the patch of tomatoes – and like half a lifetime since I had made love to Dal Bahadur in the thorn thickets at their feet.

I will not dwell further on the Brigade's failure, nor reopen old wounds by pointing out some of the reasons for it. Nor will I not indulge in recriminations about who was responsible for it. In passing over these events, however, it would be less than candid not to admit that one of the principal reasons for our defeat was the failure of 14 Brigade and the West African Brigade to reach us.

Defeat or failure notwithstanding, at Mokso Sakan Jack Masters immediately performed another of his redoubtable feats of magistery. He ordered that the famous Sunderland flying-boats be brought it and landed on Indawgyi Lake. This actually happened, although they had to be withdrawn from anti-submarine patrol in the Indian Ocean for that purpose. How strange those huge, clumsily proportioned planes must have looked flying inland over the mountains of Assam, several hundred miles from the sea.

It proved to be a most creative action, which allowed us to evacuate all our sick and wounded. It probably did more than anything else to re-establish the morale of the troops. Six hundred men – sufferers from sickness, starvation or shock, as well as battle-casualties – were by this means evacuated, and enormous quantities of replacement arms, ammunition and equipment flown in.

Dal Bahadur's and my share in these provisions was to secure a little outboard motor which we soon attached to a dugout. By means of this contraption we were enabled for a few tender moments to escape the feeling of eternal surveillance. We made secret daily excursions to an unfrequented inlet where we experimented with underwater gymnastics.

A big church parade was held during which God was not only invoked, but also actually congratulated for having in so conspicuous a manner intervened to save us.

I wrote an epic letter home. Rather an interesting episode ensued from it. Naturally I had spilled the beans in this letter, and it never got past the censor. I hadn't really expected it to, and, of course, I only wrote it at such length in order to give rein to my feelings. It achieved its objective better than I could have expected. Something of the smell and the mud and corruption prevailing at Mokso Sakan must have adhered to its pencil-scrawled pages. It found its way to New Delhi and was deposited with G II (Camouflage) at General Headquarters, who was responsible for me. Instead of reprimanding me as I deserved, he consulted the Deputy Chief of Staff. They both agreed it was too good to destroy. They had it cyclostyled and circulated it, in the form of an anonymous communication from an active-service solider, to all the officers attached to GH. It was to serve as an object lesson in what the eastern operations were like. I learned about this from my G II himself. He told me of it during my interview with him when he was making my final report.

***

Dal Bahadur and I performed twice daily under water. We were becoming positively proficient. However one afternoon this playtime period was terminated – and our peculiar practices interrupted – by Mike MacGillicuddy officially approaching me. He put in an appearance at my bivouac and asked – I cannot imagine why – for my advice. Jack Masters had ordered him to prepare for fortifying Mokso Sakan, should an occasion arise when we might need to defend it. MacGillicuddy was accordingly going round, examining fields of fire and establishing block-houses and bunkers which could operate effectively in the event of an attack. He sought my opinion on some aspects of these projects, and so, instead of being able to get away with Dal Bahadur and practise swimming, I was stuck with MacGillicuddy, trailing around after him in the heat, making an ass of myself.

I trailed around after him in the heat, making an ass of myself. We ended up having a blazing row, largely, I fear, because I still hadn't forgiven him for his exhibition of showmanship at the crossing of the Irrawaddy.

In the event, Masters received new orders and the idea of fortifying Mokso Sakan was abandoned. We moved north and later east.

# CHAPTER THIRTEEN

# On the March Again

It was at about this period that the local people suddenly became rather friendly and eager to help. In the early stages of the campaign, it had been quite the reverse: the villagers had been shy and keen to avoid us. Now, if they did not quite arrive in droves, it was no longer difficult to establish contact with them. The very beautiful daughter of a local headman developed a girlish crush on Chesty Jennings and followed him about like a tame sheep, and our Burma Rifles parties succeeded in sequestering a squad of half-a-dozen elephants with their oozes (mahouts). These proved indispensable in transporting supplies and the sick – for yes, in spite of our having flown out all casualties in the Sunderland flying-boats, the men were again succumbing to various illnesses.

This new willingness on the part of the villagers was a good sign.

No-one is more sensitive to the ups and downs of war than subject populations, which are always rushing off to transfer allegiance at the first hint of fluctuating fortunes. The present friendliness demonstrated an instinctive awareness on the part of the locals that the Japanese hegemony in this piece of territory was finished.

I wish I could have taken a similarly sanguine view of the health of the troops. Jack Masters confessed afterwards that the operations undertaken for the purpose of capturing Point 2171 were as hard on the soldiers as anything he had known. They certainly possessed a horrific quality which was unsurpassed in my own experience.

I attribute this impression to the fact that we were all so desperately ill. The troops' health was failing rapidly. They were also becoming markedly unstable.

Now this vast column of ours – men, mules, elephants, camp followers, Chesty Jennings' girlfriend, *ghora paltan* (white regiment), *desi paltan* (country regiment) – moved north along the shore of Indawgyi Lake. For several days we cut a swathe through the swamps bordering the shoreline. To our right rose the cloud-encapsulated hills; to our left rippled the water. From above, it poured with rain. They were the worst marching conditions I can ever remember.

Masters again found occasion to employ me.

It was a measure, I think, of the sickness and exhaustion of the British troops at this period that they could no longer be trusted to remain in the column. As a result, many soldiers' lives had been needlessly forfeited. The simple act of sitting down by the track-side to smoke a cigarette and nurse your lacerated sensibilities without permission seemed sufficient to break a rhythm and thereby start a whole sequence of disastrous consequences. Soon these desperately tired individuals – tired not only physically, but also of their very existence – would surrender to sleep. This gave way to kind of coma, from which often they never recovered consciousness.

Such a situation could not be permanently tolerated. I was the one chosen to circumvent it. While we continued thus slogging along slowly through the swamps of Indawgyi Lake, Masters ordered me to bring up the rear, accompanied by one of my defence platoons. I was to be the last man in the whole column. Even my own defence platoons were to go ahead of me. My job was to rally and collect the stragglers.

Away ahead, the surface of the path through the tic-typhus jungle, the elephant-grass, and the cane-breaks was comparatively undisturbed. After two thousand five hundred men had passed along it, however, accompanied by eight hundred mules and six elephants, it was in an appalling state. In addition, it was covered in six inches in water.

The elephants made huge pot-holed footprints in it, eighteen inches across and two feet deep. Into these deep indentations I plunged up to the knees every few paces, sometimes even falling flat on my face and almost disappearing from sight. It rained ceaselessly. Psychologically exhausted by rage, frustration and despair, weakened by fatigue, and racked with malarial and rheumatic pains, I was in no condition to be pleasant to the delinquents I was supposed to cherish.

We generally came upon the first one or two of them after the long halt at midday. As we were the rear-guard, my defence platoons and I lagged about a quarter of a mile behind the last man in the main body. This space was sufficient to give any prospective drop-out the impression that he would be overlooked. The bliss of sitting quietly in the lonely silence could be deceptively lulling and dauntingly sweet.

Then the malingerer would see my Gurkhas as they hove over the horizon. He still wouldn't know whether they were accompanied by a British Officer and he might consider himself reasonably safe. As they passed, he would throw them a slightly self-conscious and guilty greeting: 'Hello, Johnny.' Then the poor bastard would see me.

They came in all shapes and sizes, from the pathetic to the aggressive, and they exploited every device from tears to downright bullying in order to persuade me to let them be. One man even threatened to shoot me, and I truly believe he would have done so had not Dal Bahadur whipped out my revolver.

The way to deal with each one became a matter of trial and error. My approach differed according to experience and the temperament of the individual sufferer. However, I never lost sight of the purpose of the exercise, which was that all them, regardless of rank or physical condition, had to be cajoled – or, if necessary, driven mercilessly – onward. If they were abandoned, they would die.

I would start off fairly guardedly. 'Having trouble with your feet?'

The wretch has his right boot off, the sock in his hand, and is examining his toes. The flesh there is white and pulpy and I can tell at a glance that he has foot rot.

He looks at me with a gaze full of hang-dog anxiety and I realize at once that he is desperately worried about his physical state. If the lacklustre expression in his eyes is any indication, he has good reason to be. He bears the unmistakable mark of one near death, but he is, thank God, not fighting sick, but maudlin. Thus he is comparatively easy to encourage and coddle on his way.

The next one is a very different proposition. He is reclining comfortably on one elbow, smoking a cigarette, and the look he gives me in reply to my interrogation is cool and level.

'Come on, Sonny Boy,' I say to him (quite a different technique, you notice). 'Get going.'

'You fucking bastard,' he whispers venomously. 'Don't you Sonny Boy me! I'm staying here! Neither you nor your bloody Brigadier is going to get me to move till I want to.' He glances about him aggressively. The defence platoon has moved onward, leaving me alone with him. 'I'm still armed, y'know. It's you an' me.'

'Uh-hu.' I nod to Dal Bahadur, and he trots off. We have met this situation before. My signal meant 'Go and get 'em!' I did not bother, therefore, to reply to the soldier's remarks or respond to his rudeness. I act as if I have not even heard him. While I wait, I light a cigarette myself. It helps to emphasize my moral ascendancy and supplement the suggestion that I am invincible, serving to undermine the soldier's self-confidence.

The defence platoon soon double back and surround him. Their mud-plastered faces and air of indifference as to whether or not they shoot him carry complete conviction. It is such a God-forsaken place – under that leaden sky – that anything could happen.

'Yes,' I say. 'It's you and me. Get going!'

He stumbles to his feet with remarkable alacrity and without a murmur.

Some of them, of course, just sat by the side of the track, picking their noses. They were as tame as sheep. Others pretended they had dropped out of to have a shit. To all of them I was as kind and considerate, or as aggressive and brutal, as their condition seemed to warrant. But I must say, the worst ones to deal with were the emotional ones – the ones that appealed to your softer side and made you weep. Tears, on these occasions, were by no means uncommon. These men were the ones who had arrived at the point where death was infinitely more desirable than their present condition, and who were in effect consciously committing suicide. They were difficult to deal with because I felt a certain sympathy for them. Indeed I had, in my madder moments, considered taking such a step myself.

'Here's a funny one, sahib,' Dal Bahadur said, having learnt by experience to interpret the symptoms, which were plainly distinguishable on the face and characteristic of mental anguish and moral indecision. In this instance they were accompanied by a *tic douloureux* or involuntary *rictus*, exacerbated by a St. Vitus-like twitching of the limbs.

I approached the man sympathetically but with an inner dread. Such confrontations often involved a mental struggle for me. They were often more than just a simple matter of life and death, and I was not always qualified to resolve them. It was like trying to rescue a drowning man while being yourself a very indifferent swimmer. Furthermore, I was never entirely free from the fear that, instead of overcoming the man's negative emotions, they might succeed in overwhelming me. To prevent such a possibility, I always kept Dal Bahadur very close beside me. Now I signalled to him, 'Don't leave me!'

The soldier, sitting hunched beside the track, his head buried in his hands, took not the slightest notice. Although he must have heard us approaching – for we did not walk but wallow – he did not raise his head or give the slightest intimation that he was aware of our presence. This was a telling indication of his condition.

He was a rifleman of the King's Own. I could tell immediately that he was not a Lowlander, let alone a Glaswegian. He had some indefinable quality – a sort of softness of psychic silhouette – which those north of the border, with their rugged outlines, do not possess.

I stood beside him quite closely, yet fearing to put a hand on his shoulder as I had originally intended, in case he should do something rash.

'We all feel like this at times,' I said, perhaps a bit sententiously, 'but it does no good to give way to it.'

He jerked his head up so suddenly that he made me jump. My reactions in dealing with these malingerers had become pretty quick, for in many ways they were more treacherous than the Jap.

He still failed to speak, but I could see that he was struggling to formulate words. When they came, they came in a voice that was completely muffled. He simply said, in heart-broken accents, 'I can't make it – it's no use. I can't make it,' and then fell back.

I had bent double with my ear levelled to his mouth in order to hear him. Now I straightened up and glanced around. The scene was one of unredeemed desolation. It was relieved neither by sight of human habitation nor, except for ourselves, by any human presence. At a little distance the defence platoon had halted. The men were squatting on their packs and waiting for orders. Squally gusts blew shorewards from the centre of the lake, where a rainstorm was brewing, and among the thickets of pampas grass and in the cane-breaks the tall, feathery grasses – seven feet high – were bending and whipping to the wind. On the tops of the mountains to the right of our line of march, the clouds squatted, grey and solid, and as heavy as lead.

'Do make an effort.'

The rain began. It needled into my flesh as piercingly as pins. For all the response my appeal elicited, I might have been apostrophising my shadow. At that point I completely lost my self-possession.

'For God's sake get up and get on with it!' I said, aiming a well directed but not very vicious kick at his ribs.

I had expected some sort of retaliation. Instead he rolled over drunkenly, extended his arms and said 'Shoot me!' I was so furious that I could willingly have done so.

Dal Bahadur and I exchanged a baffled look. It was plain that we should have to carry him. Neither of us, however, felt much enthusiasm for the project. Never was the succour of a fellow human undertaken with such reluctance.

'Leave me alone!' he screamed as we muscled him up and draped his nerveless arms round our quaking shoulders. 'Let me die!'

I would willingly have done so! However, I had my orders, and I was determined to fulfil them.

On that occasion we staggered into camp well after midnight. Every member of the defence platoon had taken a hand. Jack Masters was so worried about us that he was on the point of sending out a search-party. We collapsed, sobbing with exhaustion and relief, in a heap. During all the hours that the defence platoon and Dal Bahadur and I had supported him, this poor, broken wretch never for an instant ceased abusing us for saving his life. I never even knew his name.

This experience was so unsettling that I began to have serious doubts about was I was doing. The following day, however, we came upon something which gave validation.

It happened during one of our hourly halts. The defence platoon, true to their incorrigible restlessness, was poking about among the reeds, pursuing a snake. They stumbled upon a boot. It was sticking out of a clump of marsh grass, and it was attached to a leg. Further investigation revealed a corpse – one of the King's Liverpools. Faint traces of warmth lingering in the torso testified that the man was only recently dead.

It was a nasty enough thing to encounter, even if the circumstances had been entirely straightforward, which they weren't. The King's Liverpools were one of 77 Brigade's battalions, and what one of their soldiers was doing here, in this part of the world, alone, and fifty miles from his headquarters, was never to be satisfactorily explained, unless he was a deserter. What was so shocking about the discovery, however, were the hundreds of leeches which clung to the body. They immediately raised doubts as to the cause of death. In the face of such an unusual event, I did not feel confident enough merely to report it. Instead I took the unusual step of sending a message to Doc Whyte.

When he arrived, we examined the body. The first thing we had to do was remove the gorging leeches from the orifices of the head. Ears, eyes and nose were entirely obscured by them. Two voracious specimens had taken up residence in either nostril, and were swollen to such an enormous size that it proved almost impossible to dislodge them. The inside of the man's mouth was also full of leeches.

We then unbuttoned his trousers and submitted the lower limbs to examination. A number of leeches, bloated with blood, were clustered in the aperture of his anus. Another's tail wiggled from the eye of his prick.

'Could it be,' I stammered, 'I mean, his death – what about the leeches? Can he have bled to death?'

'A distinct possibility,' Doc Whyte concurred. 'Having regard to his weakened condition.'

A second incident occurred a few days later. We had left the swamps and were proceeding through tall trees. Above our heads, in their upper branches and cushioned among swags of Spanish moss and encapsuled in wads of lichen, there flowered sumptuous sprays of purple orchids, like luscious bunches of magenta grapes.

I was marching behind a bunch of British Other Ranks. They constituted that group of specialists attached to Brigade Headquarters, such as Signallers and like experts, who were not commissioned.

The scene was informal and the atmosphere animated and relaxed. Snatches of conversation drifted back to me. They were joking about booking a houseboat near Dhal Lake in Srinagar via Briggo's radio network to Rear Headquarters, in readiness for leave. It was generally assumed that our evacuation from the battle-zone could not now be long delayed. Doc Whyte was marching only a little distance ahead.

Suddenly the homely badinage and jesting companionship of this group of idly chattering soldiers collapsed, caving in upon itself like a hollow object disintegrating under pressure.

One of the men fell to the ground.

As if in a set of flashlight stills, I saw a series of tableaux. Each one was distinct, completely uncommitted to continuity of movement. A man stood with distraught gestures and an anguished expression. A second man, his face magnified in my memory into a monstrous mask of incomprehension, was caught napping, his eyes as vacuous and sightless as those of a Greek statue. A third, the subject of a quicker reaction, started away horrified, his face mottled by disgust and shock. Another grasped his rifle grimly and took first pressure on the trigger, searching the distance for the source of the onslaught. We all assumed that the man to whom the injury had occurred must have been shot – picked off by a sniper.

Some soldiers took up defensive positions facing outwards. Others bent down to help their comrade, now lying on the ground. Yet more remained transfixed, incapable of coherent action.

More vividly than all of this, however, I recall the slightly stupefied expression on the face of the man on the ground, and his half-startled, half-instinctive movement to put his hands up to his neck. They never got there.

The expression died stillborn. The stupefaction of his features faded and the tide of life which they had represented subsided.

A gash had opened in the side of his neck, just behind his throat. Out gushed his life's blood. It pumped and squirted in spasms, staining the carmine-coloured mud a brighter red. By the time Doc Whyte arrived he was dead.

It was difficult to take in the finality of what had happened. Inadequately we stood around the blood-saturated corpse, now hideously disfigured. We gazed down at the drained white face of the man who only recently – less than three minutes ago – was planning how to spend his furlough. Doc Whyte made his examination.

The results of this post-mortem carried out at the scene of the accident and in the blood-drenched mud, together with a few brief facts pieced together from the man's medical history, were very remarkable. When they became available, they revealed a most extravagantly unlikely set of circumstances.

The man had been insignificantly wounded by a minute shell-splinter from a Japanese mortar bomb during one of our earlier actions against Kyaungle. The tiny particle of steel, sharp as a razor blade and pointed as a needle, had remained inside him, and the apparently trifling injury had remained untreated. Then the cicatrice healed over. The fragment thereupon proceeded to travel all over his body. It had finally landed up in his neck. Some incredible mischance had there caused it to sever the main jugular artery.

This incident had the most unnerving effect on all of us. We had been in Burma for more than ninety days. This was the period universally agreed upon by all parties as a maximum one beyond which Chindit troops were not expected any longer to be able to support such conditions. An incident such as the one I have just described brings many hidden disharmonies to the fore. We all felt rotten, but then we were already in a deplorable condition. Jungle sores, tic typhus, pneumonia and pleurisy were ubiquitous.

But for those of us who marched with the Brigade Headquarters at that time, I think the most distressing thing we had to contend with were the cerebral malaria cases we carried around with us. These were soldiers so desperately ill that they required constant medical attention and supervision. Doc Whyte had set up a sort of mobile dressing station for them. It travelled around with us, in order that he could give them his personal care.

The continued presence of those sufferers, quite unconscious and with fevers ranging from between 108° to 112°, was a constant source of worry. Dragged around on improvised mule-litters, fed on brandy, sugar and water by a little tube passed through the nose to the stomach, relieved by a catheter tube up the urethra and exposed to all sorts of infections by the necessity of being treated with saline drip, they presented a spectacle – with their bottles of saline solution suspended above them and their tubes and strappings – that was a dreadful reminder of what could happen to any of us.

The troops had some justification for thinking and talking about evacuation. But it was not to be. Outside the battle-zone and beyond us, another sort of war was being waged pointlessly and privately. It was the battle between our higher commanders.

Very little of this fanatical contest filtered down to the men in the field. But, on account of my close contact with the Brigade Commander in the ordinary run of business and also by reason of my occasional co-operation with ciphers, a considerable amount of it was known to me.

I was aware of the bitterness, stalemate and deadlock which existed between Lentaigne and Stilwell. Stilwell was accusing 111 Brigade of having unnecessarily abandoned Blackpool and was demanding that we move north and try again. Jack Masters was trying to prevent 111 Brigade from being sacrificed to Stilwell's egotistical mania, and as a result being completely destroyed. He was opposed to our being ordered into further action because he considered we were physically and mentally incapable of it. All such protests, of course, were of no avail.

We were ordered to take Point 2171 and push on down towards the main Jap lines of communication in the valley.

But before we arrived at this point of decision Masters did his best to adopt a bellicose stance and to occupy a position that was potentially threatening to the Japanese lines of communication. Acrimonious messages were winging back and forth between Lentaigne and Brigade. Lentaigne and Stilwell had ceased to be on speaking terms. Meanwhile Masters and Calvert (still attacking Mogaung) had entered into a lively correspondence in limerick verse of a consistently high standard, and of exceptional quality, via light plane. We had all become exceedingly light-headed.

We had now left the leech-infested swamps bordering on Indawgyi Lake and were established in the hills. From here, Masters once more started sending long-range patrols to beat up the Japs in the valley.

At one point during these activities I was pushed well out beyond Brigade Headquarters group, with my two defence platoons covering and blocking off a track intersection, and commanding the lower slopes which tumbled into the valley. It was two mile or so away from Brigade Headquarters and was just distant enough to give me once more that pleasant feeling of independence from Masters's dominant personality.

I was taking advantage of this unaccustomed liberty to have a look round. I took a section patrol in a wide sweep through the jungles, which in the monsoon rains were looking particularly magnificent. Apart from the fabulously flowering trees and shrubs, I discovered nothing of significance. When I returned to my encampment, it was late afternoon. I found a message waiting for me to the effect that a 'sahib' had passed through from 30 Column with a patrol and had asked for me. He had apparently been so anxious to make my acquaintance that he and his platoon had sat down and waited for half an hour. On my failure to appear, they had departed. They had continued on their way into the valley where, so the 'sahib' had informed Thaman Bahadur, they intended to waylay a Japanese convoy on the road. Before he left, the 'sahib' had particularly asked Thaman Bahadur to say to me that he was sorry.

I wondered who it could be. I assumed that the bit about 'being sorry' referred to some message which he had been charged to pass on to me from Brigade and which my absence from the place had constrained him not to deliver.

On the following day my forward picket reported a strong group making their way up the path through the *lantana* scrub from the plain. They were taking so little care to conceal themselves that it was assumed they must be our own troops – probably the patrol who had gone through on the previous day. This turned out to be the case.

They looked so crestfallen and bedraggled that I forbore to question them. They passed through with severe, unrelenting looks on their faces, glancing neither to left or right. To the remarks of my men they simply returned a perfunctory 'no' or 'yes'.

They were, however, unable to resist the inquisitiveness and charm of Dal Bahadur, who successfully wormed out of them the secret that they were seeking to keep safe for their own Commander and for Brigade.

Dal Bahadur passed on the information to me. They had lost their officer in a brief action during the night. Only a few shots had been exchanged. At the first enemy onslaught a bullet had entered his forehead – it made only a little hole, they said – and he had died at once. They had then disengaged from the action and retired, abandoning his body to the enemy.

That officer had been Mike MacGillicuddy. He left me with a heavy sense of regret. We had quarrelled badly and never had the chance to make up.

# CHAPTER FOURTEEN

# A Court Martial

While we were loafing about under these circumstances, we became involved in a local vendetta. A group of villagers came trooping into camp. I remember glancing incuriously at them. One of them had his hands tied behind his back. Some sort of criminal, evidently. These fellows had their own exemplary forms of justice. I do not recall feeling the slightest sense of empathy, nor did I find the situation in the least extraordinary. One's capacity for reacting to unusual circumstances had become blunted.

And what, in any case, had it got to do with me? If certain people had formed the habit of constantly coming and going – trading in rice, in lives, in lies, in hastily garnered and quite irresponsibly misleading pieces of gossip about the enemy – was I therefore obliged to pay attention to every petty informer who had simply made commerce out of these things?

The answer, surprisingly, was yes. It was part of the intelligence gathering function of every guerrilla fighter, and consequently every Chindit. I assumed that these villagers trooping into camp – abject and half starving as they were, for all that they retained a diffident dignity – were just another aspect of the underside of our operations.

Consequently it was only when the word got about that there was to be a court-martial that I sat up and took notice. Consumed with curiosity, I made my way to Jack Masters, who was interrogating the villagers. I did not put in an appearance at a particularly appropriate moment.

'Ever served on a court-martial?' Masters challenged me.

'Er – yes – as a matter of fact I have.'

'Then make ready to serve on one now. You are officially co-opted.'

'Um – er,' I gasped, 'I don't think I have the necessary qualifications.'

'It doesn't matter. I'll explain the procedures. Just help the others, please, to prepare the scenery.'

There were several of us present. I remember exchanging baffled glances with Smithy. 'What,' I whispered to him helplessly, 'does he expect us to do?'

Smithy responded to the summons with his usual resourcefulness. Under his direction we collected some ammunition boxes and *yakdans* and arranged them like a table. Over the top of them we draped a blanket. Crates of unprimed grenades provided the court's benches. The president's chair was a skilfully improvised three-inch-mortar base-plate. Masters, of course, was the president.

I forget who the others were, Briggo, Geoffrey Birt, Douglas Larpent perhaps, maybe even Alec Harper, possibly Major Henning from the Cameronians or Major Heap from the King's Own. I remember one person who was conspicuously absent, and that was Doc Whyte. He insisted that it was no part of his business. I also remember that I sat on the extreme right.

Macpherson acted as interpreter and conducted the prosecution. I don't think the poor devil of an accused (the man with his hands tied behind his back) had a defender, and there seemed hardly any point in his having one, because the case was so deceptively simple. He was arraigned upon several charges and there was really no evidence for or against, apart from the fact of the dead bodies. Macpherson and the Burma Rifles people swore and testified to having seen these personally.

The prisoner was charged with having informed the Japanese that certain villagers had provided guides for our soldiers some days previously. The Japanese had then come, crucified the wife of the headman (the headman was one of those present), shot one of his sons, and bayoneted other people. The remainder of the village had managed to run away. The accused denied having acted as an informer.

It was one man's word against another's. I believe they designate these active-service affairs, picturesquely, as drum-head courts-martial. The term is certainly evocative. It has a sort of primitive appositeness – a rudimentary rectitude – which is the very fibre of rough justice.

A shaft of sunlight shot through the branches of the teak trees with theatrical effect and illuminated the gathering. We might have been sitting down to some sort of intimate meal like the Last Supper. The prisoner was duly brought to the bar. The first action the court took was to order the guards to unbind his hands. He was then charged.

I was encouraged by this action – for it was a movement towards clemency. I thought it boded well for the prisoner's fate. It was not achieved, however, without a certain huffing and hawing. Somebody had pressed the possibility that the prisoner might take advantage of the opportunity and dart away into the jungle.

It will appear in retrospect no doubt almost incredible that we could actually have envisaged such a thing, since the man was surrounded by squads of armed soldiers. Yet such an eventuality was seriously considered, and it was not as silly as it sounds. The local people were incredibly clever at merging imperceptibly with the trees. You will readily appreciate that even a modern army, well-equipped with sophisticated weaponry and tanks, may find itself severely at a disadvantage when dealing with slippery peasants. As a consequence, as the man stood before us and shivered, an undertaking was extracted from him that he would not escape.

The ins and outs of the affair could have been unravelled without any difficulty. But the question of equity was complicated by political expediency. We were embarked on the series of actions which were going to result in the reconquest of Burma. The villagers could appreciate this and were beginning to turn in our direction. But whether Macpherson and his Burma rifles men had just stumbled on this situation, as they averred, and were acting as honest brokers; or whether they were attempting to exploit a local feud, and blow it up to proportions which impinged on the Brigade's security, merely for political ends, or to persuade the Burmese to throw in their lot with the British – these are things I shall never know.

From the point of view of our side, the whole thing seemed far too damned convenient. The Japanese army was plainly no longer able to tyrannize the local people with impunity in order to win support for their own particular partisans. Now the partisans of the other party – our partisans – were turning to us, obviously desiring, or so it seemed to me, that we in our turn should buy support and win adherents by likewise tyrannizing their opponents.

Sometimes human nature, in all its twists and turns, seems past redemption. The entire proceedings were concluded in about half-an-hour. Although we heard evidence and banded questions back and forth, thus doing our best to make it look as if we were striving to arrive at the truth, there was really nothing to argue about.

I, myself, had propounded, artlessly, the fundamental question at the very outset of the proceedings by asking, 'Is not the prisoner a Burman?'

'Yes.'

'And are not his accusers Kachins?'

My remark was greeted with an uncomfortable silence. Of course it is well known that the Burmans, or plains folk, had always been anti-British, pro-Japanese and anti-Kachin. The Kachins, on the contrary, or hill folk, were pro-British, anti-Japanese and anti-Burman.

The prisoner's fate had been sealed as soon as he was brought into camp. No one doubted – not even I, who was quite sympathetic to him – that if he were released from custody he would rush off to the Japanese and tell them all about us.

'Well,' demanded Jack Masters, in summation of all these intangibles, 'is the prisoner innocent or guilty?' He posed the question to each of us in turn, personally interrogating every member of the court separately.

The answer was a foregone conclusion.

'Guilty.'

'Guilty.'

'Guilty.'

Finally he came to me.

I made a determined if not very prolonged effort to assert my independence.

'What happens if I disagree?'

'I don't see how you can do, in face of the evidence.'

'No – but I want to know.'

'It would simply mean I should have to convene another court-martial.'

'You don't intend to let him go,' I said, half-accusingly and half as a factual statement.

'No.'

'If he were acquitted, he would simply go and tell the Jap, I suppose.'

'That is so,' Masters conceded, bleakly.

'Of, course, it's unthinkable,' I supplemented, pursuing my train of logic with remarkable slowness. 'But what's the alternative? Is the penalty death?'

Briggo was about to put in a word, then choked on it, and Masters nodded.

All during this interchange the prisoner, who had turned a mud-grey in colour at the inception of the proceedings, began to look towards me with a renewal of hope. His complexion perceptibly brightened as his prospects improved. I glanced at him furtively. Our eyes met. I was unable to prevent a charge of understanding from passing between us. He was not young – about forty – and quite unlovely to look at. His head was closely shaven and demonstrated the markedly Proto-Malayan, brachycephalic cranium with its strikingly bulging protuberances at the rear quarters, which is so characteristic of South-East Asia man from Bengal to Southern China. I examined it curiously from my place at the right of the court.

Meanwhile, the prisoner's eyes never left off observing us. They flicked back and forth persistently during my exchange with Masters.

'I suppose it's no use my making an attempt to save him,' I muttered rather miserably, and Jack Masters replied, quite mildly, 'Not in the least.'

There ensued an uneasy silence which I am sure was designed to give me time to pull myself together. I was embarrassingly aware that I had exhausted everybody's patience – perhaps including the prisoner's. Geoffrey Birt summed up the general feeling by putting in: 'You're only giving him false hope.'

I saw that they were determined to condemn him. All the same, they still couldn't do it without my concurrence.

'Well,' repeated Masters, having allowed this interval to elapse during which I might be supposed to make up my mind. 'Innocent or guilty?'

The problem instantly resolved itself into its basic components and, with horrible clarity, presented itself to me as a choice between two alternatives. It was not what was going to happen to the prisoner if I pronounced him guilty that mattered – it was what was going to happen to me if I didn't!

Without a shadow of hesitation I pronounced him guilty, and thereby salvaged my position.

The rest of the proceedings were gabbled through so quickly that I had the impression that their despatch was deliberate. Masters dealt out the death penalty – 'to be taken into the jungle and shot summarily' – and we embarked on a discussion of how to do it.

Major Henning had a man among his Cameronians, he said, who was a proven expert – 'the man who does our executions'. He would send for him immediately in the hope that he would get us out of our difficulty. Grateful to be let thus easily off the hook – for none of us felt like doing the job ourselves – we sent a message to summon this cold-blooded-killer, as I conceived him. To my astonishment it turned out to Sergeant Barker.

Meanwhile, in his own vernacular and with desperate fluency, the prisoner started to speak. He began stumblingly and as if he had only then realized the horror of his plight. During the course of the trial he had been conspicuously silent. He had merely indicated his affirmation or denial by a nod or a grunt. Now fear, and the approaching shadow of death, seemed to have lent wings to his eloquence.

Words poured out of his mouth in breathtaking profusion; they sped like arrows from between his lips – words bitter and broken – words tragic and tangled – words tender and sad. Nobody translated for him. It wasn't necessary. Indeed Macpherson, with the rest of us, appeared struck dumb with amazement and rendered speechless by the frenzied torrent. We understood him perfectly.

He wasn't pleading. He was pouring out to us in a torment of despair his whole life. We saw the dawn, in his speech, breaking over the flat plains of central Burma and glorifying, in the process, the tips of the spires on the gilded pagodas. We experienced the sun at noon and partook sympathetically of the torpor of midday when the silence in the parched paddy-fields was like a palpable presence. We passed with him from village to village, where the wind whispered tantalisingly among the dry leaves in the hot areca plantations. And we arrived with him towards evening at his destination in some hamlet. We revelled with him in the breeze, in the rice planting, and in the monsoon rains.

In his desperate outpouring of emotion – in his despairing plight – he cared as little for life's so-called beauties as he did for its horrors. He equated seed-time with the pangs of birth which had brought him into this world, and harvest with the pains of death which would take him out of it, and he denounced both. He had become transfigured.

Finally, as the passion spent itself, his elation subsided and his enthusiasm waned.

We, his judges and executioners, sat before him stony-faced. It must at last have dawned on him, as he glanced from one to another of us, that his eloquence was wasted. Suddenly there took place in him one of those remarkable transformations. It was like an access of grace.

The anguish and the agony slipped away from him and he stepped out of them. His features relaxed. From being tortured and tormented they became calm and placid. He regarded us narrowly, but with a strange look that was almost tender.

'Take him away!' said Masters. 'Baines, you are to accompany Sergeant Barker and see that the sentence is executed.'

The court then adjourned and its members hurried away, leaving Sergeant Barker, the prisoner, and I to resolve our difficulties as best we might.

'Whatever possessed you to take on such an awful job?' I arraigned Sergeant Barker without allowing a single word to pass between us in greeting.

'Well, sir,' he said 'begging your pardon an' all that, but what possessed you to become a member of a court-martial?'

'I was detailed to do it.'

'And so was I!'

'What are you going to do? How are you going to do it?'

'I generally takes them into the jungle and drills 'em full of holes with me automatic weapon from the back.'

'How many of these sorts of things have you done? You sound as if you've done dozens! Was Major Henning speaking the truth?'

'There have been several,' he conceded. 'Prisoners of war and the like – spies – which we couldn't fly out.'

'But I can't imagine the Cameronians going round the country bumping off all and sundry!'

He looked at me rather flat-faced and fish-eyed and forbore to mention what was in his mind, but I knew. His view was clearly that I was attached to the Brigade Headquarters where such things are hardly conceivable, but that in actual warfare it was different.

He merely remarked, 'You know, sir, you're not going to like it.'

The Burman looked from one to another of us questioningly, his features resuming once more their former complexion of clay-grey. I was assailed by an astonishing emotion of curiosity. It was as if I were a child who had been promised an unique spectacle, only to be denied it at the last minute.

'No – but,' I stuttered, 'the Brigadier told me to be there.'

Sergeant Barker waved aside my protest. He indicated to the Burman to proceed. A bird had started out of a bush during our colloquy and flown off terrified. Together the three of us started into the jungle after it.

'I always let 'em think they've got a chance of escape,' he whispered to me confidentially. 'After a time,' he added, nodding in the direction of the Burman who was now twenty yards ahead, his pace quickening every second, 'he'll start running. Now sir, you stop here and do as I say.'

'All right,' I said unwillingly. 'When will you be back? How far are you going? What happens if you miss?'

It was such an unlikely possibility that he didn't even bother to answer. He gave me a contemptuous look, then turned and fixed his gaze on his quarry. Step by step the two of them passed out of sight. All at once there was a long burst of light automatic fire, followed by another.

After a short interval Sergeant Barker came back.

'You fired twice! Is he dead?'

'The first time I missed,' he confessed with an insane giggle. I knew it was hysterical and did not attribute it to cruelty. The hands he put to his mouth to light a cigarette also noticeably trembled. Sergeant Barker was not as callous as he pretended to be.

'Yes,' he said, striving to control the twitching of his lower lip. 'He's dead.'

# CHAPTER FIFTEEN

# A New Objective

All protests notwithstanding, Stilwell had his way. We were ordered to descend towards the plain and put in a frontal attack.

The primary objective, chosen from a scrutiny of the maps and not from a study of the ground, was selected by Stilwell's staff at his headquarters in Ledo, over one hundred miles away. It was Point 2171. This was a conspicuous hill feature dominating the road and railway to and from Mogaung. It was within easy marching distance of the flat country and once in our possession would constitute a powerful threat to these Japanese lines of communication.

From such a tactical point of view, of course, our orders were perfectly intelligible. By an extension of the same logic, however, it was obvious they would place us uncomfortably within range of the enemy's big guns.

In the event, they had placed us within range of his little guns also, for it so happened that he had the place extremely well covered. We suffered as many casualties – if not quite as much harassing mental anguish – from his quick-firing easily manipulated 75's as we did from his medium artillery or heavy mortars. Given the mental and physical state of the troops as I have described them, it was universally conceded that our orders were tantamount to condemning the lot of us to death. This final, additional burden, coming to the top of many other crippling disabilities, was going to be the last straw for us.

I had been playing with a similar suicide concept, of course, ever since I first discovered those bits about long-range penetration at the Camouflage School. The idea of a suicide mission had at the time completely dominated my imagination. Now I experienced my first really vivid attack of premonitory terror. It is a daunting thing to descend deliberately towards self-immolation. Yet, as a consequence of having to do so, I was at last able to identify myself fully with the concept of disregard for danger. Was it not on this account that I had joined the Chindits in the first place?

But, determined as I was to reassure myself that the situation was desperate (I didn't want to be involved in any false emphasis), I subjected Doc Whyte to such a rigorous cross-examination that he must have regretted ever having mentioned it – for he it was who first disseminated the information, and it was to him I went to confirm my interpretation.

He corroborated it with such a grave face that I was persuaded to take his judgement seriously.

'Does it mean the end?'

He made no attempt to conceal his anxiety. 'That's exactly how I'd describe it.'

'But some of us are bound to survive,' I exclaimed 'surely!'

'It means the end,' he repeated, 'of the Brigade as an integrated fighting formation or unit. But yes, some of us are bound to survive, of course, although in what shape it might be better not to enquire too closely.'

'You mean – we shall be marked in some way – scarred – so that people will be able to recognize us as survivors of terrible events?'

'I imagine so – although how deeply, it will be impossible to say until later.'

'You're going on,' I persisted, 'as if we were being ordered to kill ourselves!'

'Make no mistake about it – that's exactly what we've been ordered to do.'

I found it perversely exciting to have received this unambiguously pessimistic prognosis from an expert. With grim foreboding in the forefront of our minds, therefore, and full of determined pugnacity, almost as if we didn't care, we pushed on down towards where we knew the enemy would be waiting for us.

The approach march to the objective took three or four days. They were feverish days, filled with frantic bravado and heroic gaiety.

The nights before we actually made contact were occupied in frenzied attempts to review our situation objectively, and to contemplate it without bitterness. In these attempts, I think, we achieved a qualified success. The commanding officers of the various columns had got into the habit, at the end of each day, of congregating at Jack Masters's command post. The rum bottle circulated freely. It generated a temporary and spurious companionship which, despite its *Fata Morgana* quality, was undeniably comforting. Each of us was aware, however, that we would have to face our own fate individually; accept personal responsibility for all our wrong decisions; and ultimately be prepared to die alone – no matter how many of us got slaughtered. Every man has to die personally, individually, and singly. Death, regardless of how great the love, cannot be approached in pairs, hand-in-hand. So it was lonely, during those stoically pessimistic evenings too.

The Chinese artillery were sporadically pounding Mogaung from Kamaing. Then, like a clearly articulated diapason, the Japanese guns would open up in reply. Every so often a roving patrol of Chinese troops or a column from 77 Brigade foraging for food would clash with the enemy down in the valley below us, and there would follow a spirited exchange. Sometimes such encounters lasted for several hours and involved the launching of grenades and the chatter of machine guns.

The thudding of the distant explosions, always disquieting, but under our present circumstances doubly disturbing, sounded to us in the security of our night-harbour in the hills deceptively disembodied, like dreaded vibrations vaguely apprehended from under water. All the same, they added a dimension of reality to our philosophic discourses, and imparted an edge to our discussions. It is incredible how a couple of bottles of rum can universalize one's speculation, and increase the sense of historical perspective almost to infinity.

I visualized the participants and combatants of this war rolling by in quasi-Spenglerian terms with unparalleled pomp and splendour – decked out in all the panoply of the centuries, nation giving place to nation, the palm and crown of victory falling indifferently now to one undeserving tribe, now to another.

It didn't seem to matter any more who held the sceptre. What was significant were the endless tides – the great sweep which carried the whole thing forward. Viewed in such a context, the disappearance of 111 Brigade from the scroll of history, its erasure from the roll of honour, was a trifling event of such minimal importance that it became possible to regard one's personal snuffing-out from a comparably lofty viewpoint also. I did so, and experienced the immediate lightening of anxiety which always follows from having established oneself successfully within a reasonably tenable philosophic position.

Suddenly I gave tongue. In my feverish eagerness to articulate this insight and share it with my fellows, the words came tumbling out of my mouth with indecent precipitation.

Of course, it now occurs to me that I must have been horribly drunk. I should scarcely have had the hardihood to pour out a philosophy of history in front of a bunch of colonels unless I had been inflamed with alcohol, much less on the eve of battle. However friends of mine who witnessed the scene have since testified to me that I spoke as if prophetically inspired.

My diatribe was followed by an interval of stunned silence. You know right enough when you have made an impression. The effect was so unnerving that I had no option but to get to my feet unsteadily, make my apologies, and stumble out.

The following day saw the last of such whimsical incidents. It happened during one of our hourly ten-minute halts. I can see the place in my imagination just as clearly as if it were physically present. A little stream ran purling along its bed beside the mountain path by which we were descending, adorned with ferns and all sorts of lichens and mosses. My Gurkhas had fallen out and had pulled out their ubiquitous packets of cigarettes. They were now larking about at a respectful distance, keeping a wary eye on me in case I might betray a feeling of annoyance with them by one of my guarded gestures of disapproval (for we had worked all this sort of thing out splendidly and by now had got it reduced to a drill), yet unable to suppress their roars of laughter. Dal Bahadur went over to join them.

What I am about to tell you may sound senseless. It may sound unreasonable to suppose that the Gurkhas were actually laughing at what I am going to recount. I wish to assure you, therefore, that however unlikely it may appear to those unfamiliar with the regimental Gurkha outlook, this incident was absolutely typical and true to life.

Dal Bahadur returned, also squinting with sneezing giggles.

'What on earth's the matter? Let me into it – please do!'

'Tej Bahadur's – Tej Bahadur's' and he collapsed into hoots of mirth, thereby incapable of articulating a single sentence.

'Well,' I asked again, after he had momentarily recovered, 'what is it?'

'Tej Bahadur says – Tej Bahadur says – he says, in a few days he's going to be killed.'

Unable to contain himself any longer, Dal Bahadur positively rocked with laughter and even rolled on the ground in his merriment.

I, on the contrary, was extremely put out. I failed to appreciate what on earth the Gurkhas could find so funny in this.

I dashed off to where Tej Bahadur, sitting modestly on a rock and looking magnificently embarrassed, was closely surrounded by his teasing companions.

The reason, of course, why I acted so precipitately must be plain for all to see. Once a premonition of this sort takes possession, morale, followed by personal confidence, very soon takes wing. I was terrified, therefore, lest a superstitious awe or fear of death should emasculate the troops, thus inhibiting their physical courage.

I needn't, however, have worried about these men. Their morale proved excellent. I was the one who had lost his confidence, as you shall presently hear when I describe the ensuing battle.

'What is it? What's this I hear?' I clucked officiously, very much expecting that I should have to handle a hysterical patient.

'Oh yes,' said Tej Bahadur, quite unconcernedly and evidently rather surprised that I should take an interest in it. 'Yes – it's perfectly true. I do feel that I'm going to get killed. But please don't worry about it. I promise I won't give any trouble.'

'But what on earth do you mean? How can you say such a thing?'

'Oh, it's quite simple. I am just certain I'm going to get killed!'

'But Tej Bahadur, it's pure imagination. How long have you thought this? When do you think it's going to happen?'

'I've known about it for some time. I only mentioned it by accident. We were talking about the fighting and I told Man Bahadur quite casually that I think it's going to happen in three days.'

Man Bahadur and Gopal Bahadur, meanwhile, were trying to conceal their giggles behind their hands. All the others were hanging breathlessly on the exchange – not because they thought it serious, but simply because I had chosen to make an issue of it.

I felt completely nonplussed by the admission and hardly knew what conclusions to draw. I did not for a moment think that his premonition could be correct, but it was perfectly obvious that he took it seriously. The attitude of the rest of the defence platoon was hard to define.

While I was thus cogitating, searching in my mind for some phrase or comment with which to clinch proceedings, the order to shoulder into our packs came to my rescue. The incident achieved no more than a passing notoriety. In the flurry of activity consequent upon our contacting the enemy a few hours later, it got completely knocked out of my head.

Shudderingly, somewhere up ahead, somebody suddenly encountered a Jap outpost suddenly, and put in a probing attack. I did not at the time attach a great deal of importance to it. It happened spontaneously, and a good half a mile forward of the sector where I was marching, and according to my time-and-motion calculations this was far enough away from me for it to be quite safe. For want of positive evidence to the contrary and a proper liaison between rear-of-the-column, middle-of-the-column and forward, I mistakenly assumed that all the firing which I heard going on would be drill-book stuff – something of the order of second-nature reaction, performed perfunctorily, and certainly nothing significant.

The situation, however, deteriorated so quickly that circumstances themselves disabused me. What had originally suggested itself to me simply as a series of straightforward outflanking movements deployed against the enemy's *francs tireurs* and scouts, now revealed itself as a classic rearguard action in which the Japs retreated into prepared positions. They very cleverly drew us after them.

Such was the position when our advanced guard bumped the enemy on that afternoon of 20 June. Far from being the casual affair which I had mistakenly imagined it to be, the situation grew so swiftly worse during the days that followed that we had difficulty in keeping up with events. Soon we found ourselves involved in a desperate fight on all fronts. It quickly engulfed even Brigade Headquarters. We were called upon to put forth our maximum efforts. We had allowed ourselves to become committed to that most difficult of all engagements, a running battle.

On account of the actions continually going on ahead of us where our advance elements were in almost hourly contact with the enemy, it became necessary to expend all our resources. Jack Masters was compelled to throw in his reserves. He began utilising me seriously.

As I pushed out farther and farther on patrol into unexplored territory, I awoke to the chilling realities of our position. Not only were the Japs alarmingly thick on the ground; they appeared to have completely surrounded us. They buzzed like a swarm of wasps. Even my irrepressible Gurkhas seemed temporarily quelled by this discovery.

Plodding along in their company – but all of us uncharacteristically subdued, even if attempting to conceal it – I could not but notice how my senses reacted due to the nearness of the enemy, automatically peeling off and shedding their coverings like sheaths, until my hackles prickled and every nerve-end tingled. The whole place smelt of Jap like the reek from a cat's urine.

We edged through forest clearings whose atmosphere was heavy with menace ... along jungle tracks where we faced the threat of ambush at every bend ... past lonely houses whose burnt-out rafters resembled the blackened bones of gigantic skeletons ... across the ruins of ravaged villages, derelict and untenanted even by dogs or pigs, where the bare boards of abandoned huts, choked with undergrowth, stood out against the bruised sky like broken boxes.

Such evidence of wreck and ruin were everyday experiences for those in reckless pursuit of the fugitive Jap. Thank God we didn't find him. I was in no mood for it; neither, I think, were my men. Yet strangely enough, there were indications of enemy occupation all round us. I managed to avoid contact with them so persistently, however, that I was forced to formulate a theory of divine partiality to explain it. That – or admit a much worse possibility, namely that I was being reserved for something really sinister in the future!

I remember an incident that happened one afternoon with particular clarity.

It was rather late. A thick mist had been covering the tops of the mountains since early morning, reducing visibility to near zero; the cloud-base was so low as to rest on our heads. The leaden atmosphere thus generated was debilitating.

We were following along a narrow path in thick jungle with great caution. There was a heavy sense of undefined hazard. Suddenly we debouched into an open field. I found myself on the perimeter of one of those inexplicable, tiny clearings that are rudely cultivated by the local peasants.

Behind me I could sense my men edging up uneasily to get a closer look at it, and, as I turned anxiously to tell them not to bunch together, I could feel their mass horripilation rippling across my skin. The apprehension of their physical presence was, however, undeniably comforting. The place radiated such an aura of power combined with hostility that I needed all the moral support I could get in order not to surrender to a belief in it, for there was a strong urge to collapse in the face of the irrational.

Instead, however, I summoned up my reserves of courage and began to observe the place closely. The plot of ground had been laid down earlier in the year to some species of primitive grain like sago or millet. Now the corn had been harvested but the stalks had been left. The coarse straw was collected into a pile and neatly stacked in the middle. Here a diminutive hut had been constructed. It was doubtless intended to shelter the bird-scarers while the grain was in the ear. It looked like a secondary stack.

It was this temporary shelter or refuge that concentrated all our attention. I became persuaded by a sort of instinctual extension of vision – almost second sight – that it contained something unpleasant. Nonetheless

I felt constrained to go and investigate it. It was getting dark; a cold, draughty wind had arisen and it had started to drizzle.

I was giving this hut a last-minute casing before venturing out into the open, when I chanced to look down at my feet. There on the ground right in front of me, perfectly preserved in mud and almost between my legs, was a Japanese footprint. It was one of those cloven-toed ones which are unmistakeable. It was not the sort of sign calculated to increase anyone's self-confidence under such conditions. As I marched out on my own into the middle of the field, my skin prickled all over into a shudder of heat. I felt I was being observed by a thousand eyes.

The place seemed haunted. I became aware of a strange atmosphere of superstitious dread which pervaded the place. I have since been able to identify this as a characteristically Japanese phenomenon from study of the literature, drama, art and films of that extraordinary people – but at the time I was unable to put a name to my fears.

As I approached the hut, the miasmic clouds lifted a little and I was able to examine my discovery by the aid of the increased light. There were two large slices of meat. They had been freshly cut from the buttocks of a recently dismembered corpse in the form of several rump steaks. The corpse, of markedly Japanese ethnic origin – probably a boy who had been killed in action rather than one who had died prematurely of disease – was naked except for the split-toed socks on its feet. It lay, prominently displayed yet painfully ungainly, across the small bamboo platform of the hut intended for sleeping on, which had been liberally scattered with bundles of straw. The body's posture – the pearl-white skin, its mangled quarters sprawled unceremoniously upon the improvised bed where its butchers had laid it – was so pathetic that I was for the moment quite incapable of comprehending the scene, either to condone or condemn. I had supped too full of horrors.

At a short distance a small fire was smouldering and there was evidence of an abandoned meal. There could be no doubt that a Japanese party had camped here, nor that they had hastily interrupted their horrible collation at the moment of my platoon's approaching them. It came as a surprise to realize that the Japanese were starving just as we were.

By the time I returned to the main sections, it was quite dark. I had been ordered to be back before twilight. Taking into consideration the difficulties on the way, it was a wonder I arrived at all. Attack and counter-attack by one side or the other were going in on every quarter, making

195

confusion doubly confounded, and it was more by luck than good management that I avoided getting caught up in them.

I found Jack Masters and made my report to him. He was too preoccupied to pay any attention to it. An account of Japanese cannibalism was the last thing he wanted to talk about. He looked at me in such a way as precluded any communication between us on the subject.

Up forward, apparently, our advance guard had not yet succeeded in disengaging itself from the enemy, although it was long past nightfall. It was still locked in a combat which looked like going on for another couple of hours. Elsewhere, along our whole flank, all our other components were equally being subjected to pressures, and it was not until nearly dawn that the enemy relaxed. Meanwhile, the popping, without intermission, of grenades, and the chatter, without intermission, of light machine guns within twenty or thirty yards of where we were in conference, were so disturbing that I was hardly able to concentrate.

Masters, however, did not lose his nerve. He seemed, indeed, even colder and more remote from human emotions than ever. Having arrived within striking distance of Point 2171 – this was our objective – he briefly sketched out for me the plan and prospects for our attack.

When I heard them, God knows, I realized that the position was desperate. Perched half way up the slope from the dry bed of the deep *chaung* where the majority of our soft belly was accommodated (mules, admin, the medics and all that), and without any firm base or real fortress around which to rally, there was no alternative to conquering the summit. We had to take it. Our survival admitted no other choice. If we did not succeed in scaling the mountain the next day, we would be annihilated.

Under such conditions it doesn't do to say too much. I just nodded without comment.

Our initial attack had got bogged down while I was away on patrol, so I was unfamiliar with the details. The situation amounted to this: our forward patrol had encountered the enemy earlier in the day in a forest clearing half-way up the mountain slope. It was in the dense jungle immediately beyond this clearing, still about a mile from the top of the ridge and perhaps a thousand feet below it, that our advance had been halted. Our forces were now tied down at the edge of this clearing, their aggressive spirits temporarily chastened. The enemy, it is true, were still retreating gradually up the slope towards Point 2171 at the top, but so slowly that they were obviously prepared to contest every inch.

Possession of the clearing, meanwhile, was of paramount importance to us. It was the only open space for miles which was available for receiving supply drops. Indeed, the demand for a heavy drop of arms and ammunition had already been despatched and the drop was scheduled for noon on the following day. Unless we could rapidly extend our influence so that this clearing would not be exposed to enemy machine-gun fire or mortar bombardment, we would not be able to collect the supplies vital to us, and on which the success of any drive to the summit depended.

Masters aimed to attack across the clearing at first light. He would then consolidate the ground immediately beyond it. Our troops would thereafter have to push forward up the steep declivity and seize the crest. My role in these proceedings, strangely enough, was to be pointed in exactly the opposite direction. I had to issue forth at dawn and lead a fighting patrol rearward along the track we had come by, to the place where one of our own reconnaissance units had reported a party of Japs attempting to shoot us up the back. My orders were to destroy them.

It was the sort of unspectacular assignment that had previously cost us the lives of some of our best officers.

I returned to the bed of the *chaung* in the deep valley where the defence platoons were holed-up with the remainder of the administrative section and, together with Thaman Bahadur, concocted some sort of plan for the morrow. Then I attempted to go to sleep. In the series of small actions which had led to the present engagement, the Brigade had incurred a certain number of casualties. Now, to my exasperated nerves and tormented sensibilities, the *chaung*-bed seemed full of screaming madmen and moaning wounded. One man in particular, a Rajputana Kshatriya belonging to Bombay Sappers and Miners and attached to Geoffrey Birt's engineer section, never ceased calling for his mother (ma – ma – *ma*) throughout the entire night. Round about midnight, unable to stand it any longer and thinking that a member of the warrior caste ought to be able to control himself rather better, I got up to expostulate with him.

A sleepy medical orderly was seated at the foot of the temporary bamboo platform constructed to keep the injured out of the mud. He was rocking himself backwards and forwards ferociously as if he too were in intense anguish. He gazed at me with lacklustre incomprehension. Beneath the roughly thatched roof hastily improvised that evening as shelter from the pelting rain, a dim *dipak* (native lamp) was burning. It was no more than a mere twist of cotton wool dipped as a wick into some sort of oil swimming about in the lid of a cigarette tin, but it was enough to see by.

By its feeble illumination I was able to make out Doc Whyte. He was administrating to the moaning Rajput some sort of medicament – probably morphia – and had in his hand a poised syringe. The rest of the wounded were laid out side by side, covered by torn blankets and with their feet sticking up out of the bottom as if they were already dead.

'Hullo,' Doc Whyte said. 'What's the matter?'

'I can't sleep.'

The moaning man was now making awful grunting noises and a bloody spume was issuing forth from his nostrils. He was unconscious.

Doc Whyte followed my gaze and said, not without sympathy, 'Is he disturbing you? He'll soon be dead.'

A cry of anguish extracted from a tortured individual by oppressive nightmares broke from a group of soldiers kipping near us. One of them started thrashing about in his sleep. It was such a disturbing demonstration that the medical orderly actually interrupted his rocking movements and got up to quieten him. In the generally debilitated state of all ranks, one hardly knew whether the man would be officially categorized as sick or officially categorized as 'fit for duty'. It did not matter. Either way, our soldiers were on their last legs.

Just beyond the radius of the light, sitting around like a rabble of jackals waiting for a carcase, I noticed a row of Gurkhas. Their eyes glittered rabidly in the soft glow of the lamp. Every now and then one of them cackled. They were part of that body of our troops, among whom were some British soldiers, who had gone mad. They were accommodated near the medical tent so that Doc Whyte could keep an eye on them and provide deep sedation, but every so often they would arouse themselves and sit around making caustic comments.

I retired, greatly troubled, to my bed. This was the last place on earth I should have chosen to pass the night prior to an engagement.

I lay down beside Dal Bahadur. He was awake.

The following morning, my men were stirring long before daylight. Thaman Bahadur and I ordered the placing of the men as we had agreed the previous night.

We set out. I felt sick to my stomach.

It was the third day after Tej Bahadur's premonition – which, of course, we had already forgotten about – when he had foretold his death.

The composition of the patrol was somewhat unusual. I put the two Bren-gunners, Tej Bahadur and Bhim Bahadur, right up in front. The boys had instructions, as soon as they encountered anything, to fire straight from the hip.

There were reported to be in the vicinity other bodies of our troops – Chinese from Stilwell's armies, a few predatory gangs of Burmans preying on Japanese stragglers, some Gurkhas from 14 Brigade supposed to be on long-distance reconnaissance. All or any of these were perfectly likely accidentally to shoot each other up.

It was an impossible situation. To an untrained eye, the Japanese and all these other people were indistinguishable, not least because friend and enemy had got into the habit of adopting each other's uniforms.

I received, however, no complaint, and in the event this patrol proved to be abortive. We encountered nothing; and, when we returned to the main body, I found the situation there considerably improved.

Masters had moved his command-post – together with the administrative section, radio sets, and ciphers – up forward. I accordingly proceeded up a steep incline still littered with the spoils of war: some captured rifles and an example of the curious 'woodpecker' machine-gun (the first I had seen). There was a certain amount of blood spilled in the mud, and one or two corpses. Masters had established himself on the edge of the clearing. The attack had gone in at dawn and it had been successful. The site was in our hands.

From beyond, masked by the dense jungle where the bloody business of hand-to-hand contest was still going on, there percolated, as through a thick and filtering veil, the deadly sounds of a desperate conflict. The muffled explosions, the sporadic rifle-fire and the peck-peck-peck-peck-peck of the 'woodpecker' had assumed a murderous intensity.

Masters looked haggard and worn. He had his walkie-talkie in his hand and would occasionally talk into it, alternately putting it up to his ear. He was in communication with our most forward elements. Alec Harper was with him, getting his briefing about taking over the assault from 3/4 Gurkhas. He was the commander of the column from 77 Brigade which Mike Calvert had sent over to help us in Blackpool. His 3/9 Gurkhas were intending to sweep us to the top. Ray Hulme was also with him. He had done his part by capturing and consolidating the clearing. The two of them were discussing the technique by which Ray Hulme's 3/4 Gurkhas would disengage while Alec Harper's 3/9 Gurkhas passed through them.

After a brief interval, the transfer was successfully accomplished. 3/4 Gurkhas were withdrawn to reserve. The time was about a quarter past eleven. I reported my patrol accomplished and said that our rear was clear of Japs.

'OK,' said Masters. 'Your platoons can rest. Tell them to stay in the bed of the *chaung*, but to be ready to move into action. I want you to stay here, near my command post. Keep Dal Bahadur with you, so that he can run back with a message.'

'Very well, sir. They haven't had anything to eat or drink. Can they brew up?'

'Yes.'

I sent Dal Bahadur back with this information and told him to brew himself a mug of tea and return. Then I glanced around curiously and began to observe.

Brigade Headquarters was occupying the spine of a knife-edge ridge. It was up this ridge that Ray Hulme's 3/4 Gurkhas had fought their way that morning. To our left it dropped steeply in a precipitous cliff. It was not the sort of place that would have been at all easy to storm and formed an excellent defensive rampart. All our administrative units were placed evenly along it, starting (from nearest the *chaung*-bed) with Doc Whyte's *basha* and medical tent, then Briggo's signallers, then Rhodes James with ciphers, finally Jack Masters's command post which was on the very edge of the clearing. Chesty Jennings's RAF radio was right out in the open.

The path ran twenty or thirty yards to the right of this ridge. To the right again the ground sloped away gently into a shallow, saucer-like declivity and disappeared into the trees.

The clearing extended from the edge of the precipice where some bleached rocks protruded from the ground, and stretched for about two hundred yards towards the right and into the shallow declivity. At the right-hand edge, where the jungle began, it was full of cavernous shadows. Here – a most fitting location, for it looked like hell's mouth magnified – was established our little colony of maniacs presided over by one of Doc Whyte's medics.

It had started to rain. Dal Bahadur came weaving up the slope towards where I was standing. He was carrying a mess-tin full of tea, but I never got the opportunity to drink it.

At this moment, news came via reconnaissance that the clearing was menaced – the Japanese were counter-attacking from the left. Masters grabbed me and told me to bring up the defence platoons and dig in along the ridge. I used Dal Bahadur to transmit the orders to the defence platoons.

They came toiling up the slope under the burden of their heavy packs, feet slipping backwards in the mud, led by Thaman Bahadur. I detailed the places where I wanted the sections posted and stood beside the path watching them, trying to say something funny or encouraging to each one as he passed.

Tej Bahadur brought up the rear. As he came into the open from the thick forest, I plainly noted his change of expression. His face paled perceptibly and even his lips went white. He faltered markedly and hung back.

'What's the matter?'

'It's this place. This is it!'

'What do you mean?'

'It's the place I told you about. It's where I'm going to get killed!'

Masters was watching me suspiciously, wondering perhaps why my platoons weren't trotting smartly into action as on the parade ground. Under his penetrating scrutiny I lost my temper. I had always been vaguely uncomfortable because the other officers plainly thought I treated my Gurkhas too familiarly. Now I let fly at Tej Bahadur with an ill-mannerly explosion.

'What nonsense,' I upbraided him, 'to say such at thing at a time like this!'

'But it's true,' he wailed, wringing his hands.

'Please don't cause any more embarrassment. Everybody's looking at us. Just get out there and dig your slit-trench. After a little time I'll see what I can do for you. Now go!' Unwillingly he went.

All at once three DC-3's appeared overhead and started supply-dropping. Their advent was accompanied by one or two explosions. As an artillery-man I ought to have understood their significance. Some Japanese 75's were ranging on us, but I completely failed to appreciate it. One shell went off in the bamboo thickets at the foot of the cliff where we were digging in, and another burst beyond us in the jungle near where our madmen were accommodated.

If only I had marked their fall of shot I should have realized that they straddled the clearing with deadly accuracy. I would have taken the proper precautions. But since nobody took the slightest notice of them, and Chesty Jennings continued to talk the DC's down, I too followed suit.

Now Tej Bahadur abandoned digging his slit trench and came over to me. We talked on the edge of the clearing, almost in secret, at the fringe of the wood.

'Well, what is it?' I asked him a little more sympathetically, seeing as we were no longer observed. 'What do you want me to do? I can't let you run away. We all have to do our duty.'

'Yes, sahib. I realize that. But I feel dreadfully ill. It's very near now. I know it is. It's within a couple of minutes. Will you please let me go to the rear and take shelter among the mules?'

He was so distressed that I didn't know what to do. I didn't like to refuse him. All the same I was going to find it pretty hard to justify if Masters found out.

'I tell you what,' I said, hitting on a sort of compromise. 'Go back to where Thaman Bahadur posted you. Have you finished your slit-trench?'

'No, sahib.'

'Well, finish it. It can't take you all that long. When you've done so, go back down to the mules and brew up by yourself and smoke a cigarette. Will that satisfy you?'

His face brightened considerably, and he actually smiled.

'Yes, sahib. Thank you. It will satisfy me well.'

He turned on his heel smartly and saluted. As he marched out into the open, a slender shaft of sunlight illuminated him.

Then the Jap 75's came down and he was killed.

# CHAPTER SIXTEEN

# Taking Point 2171

I couldn't for the life of me make out what was happening. Don't forget that I hadn't been in Blackpool, and consequently had not experienced that terrible shelling. In fact, I'd never been shelled in my life. I had for so long been protected by deep jungle far from any road that being subjected to artillery bombardment was something I didn't expect.

Instead of taking cover as everyone else had, I staggered about as if stupefied. Then, after the first rounds of gun-fire had descended on the clearing and subsided, everything went quiet.

The DC-3's abandoned their supply dropping and buggered off, and Chesty Jennings's RAF signallers abandoned their radio sets. Only one parachute, remote like a luminous bubble, floated gently to earth. It landed in the centre of the clearing with a thud and lay there neglected – not a soul made any attempt to go to collect it.

Even the sounds of battle from uphill in the forward zone seemed lulled. It was as if my own shock and surprise had communicated itself to nature. Gingerly I ventured out into the open. The clearing which had been so full of movement only moments ago was now completely deserted. Gone were the groups of gossipy soldiers eagerly retrieving the supply drop. Gone were my Gurkhas digging their slit-trenches among the stones and the dirt. It is amazing how closely you can hug the ground when your survival depends on it.

Only the maniacs at the bottom end of the clearing were stirring. The bangs and bursts of the explosions seemed to have excited them beyond bounds, and they showed signs of becoming unmanageable.

Then the second round of gunfire descended. I saw one of Chesty Jennings's sets disintegrate under a direct hit. The other was lifted bodily by the concussion but dropped back into its place. It continued relaying dottily. The nasal American voice of the Dakota pilot demanded 'What the heck?' through the abandoned earphones.

Suddenly the mad Gurkhas took to the limelight and rushed crazily onto the set. They started to shed their scanty garments until they were naked. Then they began to dance with a dizzying speed among the bursts.

As the projectiles from the Japanese guns hurtled into the bottom of the clearing, they exploded against the dark background of the jungle in showers of sparks. The Gurkhas, with shrieks of joy, chased after them. You could see the spray of splinters glowing red hot and pretty as firecrackers as the projectiles burst. The salvo of shots landed dead among them, but not a Gurkha was hurt.

I scrambled from my knees where I had been knocked sideways and rushed desperately back. I suspected that something was going on for which I had failed to make allowances. I wanted to find someone from Brigade Headquarters who would tell me the truth.

After a frantic search I found Rhodes James. He was crouched over his code-books in the primitive birth-and-burial position alongside some of Briggo's signallers. They had all flattened themselves into the ground and looked like a group of tomb-victims when first disinterred by the archaeologist.

'What are you doing?' I yelled, glowering at him. On his face was an expression of terror.

'I'm taking cover.'

'Why?'

'We're being shelled.'

So that was it! Now everything fell into place. Gradually I began to comprehend the various components of what until that moment had been an indistinct blur.

Soldiers were crouching here and there upon the slope and soon I had sufficiently recovered my composure to be able to distinguish them and to mark their faces and expressions. One or two began to raise their heads. Another salvo of shots, however, quickly put paid to their scrutiny.

A shell slammed into the radio sets, setting them jumping and quivering (the radios seemed doomed to attract an awful lot of punishment), and another two or three landed athwart the signallers.

The Japanese 77 millimetre gun is a quick-firing weapon of high muzzle velocity and flat trajectory not unlike the Bofors. It is easily manoeuvrable, extremely accurate and fires a shell weighing about eight pounds. As a consequence, it is ideally suited to close engagements but it suffers from compensatory disadvantages. In the present instance, these amounted to a large number of failures. On account of the sloping nature of the ground which slanted away from their line of fire, a high proportion of the shells were landing on their shoulders instead of on their noses. This resulted in the fuses designed to ignite on impact failing to trigger and the shells not going off. At least this was the obvious explanation. Alternatively, the ammunition may have been damp.

Suddenly, on the ground about twenty yards in front of me, there was a terrific thump. It was accompanied by a frightful hissing noise. Then a horrible slithery thing whooshed towards me through the bushes and came to rest in the mud. It landed plumb between my legs.

My first impression was that something revolting had aroused itself – some hitherto unrecognized creature of the jungle – some species of snake.

The object, whatever it was, kept spinning – spinning with vertiginous speed. The rapidity of its revolutions in the mud made sizzling noises like a frying egg. I was convinced that it was a living thing.

Then, all at once, it stopped. In its expiring moments it exhaled a thin spiral of smoke as from a burning cigarette. There was a pronounced smell of cordite. I was gazing at an unexploded shell.

In their dumb immobility these duds could be more dangerous than live ammunition. You could never be sure that their explosions would not be delayed. I left that location quickly and made sure not to come back.

In its way, the occurrence was just what was wanted. It aroused in me a proper appreciation of realities and alerted me to the responsibility of my position, namely a preoccupation with my men – something which had temporarily fallen into abeyance.

'My darling!' I thought. 'My beloved Dal Bahadur! What can have become of you!' It was only with my realisation that we were being shelled, that I recognized the danger he was in.

To my shame, I confess that I didn't really know where Dal Bahadur had gone. He was always very independent. The last I remembered of him had been when I sent him back to call up the platoons. Where was he? Nobody seemed to have any idea.

I dashed down to the mule-lines in the *chaung* bed in an attempt to find him. 'Where's Dal Bahadur? Have you seen Dal Bahadur?'

'He went forward, sahib. We thought he was with you.'

I began to panic. Everything pointed to the same conclusion. I urgently wanted to learn the truth, but was detained by the mule-drivers.

'What's going on up forward, sahib? Are we winning?'

'Yes – yes – I suppose so,' I answered, but my mind was on other things. 'We're being shelled. 3/9 Gurkhas are going for the top. Their storming parties are already attacking. It'll be in our hands by nightfall. Defence platoons are digging in on the plateau. If only I could find Dal Bahadur!'

I felt guilty lingering where no shells were falling and where it was safe. I sought frantically to break away. The shelling was becoming more persistent, and as the bombardment increased I set off up the slope.

A shell exploded on the ground in front of me and half-a-dozen more went off to my right and my left. They seemed to burst right in my face. But it was like peering through a plate-glass window when someone throws a bucket of water at you. Nothing happened. I wasn't wounded. I wasn't even touched. I simply slipped, made a desperate attempt to recover my balance, and fell. Perhaps it was the blast which knocked me over – perhaps it was my haste.

I picked myself up, panting with excitement, bathed in perspiration, and covered in mud.

'Dal Bahadur!' I yelled. 'Where are you? Dal Bahadur!'

I wept. I sobbed. The echoes mocked me.

'Dear God!' I prayed. There was only one alternative to his having absconded without leave and it began to occupy my thoughts to the exclusion of everything else. 'Dear God! Don't let it happen!'

I came out into the open again. The clearing was suddenly bathed in sunlight. I stumbled on Bhim Bahadur. He was crouched, with some other members of the platoon, in a shallow depression.

'Have you seen him?' I shouted. 'Which way did he go?'

No one dreamed of asking me whom I was referring to.

'No, sahib,' Bhim Bahadur articulated shakily. 'No sahib.'

'Then who's that?'

I pointed to a person in a prone position lying on his back right out in the open, his face covered with a hat.

'It's Tej Bahadur, your excellency. He fell right at the beginning.'

'Then go and help him. He may be wounded.'

'No sahib,' Bhib Bahadur interjected. 'Begging your honour's pardon – but he's dead.'

I walked towards the edge of the clearing, trying not to give away any of my feelings. It was where the stony spine of the cliff projected and the land fell steeply over a precipitous ridge. It was from such a vantage point – the most exposed one – that I could accurately assess where the firing was coming from.

I pretended to be absorbed in this occupation but my eyes were dim. I peered myopically into the misty panorama of broken country before me, but without being able to distinguish a thing.

At my back were my men. At my feet, undulating away from me in hundreds of inconspicuous hills and ridges from one of which the Japs were aiming at me over open sights, stretched the mocking and anonymous distance. It seemed to reflect the tormented state of my emotions at Tej Bahadur's death.

'Dear, pimply melon-face,' I reflected bitterly. 'So you were right – you finally bought it. And God knows how many more of you there may not be!' The prospect of sustaining many such casualties was terrifying. I turned away, muttering more such thoughts beneath my breath.

Totally preoccupied, and without really being aware of where I was going or what I was doing, I moved imperceptibly to my left.

I had searched all the most improbable places for Dal Bahadur with a sort of unyielding obstinacy – and without success. Now I approached the only spot where I was likely to find him. It was where I intended establishing my platoon headquarters. My mind was concentrated on other things. It seems almost unforgivable, yet it is often thus in moments of crisis.

But what was this? There was something there, between the rocks.

'Dear God!'

I suddenly remembered the search I was engaged upon and experienced a rush of agitation. It was so violent that I could scarcely control my trembling.

'Don't let it be true – don't let it happen!' I babbled dementedly.

A little bundle of rags was lying there as if someone had taken off his clothes. Now why, I wondered, should anybody do that? Suddenly I caught the glint of naked flesh.

I breathed his name. 'Dal Bahadur!' My words were almost inaudible among the whisk of the shells as they whammed past – for they were still coming – or the whoosh of the wind. Yet he heard me.

He stood up and stared ahead. He was quite sightless. He looked quite magnificent standing there and straddling the edge of the cliff, bare of chest, his stance lofty, his face calm, composed and unclouded, full of noble indifference.

I was at his side in an instant.

A thin trickle of blood was making its way over his chin from a corner of his mouth and two others, as black as treacle, were oozing from his nose.

In every other respect, he appeared uninjured. Yet there was something in his aspect which filled me with foreboding.

The whole thing – our meeting, recognition, and my rushing to his assistance – took place in a split second. Dal Bahadur had not had time to say anything, but his eyes were wild.

I looked down into them. They were already clouding, as I thought, with the mists of incomprehension and death. He seemed to be fighting to retain his consciousness.

He let out a hysterical shriek.

'*Murgaya! Murgaya! Murgaya!* I've been hit. I'm dying, sahib. I'm dying!'

As if beseeching me to give him back his strength, which was ebbing with every exclamation, he flung himself on me. I also was bare-chested. Our naked flesh met – touched – trembled – melted – fused.

But in that instant of physical impact another thing happened. There was a hideous bubbling noise, and I was drenched with a warm, sticky liquid, and my boots began to fill with fluid.

I held him away from me, and saw his wound. It was his blood, mixed with a sort of runny yellow mucus from the pleura, which was saturating my chest. A piece of shrapnel had torn a hole through his rib-cage. The bubbling noise was the air which was escaping every time he breathed, from a rent in his lung.

Although the urge to panic and despair was almost overwhelming, I made a supreme effort to pull myself together.

'Try to lie down,' I said; but I could not disengage myself from his embrace.

'Let me carry you. Relax. Release me, there's a good boy! Please do!'

For a moment he relented. I tried to pick him up but he proved too heavy for me. We collapsed to the ground. Suddenly, in response to some inner muscular spasm, his wound opened further and spouted a fountain of blood. It hit me full in the face.

'Lie still,' I begged him, my mouth close to his ear. 'I'm going to get help.'

'Don't leave me,' he whispered; and then much louder, 'Don't leave me! I'll soon be dead!'

His eyes were full of pleading. I became aware of his scent-glands. He smelt musky as milk.

I surrendered to his importunity helplessly.

\*\*\*

Winkling out Bhim Bahadur and his section from their fox-holes and putting them to carrying out Dal Bahadur proved more difficult than I had anticipated. The shells were still bursting all round us, and not unnaturally the men were unwilling to leave shelter. It was one of those occasions which demanded – quite literally – putting in the boot.

With Dal Bahadur lying near death at the edge of the precipice, I could not afford to be scrupulous, and, after a few kicks and cuffs, they followed me.

He hadn't moved, but in the few minutes I had been absent his condition had deteriorated. The effects of shock were asserting themselves. His eyes were open, but fixed and staring, and they were plainly devoid of vision. His frame was rigid. He appeared to have relapsed into some sort of catalepsy.

Just before we lifted him, he regained consciousness for a moment, saw and recognized me, and repeated '*murgaya, murgaya,*' – but weakly and hesitantly. It was obvious that he was slipping away.

'Quickly,' I urged, impatiently. 'Quickly!'

The urgency of my words merely stimulated the men who were trying to lift him – his weight seemed to have double or trebled – into being clumsy. Fumbling about with their great ungainly hands and awkward fingers, they caused his wound to re-open. A great hot blast of moist spume and bloody bubbles flew straight at me. It was like being subjected to an attack.

I gazed with horror. The lung was collapsed and hissing like a cat. Quite accidentally, I put my fingers on his pulse. That, at any rate, was throbbing steadily. The heart was strong and true.

Unable to bear the torture of being in his company a moment longer, and with the bearers stumbling joltingly through the mud, I dashed ahead to find the doctor. As the stretcher party emerged from the rocks, the shelling miraculously stopped.

Doc Whyte came at once.

We met on the edge of the clearing, near Jack Masters's command post. They had laid Dal Bahadur down in the middle of the path, amongst the mud and the blood and the mule-droppings.

'Can you help?' I begged Doc Whyte, with joined palms.

He seemed miraculously calm beside my state of near-frenzy.

'Of course. But first of all, what's the matter with you?'

He looked at me intently.

'Why, nothing! Absolutely nothing!'

'All that blood!'

'It's his.' I wailed hysterically, pointing at Dal Bahadur and trying to prevent myself sobbing. 'It's his. I tried to carry him.'

During this exchange Doc Whyte was preparing his medical haversack. Now he took out a great roll of adhesive dressing, tore of a strip with a noise like the ripping of silk, cut it with some scissors and slapped it right over the rent in Dal Bahadur's chest. The procedure was performed with magical skill. The bubbling and hissing of the air through the aperture ceased at once, and Dal Bahadur began to breathe normally.

'Are you going to put him out? Will you put him out?'

'Certainly,' he nodded. 'Just give me a chance.'

He prepared a syringe.

'Is that it? Will it do the trick?'

'It will do the trick.'

He jabbed with the needle, then slid it in subcutaneously.

'Will it knock him out?'

'It will knock him out.'

I felt a tremendous surge of relief. I couldn't bear that Dal Bahadur should suffer needlessly.

We both watched while he slid painlessly into unconsciousness.

After a respectful interval, I asked 'Is he dead?'

'Of course not. What a suggestion!'

'Not yet? It's been quite some time.'

'What are you talking about?'

'You said you were going to knock him out. Wasn't it lethal?'

Mercy killing was sometimes practised on the fatally wounded.

Doc Whyte looked at me incredulously.

'You're in a state of shock,' was all he said. 'Dal Bahadur's going to recover. Come down to my *basha* and I'll give you something that'll buck you up.'

He saw my anxious expression.

'Don't worry. I'll look after him.'

They carried Dal Bahadur away.

Everyone was looking at me warily. They obviously wondered how I was going to react. I felt that it was essential to return to some routine activity, so I went in search of Thaman Bahadur. Together we went round the positions, getting the men back to their duties and establishing a sense of normality. Finally we arrived at Tej Bahadur.

Nobody had touched him. He still lay there on his back. Thaman Bahadur bent down and removed his hat. The boy's face was calm and undisfigured. 'Shall I detail a burial party?'

'Yes, you'd better. Just a minute though! Let's find out where he was hit. Tell them to examine the body before they bury it.'

'Very well, sahib.'

I withdrew a little apart. The intensity of the firing was increasing on the upper slopes of Point 2171 and it looked as though a ferocious battle might develop. Some mules came up into the clearing from the rear, were loaded with spare ammunition which we had saved from the supply drop, and went trotting off towards our forwards elements. The medical orderlies started rounding up the lunatics.

I observed the scene of carnage dispassionately. Everything had returned so swiftly to normal that it was difficult to realize that anything had happened. Then quite spontaneously, I looked up. The sky was undergoing a drastic reorganisation. The cloud-layer which had borne down so heavily was dissolving. The superimposed strata were withdrawing themselves like shutters. A shaft of sunlight shot into the clearing as solidly as a streak of paint. The clouds continued to roll away.

I caught a glimpse of blue sky. The revelation only lasted a few minutes, but in that interval God was present. Despite the deceptive appearance of things, I was assured that everything was divine.

I glanced about me. At my feet, the mud was dark and bloodstained. At a little distance my men were examining the corpse of Tej Bahadur. Further away, Dal Bahadur lay wounded. Yet the message was unmistakable. God was tangibly present. God was present, not as an abstraction or a concept, not as a philosophical statement, not as a metaphysical speculation, not as an old man in a white sheet sitting on a cloud, God was present in everything around me – in the howling Gurkhas, some of whom the medics had succeeded in collecting and who were now neighing like horses; in the peripatetic mule-teams plodding patiently towards the front; in Thaman Bahadur, who was coming towards me.

'What is it?'

'We've examined Tej Bahadur, sahib. Shall we bury him?'

'Yes – but what's the verdict? What did he die of?'

'Sahib – he was untouched. There wasn't a mark on him.'

I turned away despondently. My revelation of the divine seemed to fall about me in ruins. I was going to walk off when Thaman Bahadur stopped me.

'Sahib, look at your clothes. Look at your trousers. Look at the back!'

'What about them!'

I glanced down and behind. To my amazement, the seat and legs of my trousers were in shreds. They had been torn in tatters by shell splinters. Yet I was unscathed.

Doc Whyte emerged into the clearing from somewhere back down the slope, wearing a preoccupied expression. He told me in simple, unmedical language that Dal Bahadur's prospects were bleak. He did not now expect Dal Bahadur to live. In addition to the desperate nature of his chest wound, which was itself sufficient to cause death, several ribs were shattered, and he had sustained a broken ankle and a smashed wrist.

Just at this moment there flared up a revival of activity from the hill. Jack Masters came out of his command post, where he had been in communication with Alex Harper, and told Doc Whyte that Jim Blaker had arrived in position, and was about to go for the top.

Blaker was a young officer, a Company Commander of Alex Harper's 3/9 Gurkhas and thus comparatively unknown to me. He had been selected earlier in the day to lead a detour round the Japanese flank. It was the last of such assaults which we should have the resources to mount. It was, as a consequence, critical to our survival.

All of a sudden there was an outburst of bombing and mortaring from high on the slope. The machine-guns of both sides opened up with burst and counter-burst and it became impossible to distinguish anything further.

Only Masters – still in communication by walkie-talkie with one of the forward commanders – knew what was happening. I saw him blanch and shudder.

Blaker, while leading a charge against a Jap machine-gun post which had been holding up our advances, had been hit.

The walkie-talkie brayed out the news relentlessly.

'His men are struggling to get him back – they are going to evacuate him. He's still conscious. Yes – there he is – I can see him – he's propped against a log. He is crouched in the mud. Someone's giving him a drink.'

'What is it? What's the nature of the wound?' Doc Whyte kept asking. 'For God's sake tell me – maybe I can send some instructions – maybe I can help.'

'I don't know – I can't make out,' Masters answered, and handed him the walkie-talkie. 'You take it. You talk to them.'

'No, no,' said Doc Whyte, recoiling. 'They have their column doctor up there. I'll mind my own business and not interfere.'

All at once the walkie-talkie began speaking as if it possessed an independent identity and had come under the influence of one of a mediumistic spirit: 'I can't see very clearly – it's started to rain. It looks as if they're having a conference. I can see the subedar expostulating – he seems to expostulating about something with Jim, but Jim won't have it. They're breaking up – they've decided something – yes, it looks as if they're preparing for something – I can see some of them unpinning their grenades – they're going in. Jim's wounded in the stomach. He copped a burst in the gut. He's dying – his guts in the mud. He's encouraging them forward – he's still conscious – he's encouraging 'em on – they're going – they've left him – they're going for the summit – they've gone. I can hear the firing, I can see the bomb-burst – they're going in with the kukri – they've got it – they've got to the crest – they've got to it – the crest is ours – I say, can you hear me? – Jim is dead.'

Masters yelled at the instrument, 'Identify yourself – who the hell are you?' But it also had ceased to function.

Jim Blaker was awarded a posthumous Victoria Cross for his role in this engagement.

# CHAPTER SEVENTEEN

# Holding On

Darkness descended that evening rather earlier than usual. The afternoon too had been dull and leaden. The break in the clouds which had provoked my sudden burst of spiritual illumination had been quickly dispelled, its promise dissipated. Soon it was pouring with rain as relentlessly as ever.

There is always much to do after a serious engagement. Casualties have to be attended to and evacuated; the dead have to be disposed of. If the action had resulted in ground gained or a technical victory, the advance had to be exploited and its advantages consolidated. Barbed wire must be strung out and defensive positions dug as quickly as possible and the place converted into a strong-point in order to resist the counter-attacks which will inevitably follow – and Japanese counter-attacks could always be relied upon to be extremely well co-ordinated and heavy.

Men also must clean their guns and their weapons, as well as themselves. In more ways than one, fighting is a dirty business. With his attention distracted by battle, it is astonishing what an accumulation of muck can be accommodated on one man – mud and earth thrown up by bombs and the mortars, as well as an immense assortment of body dirts like sweat, blood, shit and piss, even spunk (men have been known to ejaculate under the stimulus of the excitement).

Most of the men, in relays, chose to go down to the bed of the *chaung* to wash, where there were one or two turgid pools, now filthily churned up into foetid swamps by so much traffic. I preferred to let Dal Bahadur's blood solidify on me until it could be chipped off. It came away like nail varnish, in tarnished flakes. As for my torn trousers, I threw them away and adopted a torn strip of parachute cloth for a *lungyi*.

Long lines of mules trailed up to the top of the hill with coils of barbed wire – one coil to each side – only to return after half an hour with a wounded Gurkha in the saddle. Jim Blaker and the other dead, in spite of being heroes, were treated less ceremoniously. They were bundled over the edge of the precipice, because everyone was too tired, or too busy, to bury them. Tej Bahadur, on the other hand, lay in a decent and proper – if rather shallow – grave. I insisted on according him that much respect.

I managed, round about five o'clock, to snatch some spare time to pay a visit to Dal Bahadur. He was as comfortable as it was possible to make him, but was still unconscious. Was he sinking or was it morphia? As I returned up the slope – along that same path I had traversed a hundred times that day in various stages of dementia or hysteria – Doc Whyte waylaid me. He lured me into his *basha* and presented me with half a bottle of medical brandy. This was the 'something' he had promised me when I was begging him to 'knock Dal Bahadur out', which would put me right.

Soon afterwards I received a message that Jack Masters wanted to see me.

He looked a bit put out; or perhaps it was just the characteristic embarrassment of the typical Englishman who needs to say something emotional. What followed, however, was something I would never have predicted from someone so reserved. It no doubt cost him considerable effort and as a consequence I was – and still am – extraordinarily grateful to him. I think the incident reveals him at his most sympathetic aspect. It reflects him, moreover, in a light which I have not, in these pages, sufficiently emphasized.

'Um – er,' he began, after a short pause, at the same time doing something nervously with his hands. 'I sent for you – yes! I sent for you.'

He took a deep breath, and then the words rushed out.

'I sent for you because I want you to know – about Dal Bahadur – I'm not unsympathetic. Believe me,' he continued gently, giving me a cool and level look of appraisal which penetrated straight to my heart so that I remember it to this day. 'Believe me – I know what this means to you. I understand.'

'Thank you, sir.'

'How is he?'

I told him what Doc Whyte had said, adding that he did not think he would recover. He nodded, and then he in his turn produced half a bottle of rum which he handed to me.

I stumbled out from his presence, more muddled-headed than ever. When compassion takes over from military harshness – as when liberalism replaces repression in the mechanics of government – is always a moment of danger. The effect of Masters's kindness was singularly unhelpful. It merely served to augment my physical weakness and lack of moral fibre to the point where they became visible to everybody.

At the beginning of my narrative I had occasion to recount a similar circumstance involving Joe Lentaigne. I did so, moreover, with a certain lack of sympathy. At that juncture I observed that there would be further examples, during the course of the campaign, of a comparable nature. I certainly wasn't thinking of myself.

At about six o'clock that evening we were submitted to our first experience of heavy shelling from medium artillery. It consisted of an hour's bombardment from the plain by big calibre howitzers. Daylight was filtering away, leaving the landscape dull and undistinguished, when suddenly, from way down in the valley, there was a distant boom. Within seconds all ranks were diving for cover. The muted explosion was followed by an infernal howling noise, and then by an explosion and a concussion which shook the hillside to its core.

The projectile which landed was, in fact, far from being a piece of conventional artillery. It was, in reality, a gigantic mortar-bomb. In due course we referred to these as 'flying dustbins'.

Mortar-bombs, unlike shells, do not bore their way through the air by means of revolutions communicated to them from rifled grooves along an extensive barrel. They are fitted with fins just like aerial bombs and they are lobbed at you from a short, smooth, unrifled tube which makes their muzzle velocity extremely low. Their high trajectory assures that the projectiles can soar over hills, and in this respect they resemble howitzers.

The contrivance which imparted to our own particular flying dustbin its velocity and impetus was short and blunt. As a consequence of this, the projectile, which was cylindrical like a dustbin and not conical like a shell and was not fitted with fins to keep it straight, simply turned over and over. It was its erratic flight through the air, incorporating these uncompromising aerodynamics, which created the nightmarish screaming noise.

As it was impossible to predict on which part of its anatomy it would land, it had fuses sticking out all over it. When this incredible artefact came howling across the hills at you, containing about a ton of TNT, it landed with the sort of thud that knocked the stuffing right out of you. However, it wasn't very accurate. It didn't have to be. It achieved its objective by stunning every live creature within miles into stupefaction.

The huge howitzer shells came whizzing over at the rate of about one a minute, while the flying dustbins arrived so regularly at dawn and dusk that you could set your watch by them.

Grabbing my two bottles of rum, I ran for shelter and dived into a trench. Shells were landing with a 'crunch – crump', and every so often a giant teak tree, its roots loosened up by the explosions, would cant slowly sideways, then crash majestically to earth. I was constantly showered with mud and dirt. The birds and beasts departed, and during the interval between detonations an astonished hush settled on nature. It rained incessantly.

Suddenly my self-control cracked and my morale broke. The loneliness of enduring the bombardment in a solitary slit-trench without the comforting assurance of Dal Bahadur to support me became absolutely intolerable. I went in search of the others. On my way, I stumbled upon a trench occupied by Jack Masters and Doc Whyte. As I passed it, a shell plummeted beside them and ploughed up great fountains of clods and clay. A red-hot piece of shrapnel splinter went ripping by me with a terrific whizz, and buried itself in a tree-trunk. It was as big as my arm. I was interested to remark that both Jack Masters's and Doc Whyte's faces were contorted with rictus. It was a tremendous alleviation to my torturing guilt-complex to realize that other people were similarly affected.

I then found the trench where Thaman Bahadur and my NCO's were sheltering. They were not in much better shape. I jumped into the trench, where my two bottles of rum helped persuade the NCO's to accept me.

After about half-an-hour the shelling suddenly came to an end. The NCO's returned to their sections and sectors, but I remained behind in the trench. I wanted to talk over some of the day's events with Thaman Bahadur.

Darkness had descended and the rain had ceased. The moon arose, white and waxy and, with its gigantic halo, disproportionately huge. I was about to call Thaman Bahadur's attention to the sight, when I became aware that he was no longer listening to me. We were by now out of our trench and perched on its edge. His gaze, instead of engaging my eyes, suddenly slipped past me. It focused itself somewhere over and behind – beyond my left ear, a territory where entry was probably forbidden to me. I felt that we were in the presence of those chthonic entities – psychic scavengers, ghouls – who haunt every blood-saturated battlefield. No sooner was this thought established than a great flapping night-hawk or owl swooped low over us, hooting throbbingly.

Suddenly from the distance, incredibly far away, I heard a voice appealing for succour. It was calling plaintively, in that peculiarly garbled mixture of Hindi, Bengali and Gurkhali with which my men communicated with me – and there was no question for whom it was intended.

'Help. Save me – I'm dying. Help!'

It was intended for me. My skin pimpled into goose-prickles and I leapt to my feet.

'Help! Save me! *Murgaya – murgaya* – I'm dying!'

Thaman Bahadur had gone white as a sheet.

'It's someone who's lost,' I said. 'It's one of the wounded. He's been left out in the open. I'm going to find him.'

In spite of the fact that Thaman Bahadur was plainly terrified, he contradicted me flat.

'No, sahib!'

'Yes!'

'No, sahib!'

We confronted each other eyeball to eyeball, but he did not flinch. With marvellous dexterity – almost a sleight of hand – he grasped me by the neck. Although he was only a little man, I felt forced by his powerful grip to yield to him.

Suddenly the voice sounded nearer, right up close, pleading with heart-wrenching pathos.

'Help me! Help – help! I'm dying!'

With a rush of understanding, I yielded. Thaman Bahadur threw me down into the bottom of the trench and knelt on me. I now understood that the voice could not belong to a human agency. It would have been impossible for a wounded soldier to have so quickly covered the distance between the first far-off cries pleading for succour and this last one, so near at hand.

Thaman Bahadur had rescued me form God knows what vile contagion. He had used the same stratagem as Odysseus's sailors had employed in binding him to the mast to prevent him answering the song of the sirens.

'OK,' I said. 'I understand.'

Imperceptibly he relaxed. After an embarrassed silence, he explained: 'It's a *bhuta*, sahib – an infecting spirit – we know about such things. I've had experience of them (he had seen the action at Habbaniya in Iraq and other places), and you must never answer them. They can take possession of you. They feed on the dead.'

The great flapping nightjar, hawk, owl, goatsucker or vampire bat flew back overhead. Again the voice pleaded, 'I'm dying – dying – dying' and then sank dispiritedly away. I knew that Thaman Bahadur was right.

\*\*\*

218

Over the next few days Dal Bahadur returned to consciousness, and he gradually grew stronger. Nonetheless, on the third day after he had been wounded, my health collapsed so completely that I was hard put to it to keep myself going. Under these circumstances, I was invited to a 'medical supper'. These were special banquets prepared by Doc Whyte and his orderly, a young Gurkha called Borubdar Bahadur, who had developed a *cordon bleu* flair for high quality – if improvised – cooking.

Doc Whyte and Borubdar Bahadur had at their disposal what are called 'medical comforts', namely all those choice ingredients which come within the purview of a Chief Medical Officer of Brigade. They could afford to make these suppers fairly lavish. They were also very exclusive. To be invited meant that Doc Whyte considered you to be a genuine casualty. Evidently he saw me as such a case.

'It's no good,' I had excused myself. 'You'll simply be wasting all Borubdar Bahadur's talent. I'll not be able to keep it down. It seems a pity to go to all that trouble.'

'Never mind. You'll get the satisfaction of the taste. Don't be so bloody independent. Just accept it and enjoy it.'

So I consented. The meal came completely up to expectations and also included a glass of whisky topped by a raw egg. Even the whisky and egg, however, did not manage to meet the challenge. Fifteen minutes afterwards, I had to go outside, and was terribly sick.

Doc Whyte laughed good-humouredly.

'I'll tell you what,' he suggested. 'Why not go down to the medical *basha* and spend the night with Dal Bahadur.'

Our meeting was initially somewhat constrained. His torso was encased in plaster-of-paris. He could hardly move and barely speak. I lay down beside him. We both of us surrendered to the kind of intimacy that gradually merges with sleep.

I awoke some hours later, confused by my new location, to find the moon shining full in my face.

'Sahib! Sahib!' Dal Bahadur's whisper came urgently. 'Are you awake?'

A summons from Dal Bahadur in the middle of the night was, whatever its nature, one that could not go unanswered.

He enunciated just one word: 'Tutti.'

Now this word, in our argot, meant that he wanted to have a shit. It was certainly something to be welcomed as a sign of an awakening metabolism, but it was almost as challenging in its implications as if he had wanted to do the other thing.

Slightly stunned by the appalling prospect which his demand presented, and not quite knowing how to meet it, I remained lying on my side and initially pretended still to be asleep.

Sahib! Sahib!' his whisper came again insistently. 'Tutti!'

There was no denying his request.

Perhaps I ought to explain something of my difficulty. High caste Hindus, of whom Dal Bahadur was one, can be extremely fussy about cleanliness in fulfilling bodily functions. This is particularly so with regard to going to lavatory.

Although Gurkhas in general are much more broad-minded than are their co-religionists in the plains about the mass of observations and inhibitions which make up orthodox Hindu behaviour, I was by no means certain how Dal Bahadur would react. It was a critical situation. He had been very relaxed about love-making, but helping him to have a crap was altogether a different kettle of fish. It was impossible for me to be sure that one or other of us might not become irretrievably defiled during the process. Such an eventuality could put him off me for ever. But it had to be risked.

I sat up and examined his face by the moon's light. It had that baffled expression which very old people wear, or those who are going to die, when they realize that they are no longer capable of performing humble bodily functions without assistance.

I felt a rush of sympathy for his undignified plight. I said quietly, as if to a child, meaning to reassure him, 'Certainly – certainly. Only hold it! I'm trying to think how to do it.'

I hopped down from the improvised couch where all the wounded were lying in long rows hissing and grunting, but not a soul was about. There was no-one to advise me.

In those days I was not very skilful at nursing. I realized I would have to improvise according to the inspiration of the moment. As a matter of fact, I hate pulling sick people about; I am always afraid I am going to hurt them. It is only after long experience that you realize how ruggedly you can handle them. The human organism, moreover, is at once so unpredictable and so resilient that – on the one hand – it can die with the expiry of a tiny breath and without any sign of injury, as in the case of Tej Bahadur, or – on the other – survive the most frightful pummelling, like my little friend.

A bright metal object, rudely pushed under the bed where we had been reclining, flashed back the moon's reflections and attracted my attention with its roguish light. It was my mess tin. Before retiring with Dal Bahadur to bed, I had brewed up a weak mash of tea and persuaded him to drink it. It was pretty well the first sustenance which had passed his lips since the wounding. Perhaps it was the tea which had instigated the bowel-movement.

The use of the mess tin as an impromptu jerry in such potentially degrading circumstances was fraught with danger. I had no idea whether Dal Bahadur would accept it. However I picked it up gingerly as if it were already polluted, and presented it to his gaze with a look of enquiry.

'Do you mind?'

To my surprise he never batted an eyelid. He began raising his body painfully on his elbows so that I could shove it under him. By merciful providence, the bottom half of his body was naked, so we didn't have the awkward business of unbuttoning his trousers. I stood over him – my legs astride his body – and supported his buttocks with my hands. The procedure was a stunning success.

***

One afternoon several days later I was told to take a defence platoon up to the top of the hill. I myself was not to remain with them but to come back down. I suspected that I had lost Jack Masters's confidence.

And it is true that I was in a very curious mood for a British officer. I had quite ceased to carry a weapon, and went about completely unarmed. This could hardly have failed to attract attention.

It was the only symbol, however, which I could think of to emphasize that I bore no animosity towards anybody – least of all towards the Japanese. As a matter of fact, we had long since arrived at that point where the only people any of us felt like murdering were our own generals.

Shells had been crumping and thumping into the hillside for more than half-an-hour and, when I set out it, looked as if we were in for an attack. It would be just my luck if I got to the top while it was going in.

As I wound up the narrow path to the summit, now so churned up by the mules and ponies bearing arms and ammunition to the beleaguered garrison as to be almost impassable, I could not avoid speculating about how it would all end. One good thrust on the part of the Japanese and we would be finished. One ought to be grateful, I suppose, that the enemy was equally debilitated. But perhaps this attack would be it. At any rate, it could only be a question of time before the Japs accumulated sufficient forces. Then we should be done for!

Gazing into the leaden faces and lacklustre eyes of the lonely soldiers on guard-duty in their slit-trenches, it was impossible not to surrender to morbid emotions.

Musing thus, I passed away from the area of the fortifications (a grand word for very impoverished and improvised slit-trenches) into no-man's-land. Huge trees shot up all round me, towering towards the sky, and the ground was thick with dead leaves – the earth heavy with humus.

It was that part of the track, about three quarters of a mile in extent, which we did not have sufficient soldiers to cover, so traffic passing up and down it had to be prepared to run the gauntlet. It was indescribably lonely. It also partook of that ghostly aura which ground regularly fought over begins to possess when numbers of people have surrendered their lives there.

Leading my little band of indomitables, I felt insignificant almost to vanishing point, where all discriminations and distinctions are extinguished. The trek seemed to be taking an unconscionably long time.

As we neared the summit, the shelling became more intense. To be out in the open, under these circumstances, with no access to a slit-trench which one could call one's own, would be most unpleasant. On this occasion, furthermore, I did not make the mistake of failing to recognize that the Japs were ranging.

They were ranging, moreover, with heavy howitzers slinging huge projectiles of over one hundred pounds in weight. To be caught under such an attack without protection would be disastrous. Imperceptibly we increased our pace.

Presently we passed the place where Jim Blaker had been killed – in some odd way I was surprised to observe that it possessed no distinguishing feature (had I been expecting a commemorative tablet?) – and emerged into an open space.

The huge forest giants towered up all round it, and access was achieved via the narrow path which I had been following through an imposing barbed wire *cheveux-de-frise*. The trees inclined gently towards the centre as if silently worshipping a solemn narthex, and I have often wondered whether there might not in reality have been something magical about this place, for it, after all, was still the country of the Kachins, who were celebrated magicians.

When I first put my foot within the circle, it was still humming with activity. A huge pile of boxes occupied the centre. They were empty crates of grenades. Even as I watched, Gurkhas were running like ants back and forth from this improvised ammunition dump, distributing to their fellows its deadly eggs.

Suddenly a gigantic salvo of artillery – the anticipated one-round-gunfire – landed just beyond us on the forward slope. Its effect was instant: everyone vanished into their slit-trenches, leaving me and the platoons standing idly isolated.

I shooshed them through the barbed-wire *cheveux-de-frise* like a nanny shepherding her charges through the turnstiles at the zoo. Once inside, they still seemed completely dazed. It is a difficult situation taking over an unreconnoitred position at the inception of a powerful attack. I had to go around squeezing them into other people's fox-holes.

When I had done so, I found myself standing on my own. The tamped, naked earth of the hill feature began drumming with rain.

I had to make a decision. One option was to promenade all round the place out in the open, searching for the headquarters trench of Colonel Harper, and report that my men were distributed over his position – thus passing the duration of the attack in his company, which I didn't want to do. Without a weapon I was going to have an awful lot of explaining to do, and in any case I was going to look pretty silly. The second option was to return – I had been given my orders – the way I had come.

Another salvo of projectiles crashed into the hillside just below where I was standing. One of the great teak trees canted crazily. I knew at once where the next one would land – it would land on me. I decided then and there that I had had enough.

Little peaky faces with bright, beady eyes were peering at me from every nook and cranny. They were Alec Harper's Gurkhas. Seeing as how not one of them, either by gesture or by nodding inclination, offered me shelter – after all, I was not their officer, I was a stranger to them, and Gurkhas are incurably clannish – I turned back.

The path stretched down precipitously into the darkness of the forest. I felt sure that it was safe to follow, and I set off.

When I come to contemplate what followed, it seems almost inconceivable that I did not disappear without trace. It ought to have been one of those cases which occasion the classic, 'Missing – Believed Killed in Action' formula of the casualties lists. Instead, I sustained a miraculous escape.

105mm shells were crumping into the crest as I descended and to hear the crack and splinter of teak trees disintegrating under their impact was a tempering experience. It was like being pursued by a giant. Even more disturbing was the fact that the flying dustbin had joined in. The combination of all these noises – the wail of the passing projectiles and the howl of the mighty mortar-bomb together with the wrench and shiver of timber – was truly terrifying. It is hardly surprising that I panicked.

Mysterious explosions – or rather, explosions that presented themselves to my awareness as mysterious because at the end of their trajectory the shells were not audible – kept up hunt-the-slipper with me, and it became possible to conceive of them as endowed with a seeker-device targeted on me. Looking back over my shoulder in that characteristic gesture symptomatic of fear, I started to run.

All at once, I spied something happening just ahead of me which halted me dead in my tracks. I had stumbled on a group of soldiers. Who the hell were they? They looked indefinably different. An officer, easily distinguishable by his more confident manner and masterful attitude, was marshalling them, but the soldiers were responding to him clumsily, their face revealing them as inexperienced boys.

I was on the point of going up to them and explaining that I was lost, and asking where the hell were we, and in which direction, pray, was Brigade, when something withheld me.

Their high cheek bones, slit eyes and small stature did, indeed, make them almost indistinguishable from Gurkhas. But why the carefully camouflaged combat uniforms they were wearing – so neat and clean – which we did not have? And why the funny, flower-pot-shaped tin hats? Even if they could just possibly be confused with our own soldiers on account of facial resemblance and similar characteristics, it was inconceivable that the officer could be one of ours, for he was totally unlike anything we possessed.

Belatedly the realisation dawned on me that they must be Japs!

Several of them began coming in my direction. They seemed to look me directly in the face. The jungle, at that point, was pretty thick – but composed largely of tall teak trees with sparse undergrowth, a circumstance which, however, could be confusing to vision. But they were only twenty yards away. I was certainly convinced that they saw me.

It was nothing short of a godsend that I was not carrying a gun. Had I possessed one, I should certainly have responded by making some sort of movement. As it was, I leaned quietly against a tree.

I had discovered in myself a propensity for acting unpredictably, and in a calm and collected manner, at the moment of danger. I can only explain this in the present instance by further insisting that I had lost my bellicosity. My outlook was that of the unprejudiced observer – a sort of referee. I am convinced that this attitude had its effect.

The Japanese soldiers advancing towards me regarded me so incuriously that I might have been a statue. They were quite near enough for me to see their eyes. These remained unenlightened by any spark of recognition.

I did not move. Presently they turned to their right and disappeared up the hill.

After a short interval, the machine-guns began rat-tat-tat-tat-tatting and there was the crash of grenades. My panic returned in full force and I began running like one possessed.

Luckily this time I was running in the right direction. I landed up flat on my belly on the lip of one of our machine-gun posts. It was manned by two soldiers of the King's Own and I found myself gazing at them full in the face.

'Hullo,' I said to them stupidly, making no attempt to conceal that I was frightened.

'Come inside,' they said laconically, without demanding any explanations.

# CHAPTER EIGHTEEN

# Getting Out

Somewhere about 15 July orders arrived for us to abandon Point 2171 and withdraw. At much the same time we received news of Mike Calvert's success with 77 Brigade in capturing Mogaung. Chinese troops were also sweeping south towards that city. Such developments all made things considerably easier for us.

I had been aware for some time that Jack Masters was locked in an unprecedented struggle with his higher commanders. It revolved around the bitter controversy then raging about whether or not the Brigade was physically fit and whether we all ought to be flown out. Stilwell still insisted that we were in perfectly good shape and were simply not doing our duty.

The argument had been conducted via signal and counter-signal under the most testing conditions. It had continued throughout the whole period of occupation of Point 2171. We did not, however, foresee it resulting in such a resounding victory on Masters's part as actually to cause us to retreat.

A rustle of excitement rippled through the ranks when this news reached us, but it didn't do to let it run away with you. There still remained many intractable problems to be solved, many insuperable obstacles to be surmounted.

Principal among these, I need hardly say, was our commitment to caring for our casualties. In view of Dal Bahadur's injuries – although he was now making excellent progress – this was naturally an important priority for me. Excluding the walking wounded, we had about sixty serious stretcher cases to carry out and convey to some point where we could build a light-plane strip and get them evacuated.

The decision over our evacuation had been wrested out of Stilwell by sheer argumentative skill, but – oddly – the day set for the final execution of the project arrived almost too quickly. I was in a lather of apprehension about the whole thing. Only the preceding evening one of our patrols had returned with information that the Jap presence was still straddling our rear. It did not seem that we would be able to get away without fighting for it, yet a battle – with so many wounded to care for – was to my mind unthinkable.

At eight o'clock that night Jack Masters summoned his inner cabinet. It was the first occasion during the operations that such a Council of War had been convened. It was a measure of the desperation of all concerned that it was even considered. All the column commanders attended. Masters presented his decision to withdraw along a particular route as a calculated risk. The assembled mandarins endorsed it. It was the only path which offered the slightest prospect of success and to have hesitated over the choice would have been tantamount to surrendering the initiative.

It was as a consequence of this decision that on the following morning I found myself leading the whole bloody Brigade in its attempt to get away.

It was a beautiful day. As the sun rose, it shone with dazzling splendour upon the droplets of moisture decorating the feathery bamboo. I was three miles from the crest of Point 2171 and well on my way.

Since long before dawn the wounded had been assembled and got out onto the path escort. It was a pathetic sight. This collection of the wrecks of battle hobbled forth on their sticks and crutches and out into the night. When Dal Bahadur rode past me on his pony, however – such had been the speed of his recovery – I felt strangely proud.

As the defence platoons had been pressed into service for stretcher-bearers, all Masters could muster by way of an advance guard was one section. That section was the one led by Shiv Jung.

He and I were together, therefore – we were already high on the slope of the opposite mountain and were congratulating ourselves that the withdrawal was going splendidly – when two of our foremost scouts came rushing back and reported they had stumbled on a party of Japs.

I honestly didn't know what to do. Shiv Jung and Thaman Bahadur and I gazed at each other in consternation. Already the stretcher-bearers and the walking and mounted wounded were bunching dangerously as the momentum of our advance checked, and then came to halt. Dal Bahadur sat on his pony close to me. Just behind was Doc Whyte. If we encountered the enemy – even in the shape of a scattered machine-gun burst – it would rip directly into this vulnerable soft belly.

I consulted Doc Whyte. The varieties of tactical disposition you can make with one section are severely limited. He agreed that I should return to the bed of the *chaung* where Masters had probably established temporary headquarters and try to rustle up some reinforcements. Meanwhile, he would take responsibility for Shiv Jung's section and attempt to keep the impetus of our movement going.

I thanked him, consigned my men and Dal Bahadur to his merciful care, and hurried the two miles back. So great was my mental intensity that I seemed to make this journey in a matter of minutes. The bed of the *chaung*, however, when I arrived there, presented such a scene of disorganisation as made the slopes of the mountain which I had left seem by comparison a veritable paradise.

Alec Harper was down there. He was perched on a huge banyan root and appeared to be wrestling with a mule. He looked like Mithras in the act of killing the bull. The giant peepul tree towered above and around him, extending downwards from its boughs its aerial radicles, and at exactly the point where he was standing the floodwater of some past inundation had excavated the bank. It had exposed a tangle of serpentine roots of labyrinthine complexity. The whole tableau – a sort of Laocoön – looked like a glyph of some stupendous group of antique statuary.

Nobody took any notice of me. They were too busy rescuing the mule which had shed its load and tripped over the bank.

From the opposite incline – that incline up and down which I had pounded so many times on the afternoon of Dal Bahadur's wounding, and which stretched upwards towards the top of the hill – there extended an eerie silence. It was that slope which erstwhile had accommodated the slit-trenches of the defence platoons, Masters's command post, and Doc Whyte's Forward Dressing Station. Heretofore it had been humming with activity. Now it looked bleak and deserted. Only one or two derelict pieces of equipment and the abandoned earthworks bore witness to its former importance.

Every so often, plainly in accordance with some complicated plan, groups of Gurkhas scuttled across it, as they withdrew from Point 2171. I watched them with admiration as they retreated into their lay-backs. Neither Masters nor the Japs were anywhere in evidence.

I transferred my attention to the bed of the *chaung*. Everything seethed with chaos. The mules seemed to have taken it into their heads to behave with the temperament of prima donnas. The mule-leaders were swearing at them under their breaths, with restrained passion. The whole place was chock-a-block.

Still there was no sign from the top. The Japs, apparently, were still in blissful ignorance of the fact that we had gone. I went up to Alec Harper and asked him who was in command there. As he was the only officer it sight, it was pretty obvious he was.

'I am,' he snapped.

I apologized and told him what I wanted but he declined to grant my request. Nor did he seem, on receiving my news that there were Japs ahead, unduly put out. We were all so hard pressed to fulfil our own obligations that no-one was much concerned with those of others.

I realized that I had wasted my time and my energy and, frantically pushing past the mass of mules and men who were blocking the path, set off back to my own men.

Rather an euphoric air prevailed among my forward section when I reached them, and Shiv Jung, Thaman Bahadur and Doc Whyte were laughing – presumably from relief.

'What is it? What's happened?' I enquired, somewhat dazed.

Doc Whyte was wearing a smug expression. Smithy appeared from the rear with another officer, apparently alerted by Alex Harper that all was not well with the head of the column – and would we please get a move on!

Shiv Jung beckoned me ahead. I followed him down the path into the bamboos to see what he had discovered. It was a perfectly co-ordinated, yet quite unarmed, defensive position. Going around this strong-point where the enemy had planned, with considerable ingenuity, to receive us, was rather creepy. It could only have been abandoned, according to the indications, a few minutes before. Several cooking-fires were still smouldering and beside them, dumped from upturned eating-bowls, were the remains of the morning rice.

Shiv Jung plunged his index finger disrespectfully into one pile to demonstrate that it was hot. It seemed like a sort of miracle.

So we got out. Several days after the retreat from Point 2171, we had retired sufficiently beyond the possibility of Jap pursuit to be able to consolidate ourselves, search out a strip of paddy cultivation, construct a light landing strip, and fly out our wounded. Dal Bahadur was evacuated.

Mogaung, when we entered it, was in a condition of disorganisation and decay which was almost beyond belief. It occupied a low-lying site near the river and, as the ground seemed to be more or less permanently waterlogged, the houses were built on stilts. They were also constructed of timber. This fact alone was sufficient to account for most of them having been burnt to the ground. Those that had escaped this calamity were roofless.

Luckily the defence platoons managed to misappropriate a relatively sound Burmese-style mansion in the quarter allotted to them.

Corpses – our own and the enemy's – were lying about everywhere without any attempt having been made to bury them. They turned up in the most disagreeable places – rotting on the lavatory, for example – and were in every state of decomposition. Their putrefying smell hung over the city like a miasma.

One day I took at trip into town to inspect the Buddhist Monastery. It, also, was without a roof. The mighty teak timbers of its columns rose up all round me, looking inappropriately garish, for they were covered in gilding and red lacquer, their lower members encrusted with mirror-fragments in mosaic.

A colossal reclining statue of Buddha, using its hand as its pillow, occupied the centre of the building – now a space open to the sky. The lush vegetation of a tropical climate sprouted up all round it, and through the cracks in the pavement, liberally manured by the heaps of elephant dung which lay around –for the place had been used as a stable – there thrust seedling peepul and banyan trees, some of them ten feet high, although only two years old.

That a place of worship should have fallen into such a state distressed me quite disproportionately. I returned to my billet chilled to the bone. As daylight drained away and evening descended with its sombre invitation to deeper depression, I was visited by an onset of twitches and shivers. Every joint and tendon in my body complained with an intolerable ache.

Surrendering to the malaise, I crawled to that part of the house where the defence platoons had laid out my groundsheet. Stretching myself upon it, I pulled the blanket up over my head and went to sleep.

My temperature must have doubled as I slept, for I awoke suddenly bathed in sweat and reeking of that strange rubbery smell which characterizes the body when it is feverish. Thaman Bahadur was kneeling beside me. A ring of my Gurkhas stood at a respectful distance, solemn as owls, and I gained the impression that they were expecting my demise.

A brilliant moon shone outside, lapping the ground like quicksilver. It was plainly visible from where I lay. The place had no walls; it was simply a roof and a few pieces of floor on stilts five feet above the floodwaters.

My fever had not abated during my sleep. I was consumed with ague and thought I was dying. I did not want any witness to my passing – much less interference – and eventually managed to persuade Thaman Bahadur to leave me and take the Gurkhas away. They retired through several side rooms to a place practically opposite me, where I could observe them, and call to them if I needed assistance. It was across a great, gulf-like, central living-room which had lost its floor and from the depths of which the frogs croaked continually. I was submerged once more in the swamp of delirium.

Suddenly young Lawrence appeared – but so realistically that I forgot for a moment that he had been killed. I made a movement to welcome him and my heart dilated with joy. Instead of responding to me, he assumed a sullen and threatening mien totally unlike his real personality, and I recalled with a sensation something like a blow on the chest that he was dead.

'Why didn't you stop him,' he hectored me 'when you knew by your own confession what it meant? Why didn't you stop him?'

'Who? ' I stammered.

'The shoe-shine boy – I mean the shoe-shine boy at Jhansi station – the one who presented me the garland. You knew then that it meant I was done for. Why didn't you prevent it? Why didn't you prevent it?'

He wailed as his wraith disappeared like a mist into the glittery moonlight.

Then in his place there stood another figure, also a British officer. I recognized it as Mike MacGillicuddy. There was a little round red hole neatly drilled in the middle of his forehead, and he had taken off its hat the better for me to see this.

'Why weren't you in your platoon position?' he asked, shaking his head sadly, 'when I waited specially for you in order to make up our quarrel? Why weren't you in your platoon position?'

'It isn't fair to hold me responsible for that.' I yelled after him. 'I was on a recce. I was doing my duty.'

He vanished. Next came Tulbir Gurung.

'Why did you send me down to Brigade Headquarters?' he demanded fiercely, making no bones about his anger, and using that persuasive, conspiratorial mode of address he always adopted when speaking to me, as if making me a party to whatever cunning plot he was hatching. 'You knew it was a false message. You deceived me into carrying the instrument of my own death. They kept on putting me in the front rank of all the storming parties. They knew eventually I'd cop it. Why did you send me down with that false message?'

I started to say 'It wasn't like that.' Then I fell silent. It was true what he said. Calculatingly I had sent him down there, rejoicing in my cleverness and in this crafty way of disposing of him. I honestly didn't realize – it never occurred to me – that they would deliberately expose him to all the hazards of battle. That was too great a retribution for his trifling fault.

'Honestly, Tulbir, I didn't realize.'

But he too, without waiting for my explanations, had vanished.

I knew who the next one would be, and I was right. It was Ganga Bahadur. He was wringing his hands. I attempted to forestall his expostulations by rising from my couch pre-emptively and apologising.

'Ganga Bahadur, forgive me!'

But he would have none of it. He brushed me away. He wore that particular expression of craven pleading mingled with craftiness which had made me so dubious of his honesty in the first place. I stopped making excuses and waited patiently for him to speak.

To my astonishment he said nothing. He remained standing in front of me, wringing his hands and wearing that plaintive expression. Then he too merged into the background of the blazing moonlight and disappeared.

The next who appeared was carrying his pack. He had his Bren gun slung across the top of it and was slightly bowed, exactly as I had seen him as he toiled up the slope towards that fateful clearing near Point 2171 on that dreadful day. It was Tej Bahadur. His face was moon-shaped and pimply as ever but, instead of its perpetually pleased expression, it now looked pain-worn and perplexed.

'What's happened to me' he asked, catching sight of me for the first time and perhaps mistaking me for a fellow wanderer in the House of Shades. 'Am I dead?'

'Oh, Tej Bahadur!' I said, by now quite broken in spirit.

'Sahib!' he interjected, as if taken by surprise.

There was a short silence. Then he took up the theme adopted by all the others.

'Oh – why didn't you let me go back down the *chaung* when I asked you? I always obeyed your orders. It was a small thing to ask when it came to my moment of decision. Why didn't you? You didn't believe me!'

Then he too faded away.

I woke up with a start.

Practically no time at all seemed to have elapsed since Thaman Bahadur had knelt beside me but, now that I needed someone, they all seemed lapped in sleep. Only the moonlight burnt down outside, bathing the neglected plot of ground which had once been a garden in its incandescent fierceness.

But I was mistaken. Someone was stirring in the side-room opposite the great central chamber which lacked a floor, and I waved my arm weakly, trying to attract his attention. He was wearing a Burmese *lungyi* as were all my men, but in addition he had over his naked torso a little, short, loose linen jacket with ample sleeves such as I had seen a number of Burmese civilians wear. In spite of this, I was in no doubt whatsoever that he was one of mine.

He came obediently to my command, treading on air and walking quietly across the breached open space of the central living-room as if it was the most unnatural thing to do in the world. He looked like Christ walking on the water.

I surrendered to the phantom immediately and averted my head without saying a word, for of course I recognized him. It was the Burman with the shaven head whom we had court-martialled and whom Sergeant Barker had taken out into the jungle to shoot. He gazed at me silently, with that same reproachful expression he had worn when he gazed at me, one of his judges, at his trial. Again the same spark of sympathy shot between us. I couldn't clearly see his chest because the shadow of the loose jacket concealed it, but, as he turned round to leave me, I saw his back. Where the shoulder blades and spine should have been was simply one huge, gaping cavity. Sergeant Barker had known his business.

The final stage in this long sequence of spirits demanding retribution was the Jap Officer whom I had waved away from me during my attack on that village when I was trying to avoid sticking him with my bayonet, and he still wore his *hachimaki*. He made a gesture towards me which I can only describe as one of absolution.

*** 

On the following day my fever broke. Evidently it had only needed one person to intercede for me. But it was strange that the solitary individual capable of doing so should have belonged to the other side.

A few days afterwards we marched to Mogaung railway station. We crossed the bombed steel-girder railway bridge gingerly on foot. Against its central pier several decomposing corpses were bobbing in the swirling water. We then boarded a train for Myitkyina.

The city had been captured by the Chinese some few days previously and fighting was still going on in the outskirts, but the airstrip was in our hands, although the Japanese were shelling it. The ground was so waterlogged that every time a projectile landed it sent up a column of spray like the shelling of a ship. We stood around for hours making bets on the near misses, but many aircraft were hit.

Eventually an aircraft arrived for us and we scrambled aboard. Thunderstorms were hitting the hills beneath us and lightning licked from cloud to cloud, but the trip was otherwise uneventful. When we arrived at Tinsukia in Assam we were driven to camp. From Tinsukia they sent us by train to Dehra Dun. I was put into a hospital which occupied the old Imperial Forestry Institute designed by Lutyens.

One evening, wandering through those impressive corridors and galleries, I encountered Sergeant Barker. He also was clad in pyjamas and dressing gown and looked dreadfully haggard.

They were playing Beethoven's Emperor Concerto over the tannoy relay system and had arrived at the slow movement. Although Sergeant Barker's and my relationship had always been conducted on a formal footing, we must have reacted mutually to the emotional atmosphere generated by the music. I was emboldened to ask him a personal question.

'Do you never feel any sort of guilt for all the executions you've done?'

We were leaning together over the first floor gallery under the dome. He turned to me a face slowly being torn apart by tension.

'I do, sir,' he said intensely. 'Yes I do. I dream about them. They haunt me.'

He shuffled away in his slippers. It was as if all the hounds of hell were after him – and indeed they were. I heard that not many weeks later he tried to hang himself. Soon after that he slit his throat and died.

It was during this period that my G II at GHQ, Major Freeman, called for a report on me. It was duly compiled. According to Military Regulations an officer has to know what is said about him, so I was called in to hear this document read to me. Colonel Rome, Special Force's Second-in-Command, was the officer who was to conduct the ceremony, so I found myself one afternoon in his almost luxurious office.

He invited me to sit down and began to read.

'Owing to the exigencies of the campaign, Captain Baines was not able to do much camouflage. In action, however, he did well. Signed, J. Masters, Commander.'

There was a long pause. Colonel Rome and I regarded each other quizzically.'

'Is that all?'

'Yes. How much more did you expect?'

I was not prepared to make a fool of myself by revealing that I had expected a definitive biography. The silence continued for so long that it became quite uncomfortable.

Finally Colonel Rome broke it.

'Aren't you satisfied? Did you expect something better?'

I found myself incapable of articulating a word.

'I want to know what you think about it. If you're dissatisfied, don't be afraid to say so. That is the purpose of this interview. Say something. I want to know.'

After a good deal of hesitation, I finally managed to say something.

'But – it's so inadequate.'

'This is a good report!'

'Surely it's what anyone would be expected to do? To do well is merely to do one's duty.'

Colonel Rome paused for a moment and then looked me full in the eye.

'You'd be surprised,' he said.

So this, I reflected sourly, as I made my way back to my quarters, was what my pain and anguish had amounted to. Captain Baines had done well! He might have saved himself the trouble.

***

Almost two months to the day after Dal Bahadur had been wounded, he returned.

It was some time towards the end of August. I had already decided that I could not postpone my departure on his account any longer. I had been under pressure to take the leave due to me and return to my staff duties with another formation. I had packed my luggage, reserved my train compartment, and was off on furlough.

Bhim Bahadur came rushing into my presence and announced, 'Dal Bahadur's back!'

I ran breathlessly to the defence platoon lines. I found him looking more beautiful than ever. It was a great joy to me to find that he had lost none of his allure.

So we went to Kashmir.

I was due to join Twelfth Army Headquarters in Rangoon – in fact, the notorious Force 136 – for forward planning with regard to the future campaign in Malaya. Movement Control in Calcutta was having some sort of difficulty regarding transhipments. Rangoon had only just fallen, but I never anticipated such a disaster as the end of the war. I was advised to go by train to Chittagong, where a lift by plane could be begged fairly easily.

We were booked on the Midnight Mail from Sealdah station to Dacca. When we arrived at Sealdah, the luggage coolies were in a flurry of excitement. We had difficulty in securing one to carry our bags. They were clustered round a radio in a *pan-wallah's* kiosk listening to a transmission of, apparently, epic importance.

Eventually one of them detached himself and came across. 'The war's over, sahib,' he announced. 'Were you going to the front? Then you can return to your hotel.'

When Dal Bahadur and I landed at Mingladoon aerodrome near Rangoon, the aircraft bearing the Japanese envoys who were to sue for surrender had just arrived. We realised that we too would have to surrender to the inevitable; bow to circumstances; and say goodbye. Soon afterwards we were put on a troopship bound from Rangoon to Calcutta for demobilisation.

The final stage can be described in a few lines. We boarded a train to Lucknow, where I needed to transact some private business. Then I was to go on to Bombay to board the troop-ship *Reina del Pacifico* for Liverpool. Dal Bahadur was going on to 9th Gurkha depot at Dehra Dun.

At every wayside halt and station the regimented bands were out in full strength in their most gorgeous uniforms, playing the heroes from the front home to depot and barrack.

We arrived at Lucknow about noon. The Local Area Headquarters had put on an especially magnificent display. There were regimental bands of all descriptions and colours keeping up an uninterrupted public musical entertainment all day. As the fifteen-car express pulled in, they struck up *Lilliburlero*. The train was crammed with returning soldiers who kept up an uninterrupted hullabaloo. It was terrifically exciting – euphoric almost.

Dal Bahadur and I left the first-class compartment we had been occupying and raced up the platform to find him another place. Gradually the crowd thinned out and I was left on my own on the platform facing the train. The engine let out a scream of steam. The pistons began to push at the huge connecting rods and the driving wheels turned. The train gathered pace.

I saluted him.

All the accompanying soldiers cheered wildly. The bands, I remember, were playing *The Flowers of the Forest.*

# CHAPTER NINETEEN

# Postscript – Farewell to Dal Bahadur

My final meeting with Dal Bahadur was profoundly sad. It occurred in December 1951, as I was contemplating leaving India for ever.

Although I had continued to get news about him through the good offices of a friend, I had preferred to keep my enquiries a secret and remain in the background. I thought that he should have the opportunity to get shot of me and develop without interference along lines of his own.

I had not seen him since we said goodbye on Lucknow station in December 1944, but, of course, I knew his address. It was: Village Lamma Gaon Busti, Post Office Phulbazaar, District Darjeeling, North Bengal.

And I went there.

I had been to Darjeeling several times before, but on this occasion the landscape looked particularly magnificent. As the little puff-puff came to the top of the hill at Kurseong, where the Hindu monastery is, it was evening. The setting sun was shining full on Kanchenjunga, ruddy as an apricot, and the mountain stood up before me tall and powerful, obscuring half the panorama with its bulk. Then the train ran slowly down the incline and came to rest.

On the following morning I started out on my investigations. Finding the actual whereabouts on the ground of Dal Bahadur's address turned out to be comparatively easy. When I enquired at the General Post Office where the Sub-Post Office of Phulbazaar was, an obliging counter clerk accompanied me outside onto the street and showed me. It was right down in the bottom of the valley, six thousand feet below.

'And Lamma Gaon Busti?' I enquired hopefully. 'Where is that?'

My informant pointed to practically dead opposite. It was, as the crow flew, only about five miles distant across the intervening valley. To get there, however, I would have to descend six thousand feet to the valley floor, cross the river by rope bridge, and then climb back up another ten thousand feet.

As I did not have much time at my disposal, I started out right away.

Phulbazaar proved comparatively easy of access. The walk there, through fruiting orange and tangerine groves and sometimes between terraces of tea-garden cultivation, was entirely delightful. A heady scent of citrus fruit was in the air and the turpentine tang from the pine plantations and the forests of cryptomeria was almost overwhelming. As I descended deeper into the valley, it got hotter.

I arrived just before mid-day at the little cluster of wooden houses, with their balconies from which flowered a riot of geraniums. I stopped at a tea-house to refresh myself, and then went along to the village store which served as Post Office, in order to pursue my enquiries.

This time I actually mentioned Dal Bahadur by name. As I knew not only his caste designation, namely Chettri, but also his patronymic, namely son of Tensing Bahadur, I was reasonably certain of getting fairly near my target. I succeeded beyond my wildest expectations.

My questions as to Dal Bahadur's whereabouts and the best way of getting to Lamma Gaon Busti were greeted with a curious sense of expectancy. I was told readily enough what to do and which was the easiest path to follow, yet I was left with the strange feeling that they knew all about me. Quite soon the entire community seemed to have foregathered and to be regarding me with what was plainly considerable respect.

As I was unaware of having done anything to deserve such V.I.P. treatment, I began to feel very uncomfortable.

I was asked if I would like to rest. A chair was produced and I was practically forced to take a seat. Then there appeared before me the village elder. This gentleman, being endowed with the communal authority, came to the point at once.

'Are you,' he asked politely, 'Dal Bahadur's sahib?'

'Well ... er ... yes,' I assented. 'As a matter of fact I am.'

'Are you,' continued the old man relentlessly, 'the officer who gave him the beautiful inscribed cigarette case?'

'Er ... yes!' And fancy him knowing *that*!

'Are you,' he continued with mounting enthusiasm, 'the same officer who gave him the priceless gold amulet inscribed with the sacred letter "Om" and containing a miniature copy of the Lord Krishna's song called Bhagavad Gita [powerful magic]?'

'Yes!'

'Then, sir,' chanted the old man, by this time positively lyrical – and the whole community standing behind him seemed to concur – 'you are truly welcome!'

They all bowed down before me in an elaborate prostration.

Absolutely horrified, I sprang to my feet. It was too late. I was already launched into a full civic reception. A garland of French marigolds was produced, and from somewhere behind my left elbow somebody thrust into my hand another glass of sweet tea.

'You saved his life!' said the old man, coming up and whispering into my ear affectionately. 'He told us himself. You saved his life!'

Such was the welcome. I believe I might have stayed in that place the rest of my life. I think I would have been happy there.

Somehow, however, I managed to struggle away. I crossed the river torrent by the rickety string bridge which was strung across it, and the whole village waved me goodbye.

The ensuing climb up the hillside in the heat of the day cost me an enormous effort. The sun blazed down unremittingly and, being out of condition, I poured with sweat. I was relieved, however, by my every so often encountering a Gurkha villager who greeted me with the most dazzling smile as well as a profound obeisance, indicating that my reputation and the news of my presence had in some mysterious way gone before.

At about nine thousand feet, with the sun striking behind Tiger Hill above the cantonment of Darjeeling to the west, and the mist on top of my mountain getting lower and lower, I began to have doubts as to whether I should make it before night. A bitter cold had descended.

Suddenly, above me, I spied a little procession. Made up of youths and maidens, it was like something which you would not be surprised to have found in Ancient Greece.

It was him all right. I would recognise that figure anywhere.

We met in the middle of an open hillside that was quite bare of cultivation. It had started to rain. And in the rain, on that bare hillside, we embraced.

He had become subtly older and wiser. In fact he had grown up and become a man. Yet I knew that he was the same.

He didn't say anything. He simply took me by the arm and led me forward. Indeed, as it transpired afterwards, he had prepared a stunning reception. He had despatched messengers to bring elegant dancing-boys to entertain me from far and near.

We sat under a thatched awning outside a sort of hut. His own house had been destroyed in the recent Darjeeling earthquake and there was nowhere else to receive me. It turned out to be the local shop and to belong to him. I was glad to learn that he had always been a rich man and owned such important property.

When we sat down, I was able, for the first time, to steal a close but covert glance at him.

He had aged considerably. That is to say, although still young and handsome, he was no longer a boy. A dashing, Kshatriya-style moustache sprouted from his upper lip in silken splendour, and he looked like the young Buddha of the Gandharan sculptures.

Huge bonfires were lit. The whole village came up to be presented to me and then sat round me in a circle. Several beautiful boys appeared, bearing gigantic earthenware pitchers of wine, for Dal Bahadur well knew my tastes. In the background, the women-folk began preparing the rice. We were all so tensed up by the solemnity of the occasion that none of us needed much persuasion to eat and drink.

Throughout the whole of that misty night, Dal Bahadur and I sat cross-legged together, leaning shoulder to shoulder. Quite early on in the proceedings his mother had come up and covered us with a single blanket. It was like a sort of wedding symbol. Under cover of it our arms entwined.

Within the circle of the firelight the dancing-boys twisted, stamped and pirouetted; the drums and *tablas* sobbed; the viols moaned.

Gradually the spectators got more and more drunk and finally flopped on the ground, fast asleep. Towards dawn, the dancers and the instrument players departed for their homes. The fires died down. Dal Bahadur and I remained wide awake. While the crickets chirped and rustled in the great bundles of paddy-straw, we talked of the past.

And later we returned to the present – and he revealed to me that he had developed phthisis in his infected lung, and was not expected to live much longer.

Before the sun was up, while daylight was yet seeping through the cloud-base, I left.

He was very stoical. Yet we wept and wept.

We wept for our lost youth and for our dear departed – which was us when we were young. And we wept because he was ill, and was feeling feeble and faint-hearted, and must prematurely die. We wept because I was leaving India for ever and because our passion was spent. And we wept because, although we loved each other, we were no longer in love.

During the whole of the long trek back to Darjeeling I did not encounter a single soul. Phulbazaar, when I passed through it, was deserted and gloomy. The river beneath the string bridge roared menacingly. I felt as if I were fleeing the wrath to come. The gorge had become a torrent for dead souls. Even the geraniums had withdrawn behind closed shutters.

But the landscape was a blur to me, for I was much preoccupied with my own sad thoughts; and I knew for a certainty that, far behind me in Lamma Gaon Busti, Dal Bahadur was preoccupied with his.

I never saw or heard of him again.